Mac OS® X Leopard®

PORTABLE GENIUS

Mac OS® X Leopard®

PORTABLE GENIUS

by Dwight Spivey

WILEY

Wiley Publishing, Inc.

Mac OS® X Leopard® Portable Genius

Published by
Wiley Publishing, Inc.
10475 Crosspoint Blvd.
Indianapolis, IN 46256
www.wiley.com

ISBN: 978-0-470-29050-7

Manufactured in the United States of America

10 9 8 7 6 5 4 3 2 1

For general information on our other products and services or to obtain technical support, please contact our Customer Care Department within the U.S. at (800) 762-2974, outside the U.S. at (317) 572-3993 or fax (317) 572-4002.

Wiley also publishes its books in a variety of electronic formats. Some content that appears in print may not be available in electronic books.

Library of Congress Control Number: 2008930833

WILEY

About the Author

Dwight Spivey is the author of How to Do Everything: Mac. He is also a software and support engineer for Konica Minolta, where he specializes in working with Mac operating systems, applications, and hardware, as well as color and monochrome laser printers. He teaches classes on Mac usage, writes training and support materials for Konica Minolta, and is a Mac OS X beta tester for Apple. Dwight lives on the Gulf Coast of Alabama with his wife Cindy and their three beautiful children, Victoria, Devyn, and Emi. He studies theology, draws comic strips, and roots for the Auburn Tigers in his ever-decreasing spare time.

Credits

Acquisitions Editor
Jody Lefevere

Project Editor
Chris Wolfgang

Technical Editor
Guy Hart-Davis

Copy Editor
Marylouise Wiack

Editorial Manager
Robyn B. Siesky

Vice President & Group Executive Publisher
Richard Swadley

Vice President & Publisher
Barry Pruett

Business Manager
Amy Knies

Marketing Manager
Sandy Smith

Project Coordinator
Erin Smith

Graphics and Production Specialists
Stacie Brooks
Andrea Hornberger

Quality Control Technician
Laura Albert
John Greenough

Proofreading
Nancy L. Reinhardt

Indexing
Broccoli Information Management

To my Mamaw, Faye Henderson Alexander. I love you very much and am so fortunate to have you in my life. Send more fudge!

In loving memory of my grandparents who are patiently waiting to see us again in Heaven: Mary Lou (Grandmama) and John D. (Granddaddy) Spivey, and Callie R. (Papaw) Henderson.

To their great-granddaughter and the newest addition to our family, my daughter Emi Faye. You are another gift from the Lord to Daddy, and I will always cherish you, sweetheart.

Acknowledgments

Sincere appreciation goes to Chris Wolfgang and Jody Lefevere, my project editor and acquisitions editor, respectively. Thank you both for putting up with me through the whole process and for being so good to me from start to finish.

Thanks and salutations go to my technical editor, Guy Hart-Davis, for his expertise and brilliant suggestions. This is becoming a habit, Guy!

I want to express my immense gratitude to Carole Jelen McClendon, my agent. You were instrumental in landing this assignment for me, and I'm forever grateful to you.

Thank you to all the wonderful people who helped get this book from my Mac to the store shelves. You are too numerous to mention here, but I extend my heartfelt appreciation to each one of you for your hard work.

I cannot forget to thank my wife, Cindy, who is so good about letting me get my writing done, in spite of having a house full of kids. I love you with all my heart.

Finally, kudos goes once again to Jerri Ledford and James Kenny, for getting me mixed up in this writing stuff in the first place.

Contents

Introduction xviii

chapter 1

What Are the Basics I Need to Know about Leopard? 2

System Requirements for Installing Leopard 4

Choose an Installation Method 4

Upgrade to Leopard 5

Custom Installations 6

Archive and install 6

Erase and install 7

Advanced Installation Options 8

Partition your hard drive 8

Install the Xcode Developer Tools 8

Explore the Finder 10

The Leopard Desktop at a glance 11

Set the Finder preferences 13

Moving Around in the Finder 16

Finder viewing options 16

Get information on files and folders 17

Using Quick Look 19

Working with removable media 21

Utilizing the Dock 22

Adding and removing items 22

Set the Dock's preferences 22

Exposé 23

Manipulating open windows 23

Set Exposé preferences 24

Spaces 25

Set Spaces preferences 25

Assigning applications to spaces 27

Spotlight   27
    Searching with Spotlight   28
    Setting Spotlight preferences   29
Searching with the Finder   30

chapter 2

What Applications Are Included with
Leopard?   34

Discover Leopard's Applications and
    Utilities   36
    Applications   36
    Utilities   42
Navigate Leopard's Applications   44
    How to open and close applications   44
    Common commands and keyboard
        shortcuts   45
    Easily access applications with a Stack   46
Create and Work with Documents in
    TextEdit   47
    Save your document   48
    Open an existing document   48
    A word about file formats   49
Format Your Documents   50
    Using fonts   51
    Using the Fonts window   51
    Checking spelling and grammar   52
Set TextEdit Preferences   53

chapter 3

How Do I Organize My Life
with iCal and Address Book?   58

Create and Manage New Calendars   60
Add Events to Calendars   61
Edit Calendar Events   62
iCal Preferences   63
Share Your Calendars with Others   65
    Publishing a calendar   65
    Exporting a calendar   66
Subscribe to Calendars   67
Print Calendars   68
Create Contacts in Address Book   69
    New cards   69
    New groups   71
Import and Export Contacts   72
    Import Contacts   73
    Export Contacts   74
Address Book Preferences   74
    General   74
    Template   76
    Phone   76
    vCard   76
    LDAP   77
    Sharing   77
See Detailed Maps of Addresses   77

Connect a Device to Your Mac 78
    Supported devices 78
    Bluetooth 79
    USB 81
Use iSync 81
    Add a device to iSync 81
    Sync devices with your Mac 82
    The Data Change alert 83
    iSync preferences 84

chapter 4

How Do I Master the Web
with Safari? 86

Getting Around in Safari 88
    Browsing basics 88
    Tabbed browsing 88
Using Bookmarks 89
    Organizing bookmarks 90
    Importing and exporting bookmarks 92
Private Browsing 92
Viewing Windows Media Files 93
Finding Text on a Web Site 94
Setting Safari Preferences 95
    General 95
    Appearance 97
    Bookmarks 97

Tabs 97
RSS 97
AutoFill 98
Security 99
Advanced 100

chapter 5

How Can I Communicate
with Mail and Chat? 102

Getting Around in Mail 104
    Customize the main toolbar 105
Creating a New Account 106
    Automatic setup 106
    Manual setup 108
Composing and Sending New E-mail 110
    Using Stationery 111
    Adding attachments to e-mails 111
    Formatting your e-mail's contents 112
Receiving, Replying to, and Forwarding
  E-mail 113
Organizing Mail, Notes, and To Dos 113
    Mailboxes 114
    Notes and To Dos 115
Using RSS Feeds 117
Getting Started with iChat 118
    Set up an iChat account 118
    Add buddies to your Buddy List 119

Chat with Friends, Family, and Coworkers 120
    Text chats 120
    Audio chats 121
    Video chats 121
Advanced iChat 122
    Tabbed chatting 123
    Send files to buddies 123
    Receive files from your buddy 124
Make Presentations with iChat Theater 124

Store 137
Advanced 137
Parental 138
Apple TV 138
Syncing 138

chapter 6

What Are iTunes' Coolest
Features? 126

Getting Around in iTunes 128
    Understanding the iTunes window
      layout 128
    Full Screen mode 129
Organizing Media 130
    Importing music 130
    Creating playlists 131
    Burning CDs 133
Using the iTunes Store 134
Setting iTunes Preferences 135
    General 135
    Podcasts 136
    Playback 136
    Sharing 137

chapter 7

What Can Leopard Do with
Digital Photography? 140

Get to Know Photo Booth 142
Take Snapshots 142
    Single snapshots 143
    Take a four-up snapshot 144
    Creating video 144
    Viewing your snapshots 144
Use Special Effects 144
    Snapshot effects 144
    Video backdrops 146
    Adding custom backdrops 147
    How to Use Your Pictures and Videos 147
Working with Image Capture 148
    Set Image Capture preferences 149
    Connect your device 150
Using a Digital Camera 150
    Transfer images to and from
      your camera 150
    Delete images from your camera 153

Using a Scanner   154
   Scanning images   154
   Sharing Devices   156

chapter 8

How Do I Work with PDFs
and Images?   158

File Types Supported by Preview   160
Open and Save Files in Preview   160
Set Preview's Preferences   162
   General   163
   Images   163
   PDF   163
   Bookmarks   163
View and Edit PDFs   165
   Mark up and annotate PDFs   165
   Delete pages from a PDF   166
   Rearrange pages in a PDF   167
View and Edit Images   167
   Resizing and rotating images   168
   Adjusting color in images   170

chapter 9

How Can I Print with Leopard?   172

Set Up a Printer   174
   Install your printer's software 174
   Connect your printer   176
   Create a print queue   178
Print Documents   183
   Discover Leopard's print options 184
   Create your own PDFs   187

chapter 10

Can I Customize Leopard?   192

The Appearance Preferences Pane   194
   Color modifications   194
   Scrolling options   196
   Accessing recently used items   196
   Viewing fonts   197

Desktop Pictures and Screen Savers 197
    Choose a desktop picture 197
    Select a screen saver 199
Customize the Finder 202
    Finder windows 202
    Changing icons 207
Open and Close Widgets 209
Widgets Supplied with Leopard 210
Advanced Dashboard 212
    Managing widgets 212
    Setting preferences in widgets 213
Where to Find More Cool Widgets 214
Create Your Own Widgets Using Web Clips 215

chapter 11

How Do I Change Leopard's
System Preferences? 218

Personal 220
    International 220
    Security 222
Hardware 225
    CDs & DVDs 225
    Displays 225
    Energy Saver 226
    Keyboard & Mouse 227
    Sound 228

Internet & Network 229
    MobileMe 229
    Network 229
    QuickTime 231
System 232
    Date & Time 232
    Software Update 233
    Speech 234
    Startup Disk 235
    Universal Access 235
Other System Preferences 236

chapter 12

How Do I Configure User
Accounts? 238

Types of Accounts 240
    Administrator 240
    Standard 240
    Managed with Parental Controls 240
    Sharing Only 241
Creating New User Accounts 241
    Password assistance 243
    Modify account settings 243
Logging Into Accounts 246
    Login Options 246
    Login Items 247

Enable Parental Controls   249

Simple Finder   250

Limit Access to Specific Applications
  and Functions   252

Restrict Internet and E-mail Access   254

  Web site restrictions   254

  Mail and iChat limitations   256

Set Time Limits   257

Keep Account Activity Logs   258

chapter 13

How Can I Share Files and
Other Items?   260

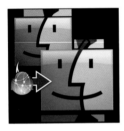

Using the Sharing System Preferences   262

  Sharing preferences at a glance   262

File Sharing   264

  Add shared folders and users   265

  Enabling file-sharing protocols   267

Printer Sharing   267

  Sharing with Mac OS X users   268

  Sharing with Windows users   268

Remote Management   269

Sharing through Bluetooth   270

  Using Bluetooth File Exchange   271

chapter 14

How Can I Automate My Mac?   274

Getting Around in Automator   276

Using Workflows   277

  Designing a workflow   278

  Saving your workflows   282

Recording Your Own Actions   282

Discovering Time Machine   284

  Why it's important to back up
    your files   284

  Hardware requirements for using
    Time Machine   284

Set Up a Backup Disk   285

  Formatting a hard disk   285

  Tell Time Machine about the
    backup disk   286

Select the Files You Want to Back Up   288

Working with Backups   289

  Manual backup   289

  Pause and resume a backup   290

Retrieve Information from Time Machine   290

  Restore individual files   290

  Restore an entire disk   291

chapter 15

What Can I Do with UNIX
Commands in Terminal?   294

Tinkering with Terminal   296
   Terminal preferences   296
   Tabbed windows   300
Entering UNIX Commands   301
   Navigating a CLI   301
   Common commands   302
   It's a bird! It's a plane! It's superuser!   303
Where to Find Additional UNIX
   Information   305

chapter 16

Can I Install Windows on My Mac?   306

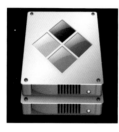

Understanding Boot Camp   308
   Benefits of installing Microsoft
     Windows   308
   What you need in order to
     install Windows   309

Using Boot Camp to Install Windows   309
   How to partition your hard disk   310
   Windows installation   312
Choosing a Startup Disk   313
   From Windows   314
   From Leopard   314
Removing Windows from Your Mac   315

chapter 17

Do You Have Any
Troubleshooting Tips?   316

Problem Solving 101   318
Make Sure You Are Up-to-Date   318
Startup Issues   319
   Your Mac won't power up   319
   Your Mac is hung at startup   320
   Handy startup keyboard shortcuts   321
Isolating Software Troubles   322
Permissions Problems   323
When All Else Fails, Reinstall   325
Index   326

Introduction

Thank you, Apple! Once again you've raised the bar for your competitors and knocked the socks off the rest of us. Leopard isn't only the best-looking operating system around, it's also the most functional and easy to use.

Some of you may be rolling your eyes right now; all computers use the file and folder concept and some sort of colorful user interface, so there couldn't be that much difference between Mac OS X and its competitors, right? Wrong. I don't just say this because of some blind devotion to all things Apple; I've actually used different flavors of Windows and Linux for more than 13 years, right alongside my trusty Mac, so experience has been my teacher. If I have any devotion to Apple, there are plenty of good reasons why, the subject of this book being the first.

Readers of this book who are already Mac users understand exactly what I'm talking about. For those of you moving from other computing platforms, it's my desire that by the end of this book you will have a whole new perspective on computing and see what it means to really have fun while working with your computer.

In *Mac OS X Leopard Portable Genius* you can learn not just the basics, but the subtle nuances and little tips and tricks that make using your Mac that much easier. I've covered the gamut, from printing files, surfing the Internet and using e-mail, to partitioning your hard drive, automating repetitive tasks, and using UNIX commands, with just a little bit of geeky humor thrown in for good measure.

I hope this book will do justice to Mac OS X Leopard, which isn't just a computer operating system; it's an art form.

What Are the Basics I Need to Know about Leopard?

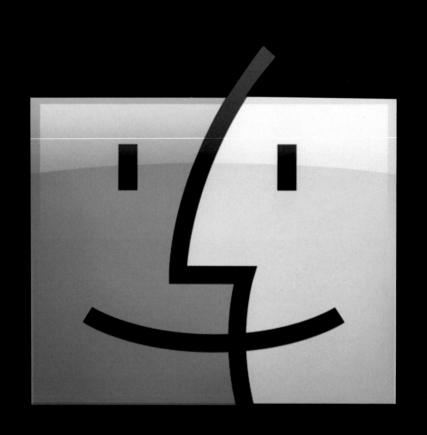

You are about to embark on the world's most advanced operating system experience, courtesy of Apple Inc. In this chapter, I show you how to get Mac OS X Leopard up and running, as well as how to navigate Leopard using the Finder application, which helps you find just about anything on your Mac.

System Requirements for Installing Leopard. 4

Choose an Installation Method 4

Upgrade to Leopard 5

Custom Installations 6

Advanced Installation Options. 8

Explore the Finder 10

Moving Around in the Finder 16

Utilizing the Dock 22

Exposé. 23

Spaces 25

Spotlight. 27

Searching with the Finder 30

System Requirements for Installing Leopard

As anxious as you probably are to get started, make sure that your Mac meets all the necessary hardware requirements for properly installing and running Leopard. Table 1.1 lists the require-ments, which are straight from Apple.

Table 1.1 Requirements for Installing Leopard

Requirement	Minimum Specifications
Processor	Intel processor or a PowerPC G4 (867 MHz or faster) or G5 processor
Memory	512MB of RAM just to get Leopard up and going
	2GB is needed to run all the bells and whistles at a decent speed
Media	DVD drive
Hard disk space	At least 9GB of free space

Choose an Installation Method

Only you can decide how to install Leopard. Should you upgrade or wipe everything clean on your hard drive and start all over with a fresh OS install? Let's look at the options.

Upgrading from a previous version of the Mac OS has its advantages, to be sure:

- **There is no need to create new user accounts for every user.**

- **You don't have to reload all of your applications and documents.**

- **The Leopard installer does all the difficult work, migrating user account informa-tion such as passwords, e-mail accounts, and Safari bookmarks.**

These are compelling reasons to simply upgrade and be done with it. However, there are also a couple of good reasons not to upgrade:

- **If you have Mac OS X 10.2 or earlier, you can't upgrade to Leopard.** You must have 10.3 or 10.4.

- **If your Mac has been exhibiting some weird behavior lately, it is most likely system-related.** It's best to start over if this is the case.

- You may want to simply start over, especially if your Mac has become bloated with extraneous application and documents that you've forgotten about or neglected to maintain.

Weigh the six points I've just listed and decide for yourself whether to upgrade or not. If you choose to upgrade, simply continue on to the next section. Should you decide to wipe the drive clean and start fresh, skip to the "Custom Installations" section to get going quickly.

Upgrade to Leopard

Let's get started with your upgrade to the newest feline from Apple:

1. **Insert the Leopard installation disc into your Mac.**

2. **When the disc mounts, the Mac OS X Install DVD automatically opens, as shown in figure 1.1.**

3. **Double-click the Install Mac OS X icon.**

4. **Click the Restart button in the Install Mac OS X window, shown in figure 1.2.**

5. **Once your Mac reboots, select the language you want to use for the installation process and click the forward arrow.**

6. **Click Continue at the Welcome screen.**

7. **Agree to the software license agreement.**

8. **Choose the hard drive on which you want to install Leopard and click Continue.**

9. **Click the Install button in the Install Summary window.**

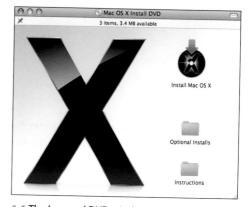

1.1 The Leopard DVD window

1.2 Press the Restart button to begin the installation process.

10. **Sit back, get a cup of your favorite beverage, read the Welcome to Leopard manual that came in the Mac OS X Leopard retail box, and when the installation is finished, you will be fully Leopardized!**

Caution

If you are installing Leopard on your startup disk, do not stop the installation process! If the process doesn't finish, you may not be able to start up from your hard drive. If you are installing on a laptop, make sure the power supply is connected before beginning the installation so that the process isn't stopped due to low battery power.

Custom Installations

Should you decide to completely start over with your Mac, you've come to the right section of this chapter. To "start over" means to completely install a fresh operating system and not upgrade over an existing one. There are two ways to start over with your Mac: archive installations and erase installations.

Archive and install

When you perform an archive installation, the Mac OS X Installer creates an archive of your existing system software and then installs an entirely new system. This prevents you from completely erasing the previous system, which will allow you to retrieve items from the archived system later if you need to. For example, you may want to find an old Safari bookmarks file and import it into Safari or some other Web browser that you use with Leopard.

The best thing about the archive installation is that you can have the Mac OS X Installer preserve all of your user accounts and their home folders, along with your network settings, and import them into Leopard. This alone can save you massive amounts of time.

To perform an archive and install:

1. **Insert the installation disc into your Mac and restart the computer.**

2. **Immediately after you hear the startup sound, hold down the C key to boot from the installation disc.** Continue to hold the C key until you see the gray Apple logo on the screen.

3. **Choose the language you want to use for the installation process and click the forward arrow.**

4. **Click Continue at the Welcome screen.**

5. **Agree to the software license agreement.**

6. **Choose the hard drive you want to install Leopard on and then click the Options button in the lower-left corner.**

7. **Select Archive and Install.** I whole-heartedly recommend that you check the Preserve Users and Network Settings check box.

8. **Click OK and then click Continue on the Select a Destination screen.**

9. **Click the Install button in the Install Summary window.**

Erase and install

The erase and install option does exactly what it states: It completely erases your entire hard disk and installs a completely new copy of Leopard.

Caution
Back up your files before performing this kind of installation! You will lose all the data on your drive when you choose an erase and install. It is almost inevitable that after the process is complete, you will slap your forehead in disgust, realizing you just erased Grandma's recipes that have been passed down for generations.

To perform an erase and install:

1. **Insert the installation disc into your Mac and restart the computer.**

2. **Immediately after you hear the startup sound, hold down the C key to boot from the installation disc.** Continue to hold the C key until you see the gray Apple logo on the screen.

3. **Choose the language you want to use for the installation process and click the forward arrow.**

4. **Click Continue at the Welcome screen.**

5. **Agree to the software license agreement.**

6. **Choose the hard drive you want to install Leopard on and then click the Options button in the lower-left corner.**

7. **Select Erase and Install.**

8. **Select Mac OS Extended (Journaled) for the Format disk as option.**

9. **Click OK and then click Continue on the Select a Destination screen.**

10. **Click the Install button in the Install Summary window.**

Advanced Installation Options

There are a couple of other things I want to show you that can help customize your Leopard instal-lation.

Partition your hard drive

If you have a large hard drive, you can partition it, meaning that you can divide the physical drive with software to make the drive appear and even operate as if it were multiple disks. This is advan-tageous if you plan to install Windows on your Mac using Boot Camp (see Chapter 16), using part of your drive for the OS and other parts for storing your documents and information, or if you want to install multiple versions of Mac OS X on one computer. Of course, there are many more reasons you would partition your drive, but you get the idea.

To partition your drive:

1. **Insert the installation disc into your Mac and restart the computer.**

2. **Immediately after you hear the startup sound, hold down the C key to boot from the installation disc.** Continue to hold the C key until you see the gray Apple logo on the screen.

3. **Select the language you want to use for the installation process and click the forward arrow.**

4. **Choose Utilities ⇨ Disk Utility from the menu.**

5. **Select the disk in the volume list on the left side of the Disk Utility window, as shown in figure 1.3.**

6. **Click the Partition tab in the window and then click the + button in the lower-left cor-ner to begin adding partitions to the Volume Scheme.**

7. **Select a format for each partition using the Format menu.**

8. **You can resize each partition by typing a size into the Size box.**

9. **Click Apply when you are ready to partition the drive.**

Install the Xcode Developer Tools

The Leopard installation disc comes with all the tools that application developers need to get started with programming for Mac OS X. These tools, called Xcode developer tools, can easily be installed from the Mac OS X Install DVD. They are found in the Optional Installs folder on the disc; the path to the installer is shown in figure 1.4.

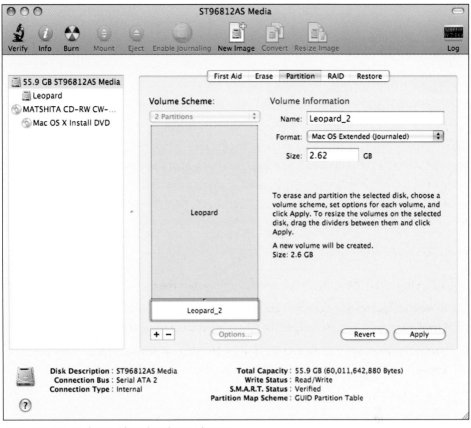

1.3 Partitioning a drive with Disk Utility is a breeze.

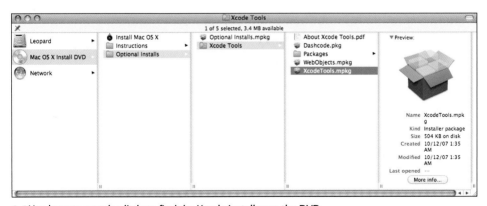

1.4 You have to search a little to find the Xcode installer on the DVD.

To install the Xcode developer tools:

1. **Double-click the XcodeTools.mpkg file to launch the installer and click Continue.**

2. **Click Continue again in the Software License Agreement window and then agree to the license agreement.**

3. **Click the Install button in the Standard Install on "Leopard" window to begin the installation (see figure 1.5).**

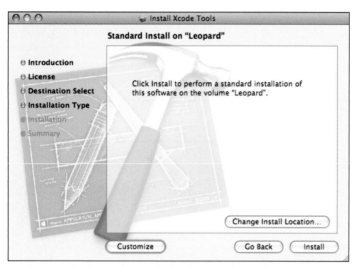

1.5 Click Install to begin the Xcode developer tools installer process.

Explore the Finder

Once your Mac has booted or when you first log in, take a look at that smiley-face guy grinning at you near the bottom-left corner of your screen. That's the Finder, and it's one of the most important items in all of Mac OS X Leopard.

The Finder is an application that always runs in Leopard, and it has been a part of the Mac OS since its inception. The Finder is what Mac fans have used for decades to browse their computers' drives and discs, and it has evolved into a great tool that I can't imagine not having (especially as you can't view the contents of your hard drive without it!). For the Windows converts in the audience, think of the Finder as the Mac OS X equivalent to Explorer (Windows Explorer, that is, not Internet Explorer). In this section, I show you how to use the Finder's basic features, and I also give you tips that I've learned to make the Finder even easier and more productive to use.

The Leopard Desktop at a glance

The Desktop is what you see when you first start up or log in to your Mac; this area is where all the action in your applications takes place. The Desktop is a major part, and is actually the starting point, of the Finder.

Desktop

Figure 1.6 should mirror your own Mac's screen very closely after you've logged in; it lists the major parts that you see when the Finder first comes up.

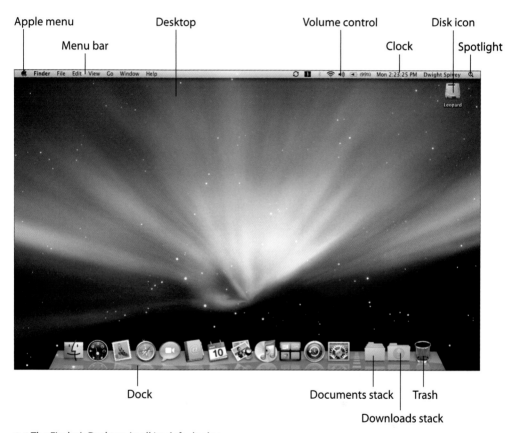

1.6 The Finder's Desktop, in all its default glory.

Now that you know the names of the items you see in the Finder, let's use Table 1.2 to decipher what functionality they provide.

Table 1.2 Finder items

Item	Function
Apple menu	Provides quick access to functions such as Sleep, Restart, Shut Down, Recent Items, and System Preferences. Windows users will find that it functions similarly to the Start menu that they are used to.
Menu bar	Use the menu bar in the Finder and in other applications to print, copy and paste, and change application preferences.
Desktop	Functions like the desktop on your desk; it's where everything else (such as documents and applications) sits while you are working on it. You can easily change the Desktop picture; see Chapter 10 for more details.
Volume control	Adjusts your Mac's volume.
Clock	Displays the current date and time.
Spotlight	Searches your Mac for files and folders. See this chapter's section "Spotlight" for more information.
Disk icon	The particular icon shown in figure 1.6 is that of my hard drive, but if you have more than one disk on your Mac, you will also see them listed here.
Dock	Houses links to applications and other items that you use most frequently. You can modify the Dock, as you'll see later on in this chapter.
Trash	Contains files and folders that you want to remove from your Mac. Former Windows users will find it similar to the Recycle Bin.
Downloads stack	Provides fast access to items in your Home folder's Downloads folder.
Documents stack	Provides fast access to items in your Home folder's Documents folder.

Finder windows

Now that you are more familiar with the features of the Desktop, let's examine a Finder window, which is the mechanism you will need to view files and folders on your disks. Figure 1.7 shows a default Finder window, and Table 1.3 gives a brief breakdown of each noteworthy item.

Table 1.3 Finder window components

Component	Description
Folders	Used to store files and other subfolders.
Toolbar	Contains tools for accessing files and folders.
Sidebar	Provides quick links to disks, favorite folders, shared folders, and preconfigured searches.
Statistics bar	Displays information about the current folder.
Hide Toolbar button	Click to hide the toolbar and sidebar from view; click again to bring the toolbar and sidebar back.
Search field	Enter a search term to look for the item in the current folder.

Component	Description
Results window	Shows the files and subfolders that reside in a folder, and also displays search results.
Vertical/Horizontal scroll bar and arrows	Drag the bars or click the arrows to navigate to areas of a window that are hidden from view.

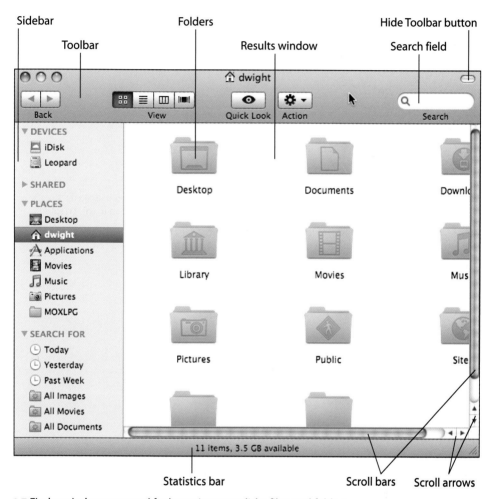

1.7 Finder windows are used for browsing your disks, files, and folders.

Set the Finder preferences

As you'll notice throughout this book, you can modify most things in Leopard to match your personal preferences and tastes (to one degree or another), and that's the way I like it. The Finder is no exception to this rule (see Chapter 10 for a lot of Finder customization tips), giving you access to its preferences by choosing Finder ⇨ Preferences, or by pressing ⌘+,. Let's take a look at the preferences that the Finder allows us to control.

General

Figure 1.8 shows the General tab of the Finder Preferences window.

1.8 Options available in the General tab.

The General tab options are fairly self-explanatory, with the exception of Spring-loaded folders and windows, which are so cool that they get their own sidebar. The other three options allow you to:

- **Show certain types of items on the Desktop.**

- **Choose which folder to automatically enter when you open a new Finder window.**

- **Decide whether to always open folders in new (separate) windows.** I do not recommend that you use this feature, unless you are someone who just can't get enough open windows on their Desktop.

Spring-Loaded Folders and Windows

Spring-loaded folders and windows are a neat feature of the Finder but are foreign to many Mac users, especially the new recruits, so I'll take a minute to mention them separately. Enabling spring-loaded folders and windows lets you move items between folders and disks with minimal effort. With this feature enabled, you can drag an item over any folder, hold it there for just a split second, and the folder automatically opens. Continue to hold the mouse button down while you position the item over each subfolder, and they will all behave accordingly, automatically opening and allowing you to drill down into the subfolders as far as you need to. Finally, drop the item into the folder you want to move it to by letting go of the mouse button. Reading a description of this feature can be pretty boring, so give it a try on your own so that you can master this nifty little trick.

You can securely empty the Trash on a case-by-case basis instead of enabling it all the time. To do so, place the item you want to permanently delete in the Trash, and then choose Finder ⇨ Secure Empty Trash from the menu.

Labels and Sidebar

The Labels tab allows you to assign colored labels to categories that you determine. You can then assign these labels to files and folders by right-clicking them (or Ctrl+clicking if you don't have a two-button mouse), and then selecting a label from the list, as shown in figure 1.9.

The Sidebar tab of the Finder Preferences window simply lets you choose which types of items to display in the Sidebar of every Finder window.

Advanced

Table 1.4 explains the options that are available in the Advanced tab of the Finder Preferences.

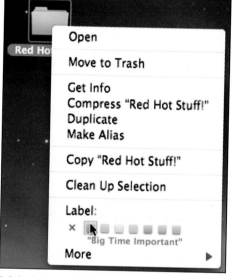

1.9 Assigning a label to a folder.

Table 1.4 Advanced Tab Options

Option	Function
Show all file extensions	Each file has an extension on the end of its name that is hidden by default. This extension helps Leopard know what type of document the file is, and what application it is associated with. Unless you understand these extensions, it is best to leave this option unchecked.
Show warning before changing an extension	Leopard warns you that you are about to change the extension of a file. This warning is beneficial so that you won't accidentally change an extension, which could cause your document to open in a different application than intended, if at all.
Show warning before emptying the Trash	Leopard prompts you to confirm that you mean to empty the Trash before allowing you to do so.
Empty Trash securely	Select this option to make certain that all traces of a file are removed from the hard drive when you empty the Trash. This is a feature security nuts will love, but it prevents you from ever recovering any files you may have accidentally deleted. Use this option with caution.

Moving Around in the Finder

Mac OS X employs the same basic navigation techniques as any other graphical operating system, such as double-clicking to open files and folders, right-clicking (or Ctrl+clicking) items to see contextual menus that can alter or perform an action on an item (like the Labels example you saw earlier in this chapter), and clicking-and-dragging items to move them to and fro. I'm sure you're all experienced at the basics of mouse operations, so I'll move on to more Finder-centric tasks and options.

Finder viewing options

You can change the way files and folders are displayed in Finder windows by choosing one of the four View options in the toolbar. Let's look at how each option displays the contents of the same folder so that you can see the clear differences between each view.

Icons

Icons view shows each file and folder as large icons in the window, as shown in figure 1.10.

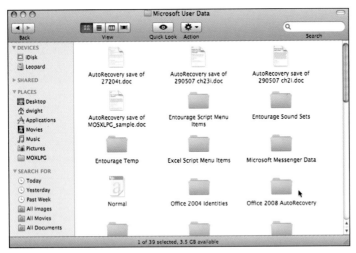

1.10 A folder as seen in Icons view.

Genius

Are the default icons too large or small for your liking? Change them by pressing ⌘+J to open the viewing options window. Drag the Icon size slider to enlarge or reduce the icon sizes in the current folder.

List

List view does just what it says: It displays the files and folders in a list. You can arrange the list by filenames, the date the files were modified, the size of the file or folder, and the kind of item it is.

Columns

My personal favorite is Columns view. This view arranges the contents of a folder into columns, with each column displaying the contents of the subsequent folder.

Cover Flow

Cover Flow is hands-down the coolest viewing option at your disposal. Figure 1.11 shows that the files and folders are displayed as they really appear when opened in an application, which can be a great help when searching for a particular document or picture.

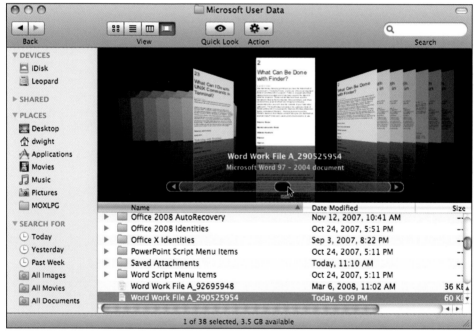

1.11 Cover Flow is really neat to use. Drag the slider back and forth to see how effortlessly the Finder zooms through the files in the folder.

Get information on files and folders

You can never have too much information, and Mac OS X is more than happy to provide you with what you need to know about your computer's files and folders. To find out what there is to know about an item:

Quickly Open Commonly Used Folders

I can't speak for other Mac users, but the Finder menu that I most wish I had discovered years ago is the Go menu. The Go menu gives you instant access to the most commonly used folders in Leopard, but for some reason I overlooked it for most of the eight-plus years I've used Mac OS X. Click the Go menu to quickly go to the Applications folder, the Utilities folder, your Network, and more.

Better yet, familiarize yourself with the keyboard shortcuts that are used to access those items (the keyboard shortcuts are listed to the right of each command in the Go menu). If an item you want to jump to isn't in the Go menu, press ⌘+Shift+G to open the Go to Folder window; then type the path of the folder you want, and click the Go button to jump over to it.

1. **Click (once) the file or folder you want information about.**
2. **Press ⌘+I, or choose File ⇨ Get Info from the menu.**

Figure 1.12 shows you a typical Info window, and Table 1.5 explains the categories that are available in the window.

Table 1.5 Information Categories

Category	Information displayed
Spotlight Comments	Enter information about the file that will help you find it using a Spotlight search (see this chapter's section "Spotlight" for more information).
General	Tells you information such as what kind of item you're viewing, its size, where it's located, and when it was created and/or modified.
More Info	The additional information shown here will vary, depending on the type of item this is. For example, for the folder in figure 1.12, you can see when the folder was last opened. If the file were an image, you might see its dimensions and color space.
Name & Extension	Allows you to change the name and extension of the file, and to hide the extension.
Open with	Select the default application that you want to open this type of file with. This option only displays when getting info about a file.
Preview	Shows a small thumbnail version of the file.
Sharing & Permissions	Allows you to change access permissions for the item. Click the lock icon in the bottom-right corner to change the permissions. Click the + or – buttons to add or remove users from the permissions list.

Using Quick Look

Quick Look is one of the best new features in Leopard. It allows you to see the contents of a file without actually opening it in its native application. For example, you can see every page of a Word document without having to open Word itself. This makes it really easy to find a document if you've forgotten its name but know the content that you're looking for, or when you're looking for just the right image but don't want to have to wait for Photoshop to load. To use Quick Look:

1. **Find the file you want to view and click it once to highlight it.**

2. **Click the Quick Look button or press the space bar to open the file, as shown in figure 1.13.**

3. **To see the item in Full Screen mode, click the arrows at the bottom of the window.** To exit Full Screen mode, click the arrows again.

4. **Close the Quick Look window by clicking the X in the upper-left corner.**

1.12 A Get Info window with most of the categories expanded.

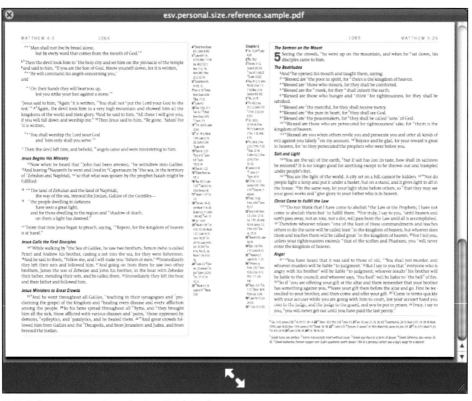

1.13 A document previewed using Quick Look.

Examine Files with the Inspector

You can use the Inspector, which is a floating version of the Get Info window, to quickly get information on multiple items without having to open separate Get Info windows for each one. To do this:

1. **Open a folder that contains the items you want to see information about.**

2. **Press ⌘+Option+I to open the Inspector window (it looks just like a standard Get Info window).**

3. **Click each file in the folder to see its information in the Inspector window.** The Inspector changes information for each file you select. You can move between files by using the arrow keys on the keyboard.

Working with removable media

When you insert or connect removable media, such as CDs, DVDs, external hard disks, and USB flash drives, Leopard automatically mounts them, making them immediately available for use. The media's icon appears on your Desktop, in a Finder window, or both, as shown in figure 1.14, depending on how you have configured your Finder preferences. Double-click the icon to see the media's contents, just as you would any other hard disk or folder.

1.14 A CD and a flash drive as they appear on the Desktop and in the Sidebar of the Finder window.

Perform one of the following steps to disconnect or eject removable media:

- **Click the Eject icon to the right of the media icon in the Sidebar of the Finder window.**

- **Drag the media icon from the Desktop and drop it on the Trash icon in the Dock.**

- **Right-click or Ctrl+click the media icon on the Desktop or in the Sidebar, and then select Eject from the contextual menu.**

- **Click the icon for the media once to highlight it and press ⌘+E.**

Utilizing the Dock

Ah, the Dock: loved by most, tolerated by some, and loathed by a few. Regardless of how you feel about the Dock (personally, I can't imagine working without it), it is an integral part of your Leopard experience. The Dock is where you keep aliases, or shortcuts, to applications, utilities, and folders that you use or access more frequently than others. It also displays icons for all your currently running applications, and even some processes, like print jobs. Currently running applications have a bright dot underneath their icons.

The Dock is divided into two sections by a divider line. Applications and utilities reside on the left side of the divider line, while folders reside on the right with the Trash icon. Right-click, or Ctrl+click, the divider line to see display options for Dock.

Adding and removing items

You can add and remove items to and from the Dock as you please, and it's really easy to do:

- **To add an item to the Dock, simply drag its icon to the Dock and drop it in where you want it to go.** You can reposition an item in the Dock by simply dragging-and-dropping it to its new location.

- **If you have an application open that you'd like to keep in the Dock, click and hold its icon (as shown in figure 1.15), and select Keep in Dock from the contextual menu that appears.**

- **To remove an item, drag its icon from the Dock and let go of the mouse button.** The icon disappears in a puff of smoke! Don't worry: the original item is still in its location; you've only removed the alias for the item.

1.15 Keep an icon in the Dock if you need to use it often.

Set the Dock's preferences

You can tame the Dock by setting its preferences to meet your needs. Open the Dock's preferences by right-clicking, or Ctrl+clicking, the divider line, and select Dock Preferences.

The Dock preferences window lets you make several changes:

- **Increase or decrease the size of the Dock by moving the Size slider.**

- **If your icons are too small to see clearly, check the Magnification check box and adjust the slider to increase or decrease the amount of magnification.**

- **The Dock can be positioned on the left or right side of the window, or at the bottom, which is its default setting.**

- **The Minimize using option lets you choose the special effect that occurs when you minimize a window into the Dock.** To minimize a window, click the yellow button in its upper-left corner.

- **Check the Animate opening applications check box to cause the icon of an item you are opening to bounce up and down in the Dock.** I leave this option unchecked; the bouncing annoys the heck out of me.

- **If you don't like the Dock cramping your style — or your Desktop space, for that matter — you can hide it from view by checking the box next to Automatically hide and show the Dock.** When you inevitably have to use the Dock again, hold your mouse pointer at the very bottom of your window for just a second, and the Dock will temporarily pop back up into view, only to go back into hiding when you're finished.

Exposé

Exposé is a great feature for helping to clear up the jumbled mess of windows that can grind your productivity to a halt. Exposé arranges your windows in one of three ways using three of the function keys at the top of your keyboard: F9, F10, and F11.

Manipulating open windows

Press F9 to arrange the open windows so that they can all be seen, as shown in figure 1.16. Move the mouse pointer over the windows to see what applications they belong to. Click the window you want to bring to the forefront, or press F9 to return to the Finder's previous state.

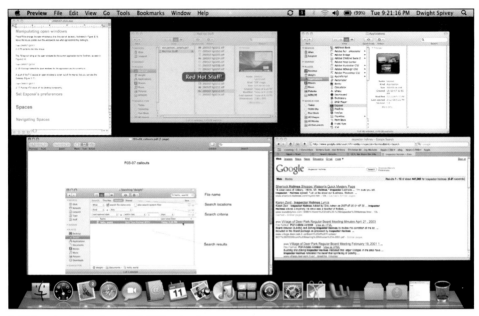

1.16 Pressing F9 performs this little miracle.

The F10 key brings all the open windows for the current application to the forefront. A push of the F11 key causes all open windows to scram out of the way so that you can see the Desktop. Press F10 or F11 respectively to return the Finder to its previous state.

Set Exposé preferences

Open the Exposé preferences by choosing Apple menu ➪ System Preferences, and then selecting the Exposé & Spaces icon. Table 1.6 explains the options available in the Exposé tab of the Exposé & Spaces preferences window.

Table 1.6 Exposé Preferences Explained

Section	Options
Active Screen Corners	Click any of the four pop-up menus to choose what actions Leopard takes when you move your mouse pointer to a corner of your screen.
Exposé	Customize the keys or key combinations that perform Exposé actions.
Dashboard	Choose which function key will cause Dashboard to open and close.

Spaces

Spaces is a new addition to Mac OS X. It is an organizational tool that lets you create multiple spaces for certain tasks. Spaces are essentially additional desktops. You could have a space for surfing the Web and checking e-mail, another space to watch your stocks, a third space to work on a spreadsheet, and so forth.

Set Spaces preferences

Choose the Apple menu, select System Preferences, and then click the Exposé & Spaces icon. Click the Spaces tab to see the Spaces preferences, as shown in figure 1.17.

To use the Spaces feature, you must enable it by checking the Enable Spaces check box in the preferences window.

Adding and removing spaces

You can have as many as 16 spaces at any one time. There's nothing magical about adding or removing spaces: Just click the + or – buttons next to the Rows and Columns options.

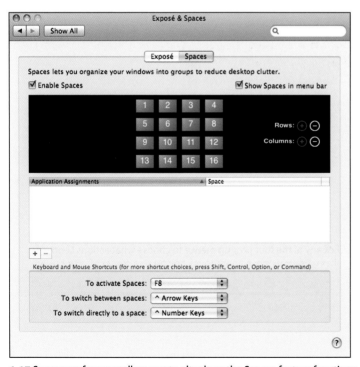

1.17 Spaces preferences allow you to alter how the Spaces feature functions.

Moving between spaces

There are a few ways to jump from space to space:

● **Press F8 and click the space you want to move to, as shown in figure 1.18.**

● **Check the Show Spaces in menu bar check box in the Spaces preferences; then click the Spaces icon in the menu bar and choose the number of the space you want to jump to.**

● **To scroll through the spaces, hold down the control key and press one of the arrow keys.**

● **I find that the easiest method is to simultaneously press the control key and the number key that corresponds to the space I want to navigate to.**

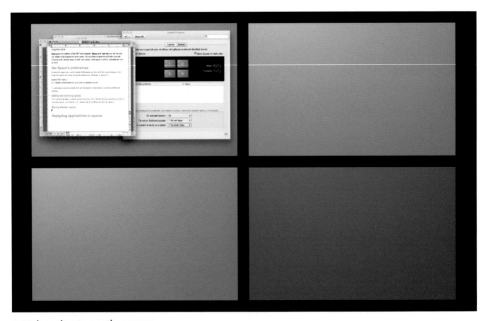

1.18 Jumping to another space.

Genius You can press F8 and then quickly move windows from one space to another by dragging them from their current space and dropping them onto the desired one. You can also rearrange spaces by clicking the blue area of a space and moving it to the location of the space you want it to trade places with.

Assigning applications to spaces

One feature I love in Spaces is the ability to assign applications to always open in a specific space.

To assign applications to spaces:

1. **Click the + button under the Application Assignments window in the Spaces tab of the Exposé & Spaces preferences.**

2. **Browse your hard drive for the applications or utilities you want to assign, select them, and click the Add button.**

3. **You can change the space that an application opens in by clicking the space selection column for that application, as shown in figure 1.19.**

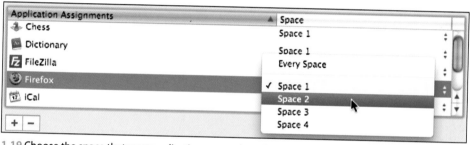

1.19 Choose the space that your applications are assigned to open in.

Spotlight

Apple introduced Spotlight in Mac OS X Tiger and instantly changed the way Mac users look for items on their computers. Spotlight finds things on your Mac much faster than you or I could if we were poking around every file and folder, and it's the quickest way to find things that I've ever seen on a computer.

When you first log in to your Mac, OS X creates an index of every file and folder it contains; Leopard knows everything there is to know about every single thing that occupies your Mac's space, whether the item is visible or invisible. Leopard stores this information, or *metadata*, and Spotlight uses the information, along with filenames and content, to find what you are looking for. Every time you add or remove an item, or add or remove something within that item (like text within a document), Leopard updates its index files, thereby keeping all your searches up-to-the-minute accurate.

You might think that with all this information to look through a search could take forever, but that's not the case at all. Spotlight can find items containing your search words almost as quickly as you can type them.

Searching with Spotlight

Chances are good that no matter how long it's been since you've seen the file you're looking for, Spotlight can dig it up for you again. Let's see how to use this amazing feature:

1. **Click the Spotlight icon (the magnifying glass) in the upper-right corner of your Mac's window to reveal the Search text field, as shown in figure 1.20.**

1.20 Enter your search words into Spotlight.

2. **Type your search criteria in the text field.** Some applications have Spotlight Search fields in their toolbars, which you can use to enter search words when specifically searching for items within that application (for example, when searching for an e-mail within Mail).

3. **Spotlight immediately begins searching your Mac, and displays the information it finds that matches the criteria you entered in step 2.**

4. **Scan the list to find the item you are specifically looking for and then click to open it in its default application.** Spotlight only shows the top matches in each category; in order to see all the matches click Show All at the top of the list.

Genius

Did you notice that Spotlight isn't just showing you items such as documents and folders that contain your search words? Spotlight literally searches every file on your Mac for your search criteria, including e-mails, Web pages you've visited, contacts, music, movies, images, and PDF files. Spotlight can even search other Macs on your network that you have connected to, if they have file sharing enabled.

Setting Spotlight preferences

You can easily modify Spotlight to search where and how you want it to, using its preferences. Choose Apple menu ⇨ System Preferences, and then click the Spotlight icon in the Personal section to access the Spotlight preferences pane, as shown in figure 1.21.

Figure 1.21 shows the Search Results section of the preferences pane. This section lists the categories of files that will appear in the search results window. Check the check box next to those categories you want Spotlight to search in, and uncheck those you want to leave alone. For example, if you don't want Spotlight to check your e-mail when performing a search, simply uncheck the check box next to the Mail Messages category. You can also click-and-drag the categories into the order you prefer the results to be displayed in.

Click the Privacy tab at the top of the preferences pane to reveal the Privacy list. This section allows you to specify directories (folders) on your Mac that you want to exclude from any searches.

To modify the Privacy list:

1. **Click the + button under the bottom-left corner of the list.**

2. **Browse your Mac for the folder you want to exclude from searches, highlight the folder, and then click Choose. The folder is now shown in the Privacy list.**

3. **You can remove a folder from the list by highlighting it and then clicking the – button under the bottom-left corner of the list.**

The two check boxes at the bottom of the preferences pane allow you to enable Spotlight keyboard shortcuts for opening a Spotlight menu or window (more on Spotlight windows in the next section of this chapter) at the stroke of a couple of keys. You can also select which keys perform these functions. See the sidebar at the end of this chapter for more on Spotlight keyboard shortcuts.

Searching with the Spotlight menu is certainly fast and easy, but it doesn't always yield the best results, as it may give you so many results that you could never realistically search them all in a reasonable amount of time. To remedy this situation, Spotlight brings in our trusty friend, the Finder.

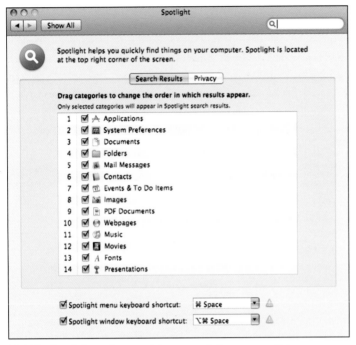

1.21 The Spotlight preferences let you search the way you like.

Searching with the Finder

The Finder gives you much more leverage to enhance your search beyond the Spotlight menu's capabilities.

To perform a basic Spotlight search within a Finder window:

1. **Open a Finder window by pressing ⌘+N while the Finder is activated (click the Finder icon on the left side of the Dock if you aren't sure the Finder is the activated, or foremost, application).**

2. **Browse your Mac for the folder that you know includes the files you are looking for or through, and click the folder to highlight it.**

3. **Type the search criteria into the Search text field in the upper-right corner of the Finder window, and you see your results displayed in the Finder.**

Any search utility worth using will allow a lot of flexibility to narrow searches, and Spotlight is as flexible as they come.

Figure 1.22 shows a Finder search window that has been assigned several search attributes, which act as filters for your search results. These attributes allow you to specify the type of file you want, when it was last modified, whether the file is visible or not, and many, many other attribute types.

1.22 Attributes narrow a search in a big way.

To add attributes to a search:

1. **Click the + button next to the Save button in the upper-right area of the Finder window.**

2. **Choose the type of attribute to use by clicking the pop-up menu on the left side of the search window, as shown in figure 1.22.** There are many more attributes preconfigured by Apple that you can access by choosing Other from the attribute list. You can also add other conditions (specifically, the "All, Any, or None of the following are true" criteria) to the search by holding down the Option button while clicking the + button.

3. **Make any setting changes to the attribute to narrow your search.**

4. **Your new filtered search results are displayed almost instantly after you add an attribute.**

5. **Continue to add as many attributes as necessary, or remove attributes by clicking the – buttons to their far right.**

Genius

Use Boolean operators such as AND, OR, and NOT to logically narrow your search. You may also use quotes around text to specify that the words in the quotes must be found in exactly the order you typed them.

Making Spotlight Even Faster

Spotlight is already amazingly fast, but you can still give it a further speed boost by using keyboard shortcuts. The keyboard shortcuts in Table 1.7 will make searching for items even easier than using Spotlight with your mouse.

Table 1.7 Spotlight Keyboard Shortcuts

Function	Keys
Open the Spotlight menu	⌘+space bar
Open the Spotlight (Finder) window	⌘+Option+space bar
Open the top search result	⌘+Return
Jump to the first item in the next heading	⌘+Down arrow
Jump to the first item in the prior heading	⌘+Up arrow
Jump to the first item in the menu	Ctrl+Up arrow
Jump to the last item in the menu	Ctrl+Down arrow
Show an item in the Finder	Click the item while holding down ⌘

What Applications Are Included with Leopard?

Leopard is more than just an operating system; it's also full of applications and utilities designed to make your computing life as productive as possible, while at the same time being simple and fun to use. From word processing to buying music online, from surfing the Web to running connectivity diagnostics on your network, Mac OS X 10.5 comes loaded with all the tools you need. Unlike competitors' operating systems, Mac OS X comes in only one flavor: fully loaded! This chapter introduces you to the myriad of programs that come with Leopard so that you will know exactly what you can do with this big cat. I also show you how to navigate most Mac applications, as well as how to use common keyboard shortcuts. For good measure, I go in-depth with one of Leopard's included applications — Mac OS X's word processing application, TextEdit.

Discover Leopard's Applications and Utilities 36

Navigate Leopard's Applications 44

Create and Work with Documents in TextEdit 47

Format Your Documents 50

Set TextEdit Preferences 53

Discover Leopard's Applications and Utilities

Leopard ships with almost 50 applications and utilities, each of which offers its unique way of handling various tasks. With so many applications, you might be wondering what in the world all these applications and utilities can do. I cover the lesser known or used applications in short detail in this chapter, going a bit more in-depth with Mac's word processor, TextEdit. Because I will cover some of the more high-profile applications in other chapters, I'll only give short introductions for them here (see Table 2.3).

Applications

Open the Applications folder, shown in figure 2.1, to see all the applications that are at your disposal:

- Click the Go menu in the Finder and select Applications.

- Press ⌘+Shift+A while in the Finder.

2.1 The Applications folder in all its glory.

Let's take a look at some of the too-often forgotten gems in Leopard.

Calculator

Calculator is not your run-of-the-mill addition, subtraction, multiplication, and division tool, although it can perform those basic functions with the best of them.

Calculator has three modes: Basic, Scientific, and Programmer. Table 2.1 gives a brief description of each mode.

Table 2.1 Calculator Modes

Mode	Function
Basic	Performs the traditional tasks of addition, multiplication, subtraction, and division.
Scientific	Expands the Basic mode to give you the ability to perform advanced mathematical calculations, such as trigonometric functions, factorial functions, and square roots.
Programmer	Performs calculations that only a true geek could love (or understand, for that matter). Programmers need to perform calculations such as hexadecimal conversion, binary computations, and logical operations; Calculator fits the bill perfectly, as shown in figure 2.2.

If you would like to see a printout of your calculations, you can use the Paper Tape function. Choose Window ⇨ Show Paper Tape, or press ⌘+T, to open the Paper Tape window. Choose File ⇨ Print Tape to print your calculations and results.

Chess

You may have noticed that Mac OS X Leopard doesn't come with Minesweeper and Hearts. No, the brainiacs at Apple prefer to include Chess, instead. Chess is one of the world's greatest games, and also one of the most challenging, making it the perfect game to include in such a classy operating system.

2.2 Calculator can also convert units of measure such as area, currency, speed, and volume.

To play a game of Chess, simply double-click its icon in the Applications folder. You can play against another person or test your wits against the Mac.

Choose Chess ➪ Preferences to change things such as the look of the pieces and board, the diffi-culty level of the computer player, and to allow moves to be spoken aloud. Refer to Chess's Help (choose Help ➪ Chess Help) for more information about this great version of a classic game.

Genius

If the board position isn't to your liking, click-and-drag one of the corners of the board in all directions, as shown in figure 2.3, until you get the view you want.

Dictionary

Dictionary, like all the other cool applications in Leopard, does more than just look up defini-tions to words. Use Dictionary as a standard dictionary (*New Oxford American Dictionary*, to be exact), as a thesaurus (*Oxford American Writer's Thesaurus*), to find terms in Apple's dic-tionary, and to discover articles on Wikipedia.

Simply type a word or topic in the search field in the upper-right corner of the window (next to the magnifying glass icon), as shown in fig-ure 2.4, to begin a search. Dictionary displays what it finds in all four sources, or only the one you select from the toolbar.

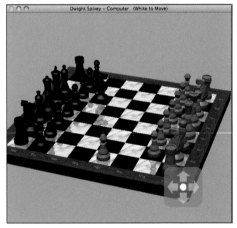

2.3 Change the board's position in the window by dragging a corner of the board.

DVD Player

DVD Player performs as advertised: It plays DVDs. Clever naming of the application by Apple, if you ask me.

DVD Player can perform all the basic func-tions of your regular DVD player. The upside to using this application instead is that you don't have to leave your Mac's side to catch a flick.

2.4 Dictionary is a great tool for students, writers, business professionals, and anyone else looking to find the meaning of a word.

You control the playback of movies with an onscreen remote, as opposed to holding one in your hand, as shown in figure 2.5.

2.5 DVD Player's remote control.

Genius

You can also control playback of your DVDs with your Mac's keyboard, using the keyboard shortcuts listed in Table 2.2.

Table 2.2 DVD Player Keyboard Shortcuts

Function	Keys
Play/Pause	Space bar
Stop	⌘+.
Scan Forward	⌘+Shift+→
Scan Backwards	⌘+Shift+←
Volume Up	⌘+↑
Volume Down	⌘+↓
Mute	⌘+Option+↓
Close Control Drawer	⌘+]
Eject DVD	⌘+E

Font Book

Fonts are very important to the look and feel of your Mac, as well as any documents you may create with its applications. Font Book is a fantastic utility that allows you to manage the fonts you have installed on your Mac.

Font Book, shown in figure 2.6, can install and delete fonts without you having to reboot your Mac. Use it to organize your fonts into collections, enable the fonts you want to use, or disable the fonts you don't want to use, rather than completely deleting them from the system altogether.

Refer to Font Book's Help (choose Help ⇨ Font Book Help) to find out more on using this exceptional utility.

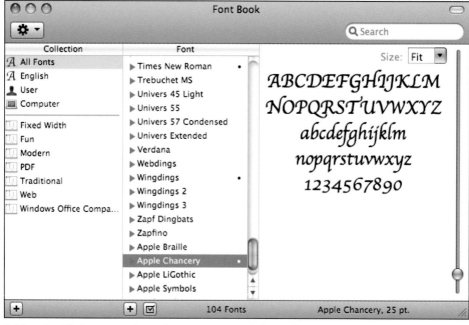

2.6 Font Book helps to organize and manage your Mac's font collections.

Stickies

Stickies is a nifty little application for keeping lists, creating reminders, and quickly entering any information you like. It uses the metaphor of the tiny yellow notes that we all have dangling off our computer monitors, with the exception that these stickies don't fall off and drift under your desk when you're not looking. Stickies automatically saves your notes. Figure 2.7 shows an example of the Stickies version of a virtual sticky note.

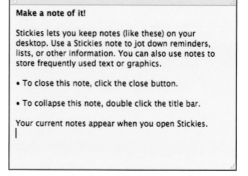

Make a note of it!

Stickies lets you keep notes (like these) on your desktop. Use a Stickies note to jot down reminders, lists, or other information. You can also use notes to store frequently used text or graphics.

• To close this note, click the close button.

• To collapse this note, double click the title bar.

Your current notes appear when you open Stickies.

2.7 An example of a sticky note.

Other applications

Table 2.3 lists other applications that come with Leopard and that are mentioned in greater detail in other chapters.

Table 2.3 More Leopard Applications

Application	Primary function
Address Book	Keeps contact information in one handy location. See Chapter 3 for more information.
Automator	Automates the tasks you find repetitive and mundane. Chapter 13 covers Automator in depth.
Dashboard	Organizes tiny applications called Widgets. There is much more on Dashboard and Widgets in Chapter 9.
Exposé	Helps organize your desktop clutter. Chapter 1 exposes much more of Exposé.
iCal	Lets you create calendars to keep up with your hourly, daily, weekly, monthly, and annual tasks and appointments. Chapter 3 goes into much more detail about iCal.
iChat	Lets you send instant messages to anyone anywhere in the world. iChat is discussed in Chapter 5.
Image Capture	Capture images from your scanners and digital cameras with this handy application. Learn much more in Chapter 7.
iSync	Synchronizes all your contacts and calendars with multiple devices. Chapter 3 goes into more detail.
iTunes	Your Mac's entertainment hub. Chapter 6 gives you the inside scoop.
Mail	Leopard's e-mail application. Discover how to use Mail in Chapter 5.
Photo Booth	Take pictures and videos using your Mac's built-in camera. See more in Chapter 7.
Preview	Capable of opening multiple file types, such as JPEGs, TIFFs, and PDFs. Chapter 8 covers Preview like a blanket.
QuickTime Player	Plays video and sound files in a multitude of formats.
Safari	Mac OS X's standout Web browser. Chapter 4 will have you cruising the Internet jungle in style.
Spaces	Lets you manage your open applications and windows in multiple desktop spaces. Chapter 1 shows you how to utilize this cool feature that's new to Leopard.
System Preferences	The one place where you can make Leopard behave the way you want it to. Make settings for your network, sharing files, changing your Mac's appearance, and much more by checking out Chapter 11.
TextEdit	Leopard's built-in word processor. Begin creating documents by perusing the "Create and Work with Documents in TextEdit" section later in this chapter.
Time Machine	Back up your Mac's files and folders to keep them safe and to restore them if necessary. Chapter 14 has all the lowdown on this very popular feature of Leopard.

Utilities

Utilities do a lot of the dirty work for your Mac. They diagnose problems with your network, help you partition your hard drive, format disks, manage color on your screen and in your documents, take screenshots, manage passwords, and much more. Table 2.4 lists the utilities that come with Leopard (as shown in figure 2.8), describes their main function in life, and lets you know whether more information on the utility can be found elsewhere in this book.

2.8 Mac OS X Leopard utilities, at your service.

Table 2.4 Leopard Utilities

Utility	Primary function
Activity Monitor	Keeps track of all the goings-on in Leopard, such as what applications are running and how much of the processor's capacity is being used.
AirPort Utility	Helps you manage your AirPort Base Station.
Audio MIDI Setup	Helps set up audio and MIDI devices that you connect to your Mac.
Bluetooth File Exchange	Transfers files to and from other devices running the Bluetooth protocol.
Boot Camp Assistant	Creates a separate partition on your Mac's hard drive for installing Microsoft Windows. Chapter 16 will give you the skinny on this awesome addition to Mac OS X.
ColorSync Utility	Manages your Mac's color profiles for devices such as monitors and printers.

Utility	Primary function
Console	Displays messages that are being generated by your Mac or its applications. These messages are generated when an error occurs. This utility is great for tracking down problems with Mac OS X.
DigitalColor Meter	Measures color values on your display so that you can enter the values into other programs, such as graphics applications.
Directory	Shares contacts, manages group services, and shares other information about people in your company or organization.
Directory Utility	Configures directory servers for use with Directory.
Disk Utility	Formats and manages hard drives, removable media such as CDs and DVDs, and disk images.
Grab	Takes screen shots of items on your Mac. Grab was used extensively in the creation of art files for this book.
Grapher	A neat utility that graphs equations, visualizing them in two or three dimensions. You can even animate your graphs with this baby.
Keychain Access	Manages your plethora of passwords in one convenient location.
Migration Assistant	Moves all the user account information from one Mac to another using a FireWire cable. You can bring over your network information, passwords, the contents of your user account's folder, and so on in one fell swoop. Will also help you restore information using a Time Machine backup.
Network Utility	Monitors network traffic and diagnoses any issues that may creep up.
ODBC Administrator	Configures applications that conform to the Open Database Connectivity standard to connect with database servers.
Podcast Capture	Allows you to record and distribute podcasts as long as you have access to a Mac OS X Server running Podcast Producer.
RAID Utility	Allows you to configure multiple hard drives to act as one contiguous drive. You must have a RAID (Redundant Array of Inexpensive Disks) card installed on your Mac to use this utility.
System Profiler	Gives you all the information you could ever want about your Mac's hardware and software.
Terminal	A command line utility for accessing Leopard's UNIX underpinnings. You will get to play around with this utility quite a bit in Chapter 15.
VoiceOver Utility	Allows your Mac to describe your screen's contents verbally. Your Mac will literally speak to you and read the contents of your open documents and windows. This is obviously a fantastic utility for anyone who has difficulty seeing what is on their Mac's screen.
X11	Lets you run UNIX applications alongside your Mac OS X applications. This is an optional utility that you can install, either during installation or later, from your Mac OS X Leopard installation disc.

Note All of these utilities have Help systems that will teach you much more about those utilities that interest you the most. To access the Help system for any application, simply click Help in the menu bar.

Navigate Leopard's Applications

Many of the basic functions and menus of Leopard's applications and utilities are accessed in the same way. For instance, opening a file from within almost any application is done by selecting File ⇨ Open. There are also keyboard shortcuts that are universally used among the applications in Leopard.

How to open and close applications

This one is really basic, so I'll keep it short and to the point.

Use one of these methods to open applications:

- **Choose Go ⇨ Applications, or Go ⇨ Utilities, from within the Finder and double-click the application or utility you need.**
- **Click the application's icon in the Dock.**
- **Choose Apple menu ⇨ Recent Items and select a recently used application from the list.**

These techniques close an open application:

- **Choose the application's title menu (immediately to the right of the Apple menu) and select Quit.**
- **Press ⌘+Q.**
- **Click-and-hold the application's icon in the Dock, and then select Quit from the resulting pop-up menu (see figure 2.9).**

2.9 Easily quit an application from the Dock.

Common commands and keyboard shortcuts

Table 2.5 lists commands that are common among Leopard's applications, as well as the keyboard shortcuts that make issuing those commands even easier.

Genius

If you are a Windows user who is converting to the Mac, many of the keyboard shortcuts you are familiar with have Mac equivalents. For example, to print a job in Windows, you would press Ctrl+P, and on the Mac you would press ⌘+P; Ctrl+C copies an item on Windows, while ⌘+C does the same trick on a Mac.

Table 2.5 Commands and Keyboard Shortcuts

Command	Function	Keyboard shortcut
Open	Opens a file or document.	⌘+O
Save	Saves the contents of a document.	⌘+S
New	Creates a new blank document.	⌘+N
Close	Closes the active window.	⌘+W
Page Setup	Selects the correct paper size and orientation to print with.	⌘+Shift+P
Print	Prints the current document.	⌘+P
Copy	Copies highlighted text.	⌘+C
Cut	Cuts highlighted text from a document.	⌘+X
Paste	Pastes copied or cut text into a document.	⌘+V
Select All	Highlights all text in a document.	⌘+A
Find	Finds words in the document or window.	⌘+F
Find Next	Finds the next instance of a word in a document or window.	⌘+G
Find Previous	Finds the previous instance of a word in a document or window.	⌘+Shift+G
Force Quit	Forces an application or utility to quit.	⌘+Option+Esc
Minimize	Minimizes the active window.	⌘+M
Preferences	Opens the application's preferences.	⌘+,
Hide	Hides the active application.	⌘+H
Quit	Quits the active application.	⌘+Q

Easily access applications with a Stack

Leopard has a neat new feature called Stacks that allows you to place folder aliases on the right side of the Dock. You can add a Stack for your Applications folder to the Dock so that you can easily and quickly access all the applications and utilities on your Mac.

1. **Open your hard drive:**

   - Double-click your hard drive's icon, or

   - Press ⌘+N from within the Finder, and then select the hard drive icon from the Devices section.

2. **Drag the Applications folder to the right side of the Dock and drop it in.**

3. **Click the Applications folder alias to open the Stack.**

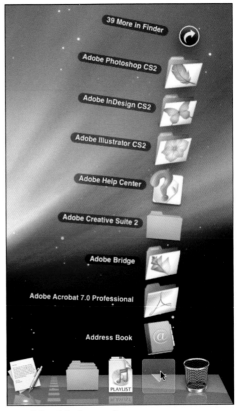

2.10 A Stack in Fan mode.

The Stack can display in either a fan pattern, as in figure 2.10, or in a grid, as in figure 2.11. As you can see, Fan mode doesn't show all the items in the folder if there are a lot in there. Notice at the top of the fan in figure 2.10 that it shows "39 More in Finder" next to the arrow. This means that there are 39 more application icons that can't be shown in the fan due to its configuration; this is where the Grid mode shines. The configuration of the grid allows you to see all of the folder's contents.

2.11 A Stack in Grid mode.

Create and Work with Documents in TextEdit

TextEdit is Leopard's built-in word processing application, and it can handle a good deal of your basic document writing needs. TextEdit is one of those names that advertises just what the application does: It edits text. TextEdit's interface is simplicity itself, as are the functions it provides. Although you don't get all the frills of a full-fledged word processor like Microsoft Word, Apple's Pages, or OpenOffice, TextEdit is surprisingly more capable than it appears at first glance (it can even open documents created by the aforementioned big boys).

47

First things first: Open TextEdit by choosing Go from within the Finder, selecting Applications, and double-clicking the TextEdit icon. TextEdit opens a new document automatically when you first start it up, as shown in figure 2.12.

Creating a new document doesn't get much easier, but what if TextEdit is already open? Simply do one of the following:

- **Choose File ⇨ New**

- **Press ⌘+N**

A shiny new document opens, ready for you to enter your information. To get started with your document, just begin typing!

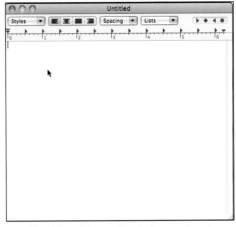

2.12 TextEdit waiting patiently for your input.

Save your document

Once you've created a document, you typically want to save it so that you can refer to it again sometime in the future.

To save a document, do the following:

1. **Choose File ⇨ Save, or press ⌘+S, to open the Save dialog.**
2. **Enter a name for your document in the Save As field.**
3. **Navigate to the location on your Mac where you want to save the document.**
4. **Click the Save button.**

Open an existing document

To open a document from within TextEdit, do the following:

1. **Choose File ⇨ Open to bring up the Open dialog.**
2. **Navigate your Mac's hard drive until you are in the folder of the file you want to open.**
3. **Select the name of the file to open, and click the Open button to display the document in TextEdit.**

You can now view, print, or edit your document as needed.

A word about file formats

You may notice that at the bottom of TextEdit's Save dialog (see figure 2.13) is a File Format menu. TextEdit's default file format is RTF, which stands for Rich Text Format. Most word processors on any computing platform (including Mac, Windows, and Linux) can open RTF documents, so you don't have to worry much about whether other computer users can view or edit your TextEdit documents. RTF allows you to make formatting changes to your document, such as adding some punch to your fonts by changing their size and color.

If you click the File Format pop-up menu, you see the other formats that TextEdit can save your document in (see figure 2.13). Table 2.6 describes the file formats so that you can decide whether something other than RTF is right for you. What is the coolest thing about the availability of these formats? TextEdit can not only save your documents in them, but it can also open any document that uses them; this gives you extreme flexibility when it comes to opening and saving files that originated with users of other operating systems and word processors.

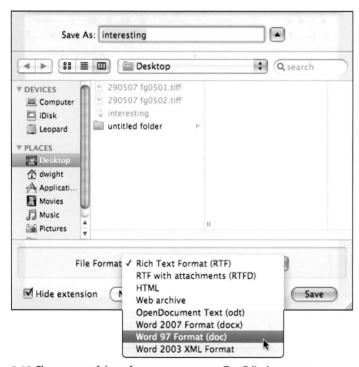

2.13 Choose any of these formats to save your TextEdit documents.

There is one more file format not listed in figure 2.13 or Table 2.6: plain text (.txt). Plain text doesn't allow you to format your documents with fancy fonts or pictures, though. So what's the appeal of plain text? First, most programming is done in the plain text format. Second, plain text is a format that all word processors, even those that run in command-line operating systems like DOS and UNIX, can open, read, and edit.

To create a plain text file, choose Format ➪ Make Plain Text from the menu.

Table 2.6 TextEdit File Formats

Format	Uses
RTF with attachments (RTFD)	This is essentially RTF with graphics included, such as pictures.
HTML	HTML stands for HyperText Markup Language, which is a programming language used to create Web pages. It allows you to edit Web pages or quickly create new ones.
Web archive	This is used primarily as a format in which Safari saves Web pages. TextEdit can open, edit, and save these files.
OpenDocument Text (.odt)	OpenDocument is a relatively new standard for word processor files that is native to the OpenOffice.org office suite.
Word 2007 Format (.docx)	Microsoft made a break from Word's traditional file format with Office 2007.
Word 97 Format (.doc)	This format should be very familiar to anyone who's used Microsoft Word in the past. It is one of the most widely used formats on the planet.
Word 2003 XML Format	Open, edit, and save files that were created from Word 2003 using XML (Extensible Markup Language), another programming language used extensively on the Web.

Format Your Documents

Sometimes simply typing text into your documents may be good enough for the task at hand, but other situations may call for something nicer, neater, and more polished. Because TextEdit uses RTF, formatting elements of your documents, such as manipulating fonts and adding pictures, is almost too easy. The look and feel of a document can be very important, even more so to the reader than the writer, and something as simple as a font choice can affect how the reader responds to the text.

Using fonts

Mac OS X Leopard comes with a wide variety of built-in fonts to spice up your life in the world of word processing. To manipulate fonts in a document, do the following:

1. **Open an existing file, or create a new one, in TextEdit.**

   - Choose File ➪ Open or File ➪ New, or

   - Press ⌘+O or ⌘+N.

2. **Highlight the text you want to change by clicking-and-dragging the mouse over it.** You can highlight all the text in the document by pressing ⌘+A, or choosing Edit ➪ Select All.

3. **Choose Format ➪ Font to change the fonts used in your document.** You can change the font size, make the letters bold, underline words, change the color of the text, and much more. See the upcoming section for information on the Fonts window.

4. **Choose Format ➪ Text to manipulate text on the page.** Move the alignment of the text to the left, right, or center. You can also change the spacing widths between lines, change the direction of your writing from right to left (necessary for text in some languages, such as Hebrew), create tables from existing text, and even more.

Using the Fonts window

The Fonts window, as shown in Figure 2.14, gives you a central location in TextEdit where you can choose and stylize fonts. Open the Fonts window by choosing Format ➪ Font ➪ Show Fonts.

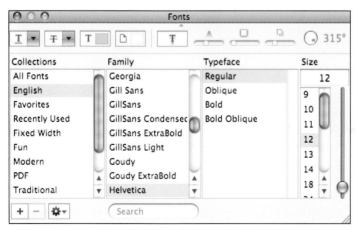

2.14 The Fonts window in TextEdit makes it easy to change the look of your document's text.

The toolbar at the top of the window allows you to make changes to the appearance of the text, such as the following:

- **Text Underline and Text Strikethrough.** Decide whether to use a single or double line for the underline or strikethrough, as well as what color the line should be.

- **Change the color of the text.**

- **Add a drop shadow to the text.** You can also change the way the drop shadow is displayed, by changing the shadow's opacity, blur, offset, and angle.

Select the fonts to use in your document by browsing the list in the Fonts window. You can change the size of the font, as well as change its typeface characteristics (such as making it bold or italic).

Checking spelling and grammar

No matter who you are or how well educated you may be, at some point, someone will catch you in a spelling or grammatical error. Thankfully, we writers have brilliant editors who come behind us and clean up our frequent messes, but most folks aren't so blessed. It is to those unlucky enough not to have editors that I dedicate this section of the chapter.

TextEdit may be a simple program, but it's quite a smart one, too. Do you have a problem spelling words like "millennium" or "weird?" Does "I am doing well" come out as "I is doing well?" If so, TextEdit has your back.

To check spelling and grammar in your documents, do the following:

1. **Choose Edit ⇨ Spelling and Grammar ⇨ Show Spelling and Grammar to open the Spelling and Grammar dialog, as shown in figure 2.15.**

2. **Click the Find Next button, and TextEdit goes one by one through each spelling or grammar violation.** It is even so kind as to make suggestions for rectifying the problems.

Genius

TextEdit can check your spelling and grammar on the fly too. Choose Edit ⇨ Spelling and Grammar, and click Check Spelling While Typing to have TextEdit check each word as you type it. Choose Edit ⇨ Spelling and Grammar, and click Check Grammar With Spelling so that TextEdit checks your grammar along with the spelling of your words. To have TextEdit look over your document at any time, press ⌘+;.

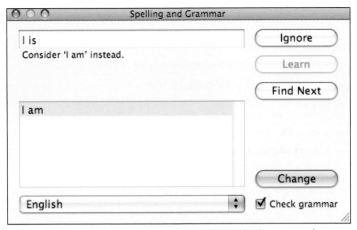

2.15 You have no more excuses for poor spelling or bad grammar if you use TextEdit.

3. **Click the Change button if you agree to the suggested changes, click Ignore to skip and move to the next violation, or click Learn to teach TextEdit the spelling of a word that may not be in its vocabulary.**

4. **Close the Spelling and Grammar window by clicking the red dot in the upper-left corner when finished.**

Set TextEdit Preferences

I am a big fan of making things work the way you want them to on your computer, not the way Apple or anyone else says you have to. The way I work may do wonders for my production, but may cause you to groan with frustration or yawn in tedium. Most applications allow you to change their default behaviors to match your style of working (or playing, as the case may be), and TextEdit is thankfully no exception.

To alter TextEdit's default behaviors, choose TextEdit ⇨ Preferences from the menu, or press ⌘+,. The Preferences window opens and permits access to two tabs: New Document, and Open and Save. Tables 2.7 and 2.8, in conjunction with figures 2.16 and 2.17, respectively, let you see what these two tabs offer in the way of customizing your TextEdit experience.

Table 2.7 The New Document Preferences

Preferences	Functions
Format	Lets you select Rich text (RTF) or Plain text (txt) as your default format for new documents.
Wrap to page	Causes text to wrap to document margins instead of window margins.
Window Size	Sets the default window size for new documents.
Font	Lets you choose the default font to use for new plain text or rich text documents.
Properties (RTF only)	Enter information you want to include with each document you create, such as your name, the company you work for, and any copyright information that may be legally necessary for the document.
Check spelling as you type/Check grammar with spelling	Activates the spelling and grammar checkers.
Show ruler	Displays a ruler at the top of each window.
Smart copy/paste	Automatically adds any necessary spaces when text is added or deleted.
Smart quotes	Uses curly quote marks instead of straight ones.
Smart links	Automatically turns Internet addresses into links that open to the appropriate Web site when clicked in the document.
Restore All Defaults	Reverts back to TextEdit's original default preferences.

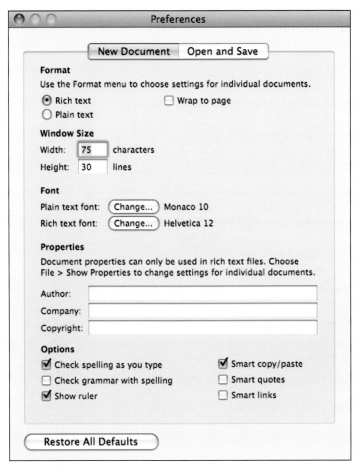

2.16 TextEdit's New Document preferences options.

Table 2.8 Open and Save Preferences

Ignore rich text commands in HTML/RTF files	Opens HTML and RTF files automatically as plain text, retaining no formatting at all. This is beneficial to Web developers who need to edit their code.
Delete the automatic backup file	TextEdit saves a backup of your file as it is saving it. Check this option to delete that backup once the save is complete.
Add ".txt" extension to plain text files	Automatically tags plain text files with the .txt extension at the end of their filenames.
Autosaving	Lets you select the time increments for automatically saving documents that you modify.
Plain Text File Encoding	Lets you decide which text encoding to use by default when opening and saving plain text files. I suggest sticking with Automatic unless you really know what you are doing with these settings.
HTML Saving Options	Lets you choose the default document type, styling, and encoding to use when saving documents as HTML files.
Preserve white space	Preserves blank areas that are already in your document so that they aren't lost during formatting.
Restore All Defaults	Reverts back to TextEdit's original New Document and Open and Save default settings.

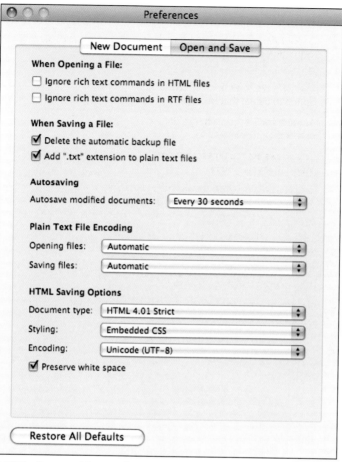

2.17 The Open and Save preferences options for TextEdit.

How Do I Organize My Life with iCal and Address Book?

If your life is anything like mine, you need as much organization as you can get, and iCal and Address Book will come to your rescue. iCal helps you create calendars for different subjects, such as Family or Work, and Address Book can keep all your contacts in a central location. You can create events in iCal so that you can schedule all your important dates and organize your time throughout the day, week, month, and year; Address Book allows you to access your contacts through any application programmed to use it, like Mail or iChat. iCal can also remind you of your scheduled events, so you guys reading this don't have any more excuses to forget your anniversary! In this chapter, I'll show you how to make iCal and Address Book essential to your Leopard experience.

Create and Manage New Calendars 60

Add Events to Calendars 61

Edit Calendar Events 62

iCal Preferences 63

Share Your Calendars with Others. 65

Subscribe to Calendars. 67

Print Calendars 68

Create Contacts in Address Book 69

Import and Export Contacts 72

Address Book Preferences. 74

See Detailed Maps of Addresses 77

Connect a Device to Your Mac. 78

Use iSync. 81

Create and Manage New Calendars

Open iCal to get started; click Go ➪ Applications in the menu and double-click the iCal icon.

You can create calendars that reflect the different areas of your everyday life, such as a calendar for your work schedule, another for bill due dates, and one for school events. Having a separate calendar for each area of your life will make it easy to organize your time.

There are three ways to create a new calendar:

- **Choose File ➪ New Calendar.**
- **Press ⌘+Option+N.**
- **Click the + button in the bottom-left corner of the iCal window.**

Performing one of these three actions creates a new calendar in the calendar list on the left side of the window. Name the calendar by simply typing its name. Continue to create as many calendars as you need before proceeding.

Your calendars are now ready to be put to work. There are a number of ways in which to manage the calendars themselves:

- **Arrange calendars in the list by simply clicking-and-dragging them into the order you prefer, as shown in figure 3.1.**

- **Rename a calendar by right-clicking, or Ctrl+clicking, it in the calendar list, and selecting Get Info from the pop-up menu.** Type a new name for the calendar in the Name field.

- **The events you enter in your calendars (more on that just a bit later in this chapter) are represented using the color of their respective calendars.** You can change the color of a calendar by right-clicking, or Ctrl+clicking, it in the calendar list, and then selecting Get Info. Click the color button in the upper-right corner of the window and select a color from the list.

- **Notice the check box that's just to the left of each calendar you've created.** That check box determines whether the events are displayed for the calendar in question. Unchecking some of these check boxes can help make sense out of a particularly busy schedule.

- **Create groups to arrange similar calendars together in the calendar list.** Create groups by choosing File ➪ New Calendar Group, or by pressing ⌘+Shift+N, and then give the new group a descriptive name. Arrange calendars into groups by simply dragging-and-dropping them underneath the desired group.

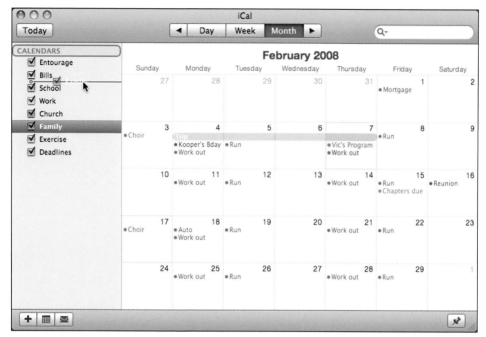

3.1 Click-and-drag calendars into the order you prefer.

Genius

You can change the way your calendars are displayed in the iCal window by clicking the Day, Week, and Month buttons at the top of the window. Click the right or left arrows on either side of those buttons to scroll to the previous or next day, week, or month. If you choose to use Day or Week view, you can always see a miniature monthly calendar in the window by clicking the View or Hide Mini-Month button in the bottom-left corner of the window.

Add Events to Calendars

A calendar without an event is about as useful as a car without tires, and it probably won't even get you as far. Events are the items that you add to your calendars to make them come alive; they are your life, only organized.

To create a new event:

1. **Select the day the event begins.**
2. **Press ⌘+N to create a new event for that day.**
3. **Type a descriptive name for the event.**

You now have your first event, but you will most likely want to edit the contents of the event before considering it a done deal, so please continue on.

Edit Calendar Events

Once the event is created, some tweaking may be in order. To edit your event:

1. **Open the event information window by double-clicking the event, or by clicking the event to highlight it and then pressing ⌘+E.** If this is not a new event, but a previously created event that you need to edit, simply double-clicking the event only displays its basic information; click the Edit button to gain access to its details, as shown in figure 3.2.

2. **Click to the right of each item in the event information window to edit it.** Table 3.1 lists the available items and their functions.

3. **Click Done.**

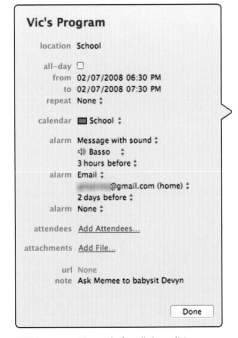

3.2 Your event is ready for all the editing you need to do.

Table 3.1 Event Information

Item	Function
Location	Where the event is to be held.
All-day	Check this box if this event will take up a day, as opposed to an hour or two.
From and To	Select the beginning and end dates and times for your event.
Repeat	Click the options menu next to this item if you want the event to be repeated sometime in the future, such as a reoccurring event like a birthday or holiday.
Calendar	Choose which calendar in your calendar list this event belongs to.

Item	Function
Alarm	Select from several different alarm types, such as e-mail, onscreen messages, and sound. You can set multiple alarms for each event.
Attendees	Invite others to add this event to their calendar.
Attachments	You can attach documents and other files to your events. For example, you could attach a grocery list to a scheduled shopping trip.
URL	Place a relevant Web site address or shared calendar address.
Note	Enter any additional information you may need for the task.

iCal Preferences

You can change the iCal preferences to customize how iCal works. Choose iCal ⇨ Preferences to see what options are available to you (see figure 3.3).

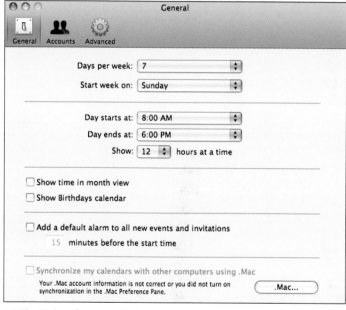

3.3 The iCal preferences window.

The General tab let's you make the most basic of setting adjustments; those settings are listed in Table 3.2.

Table 3.2 The iCal General Preferences Tab

Setting	Function
Days per week	Set the number of days for your normal week. You might change this setting to 5 to reflect a 5-day workweek.
Start week on	Choose which day to start your week.
Day starts at	Decide what time your typical day begins.
Day ends at	Set what time your typical day is over.
Show x hours at a time	For use in Day viewing mode.
Show time in by month view	Shows appointment times when in Month view. These are hidden default due to space restrictions.
Show Birthdays calendar	Displays a calendar that lists birthdays from your Address Book.
Add a default alarm off to all new events and invitations	Every new event or invitation will be assigned an alarm that will go in the time you specify.
Synchronize my calendars with other computers using MobileMe	If you have a MobileMe account, you can synchronize your calendars.

The Accounts tab allows you to subscribe to CalDAV servers, which some companies and organizations use to share calendars among several users. To subscribe to your company's or organization's CalDAV server, click the + button in the lower-left corner, and enter the server's information (contact your IT department for this information, if needed).

Table 3.3 lists the Advanced preferences available for iCal.

Table 3.3 The iCal Advanced Preferences Tab

Setting	Function
Turn on time zone support	Allows you to view your schedule as it would be in a time zone other than your default. When you check this box, a time zone pop-up menu becomes available in the upper-right corner of the iCal window; select the appropriate time zone from this menu.
Hide To Do items with due dates after the calendar view	To Do items that you've created won't appear in the To Do list (displayed by pressing ⌘+Option+T) if their dates are after the current view being used for your calendar.
Hide To Do items x days after they have been completed	Select the number of days it will take for a To Do item to be hidden from view after it has been completed.

Setting	Function
Delete events *x* days after they have passed	Automatically removes events from your calendars after the number of days you specify past their completion.
Delete To Do items *x* days after they are completed	Automatically removes To Do items from the To Do list after the number of days you specify past their completion.
Turn off all alarms	Prevents any alarms from occurring.
Turn off alarms only when iCal is not open	Prevents alarms from occurring only when iCal isn't running.
Automatically retrieve invitations from Mail	Check this box to have event invitations show in iCal instead of just Mail.
Clear Attendee Cache	Empties the names and addresses of attendees you've sent invitations to in the past.

Share Your Calendars with Others

Life is much easier when everyone is on the same page, be it your company or your family. iCal offers two different ways to share your calendars with others: publishing your calendar and exporting your calendar.

Publishing a calendar

When you publish a calendar, you are placing a copy of it on the Internet or a local WebDAV server. Other users can then access it through iCal, another third-party calendar application, or a standard Web browser using any computing platform. To publish a calendar:

1. **Click the calendar or calendar group you want to publish in the calendar list.**

2. **Choose Calendar ⇨ Publish from the menu; the Publish calendar (shown in figure 3.4) appears.**

3. **When the menu opens, type in a name for your calendar if you don't want to use the default.**

3.4 Publish calendars to share them over a network or through the Internet.

4. **Select where to publish your calendar (your .Mac account or a private server) using the Publish on pop-up menu.** If you select Private Server, enter the server information, along with a login name and password to gain access to it.

5. **When the options are all set to your liking, click the Publish button.**

Exporting a calendar

Exporting a calendar is a good way to move calendars from one computer to another. You can also edit calendars that you've exported, although you cannot edit published calendars.

To export a calendar:

1. **Click to select the calendar or calendar group you want to export from the calendar list.**

2. **Choose iCal ⇨ Export to open the Save As window, as shown in figure 3.5.**

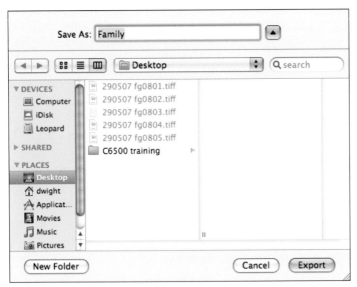

3.5 Export calendars from iCal and import them on other computers.

3. **Give a descriptive name to the file, choose a location to save it, and then click the Save button.**

4. **Share the exported calendar by e-mailing it to others, placing it on a server that can be accessed by other users, or any other way you can think of.**

Genius The default format of exported calendars in iCal is ICS. ICS files can be imported into almost any third-party calendar application, and so you don't have to worry about your Windows or Linux pals not being able to view your calendar; likewise, you can use their calendars in iCal if they export them from their application using the ICS format.

Subscribe to Calendars

It stands to reason that if some people are publishing their calendars, then there must be others subscribing to them. Follow one of these two ways to subscribe to calendars:

⦿ **This is the easy way:**

1. Choose Calendar ⇨ Subscribe from the menu.

2. Type the URL (the Web address) of the calendar you want to subscribe to in the Calendar URL field.

3. Click the Subscribe button to see the information window for the calendar, as shown in figure 3.6.

4. Decide whether to remove Alarms, Attachments, and To Do items (which I recommend if you don't know the person who created the calendar), and how often to have the calendar automatically refreshed in case there are any changes made to it by its creator.

3.6 Subscribing to calendars is a snap with iCal.

5. Click OK to complete the subscription process.

⦿ **This is even easier:**

1. If someone sends you the link to their calendar in an e-mail, or if you click the link to a calendar from a Web page, iCal automatically begins the subscription process.

2. You can pick it up from step 3 in the previous steps to finish the subscription.

Find Calendars on the Web

Can't find calendars to subscribe to? Try one of these links to find tons of calendars just begging for your subscription:

- **www.apple.com/downloads/macosx/calendars/**
- **http://icalshare.com/**

Print Calendars

If you're like me, you understand that, while the concept of a paperless office sounded pretty cool in the 1980s, it most certainly — and to some degree, thankfully — hasn't come to its fruition. Sometimes I just like to have a printed page in hand, as opposed to being tied to my desk or lugging around a laptop. I love my Mac but not permanently attached at the hip. iCal can provide you with great printed calendars to use for yourself or that you can print out and give to others. This is a great tool for offices and schools or any other organization or team for that matter. Another plus to printed calendars is that you will have a much easier time hanging them on your fridge than you would hanging your computer's screen.

To print your calendars:

1. **Choose File ⇨ Print.**

2. **Select from among the myriad options shown in figure 3.7, and then click Continue.**
   Table 3.4 lists the printing options and gives brief explanations of them.

3. **Click Print in the print window to send the job to your printer.**

Table 3.4 The iCal Printing Options

Option	Function
View	Choose what view to use for your printed calendar from the pop-up menu.
Paper	Select a paper size to print your calendar on.
Time range	Decide when the printed calendar or calendars should begin and end using the Starts and Ends pop-up menus.
Calendars	Check the boxes next to the calendars whose events you want to include.
Options	Determine whether to print all-day events, timed events, mini-months, calendar keys, or if you want to print in black and white only, instead of color.
Text size	Choose what size font to use when printing your calendar's text.
Zoom	Drag the slider to enlarge the preview image.

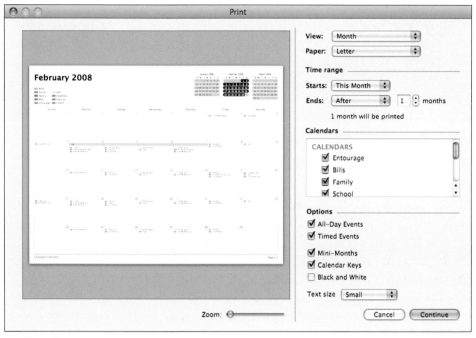

3.7 The iCal printing options.

Create Contacts in Address Book

Have you ever needed to find that elusive phone number or address for a prospective client and had to thumb through ten different devices and books to find it? Apple created Address Book just for you. Creating contacts in Address Book can sure make rounding up all those Christmas card addresses a lot easier.

Contacts are files that contain information for people in your life, such as street addresses, e-mail addresses, birthdays, and even their picture. To get started, let's open Address Book:

1. **Click Go ⇨ Applications.**
2. **Double-click the Address Book icon to open Address Book.**

Address Book is fairly useless without contacts, so let's start adding a few.

New cards

A card contains all of the contact's information, and so you need to create a new one to get started. There are a few ways to begin creating a new card:

- **Choose File ⇨ New Card from the menu.**

- **Press ⌘+N.**

- **Click the + button underneath the Name column in the Address Book window.**

Any of these actions creates a new blank card that's waiting for input from you, as shown in figure 3.8.

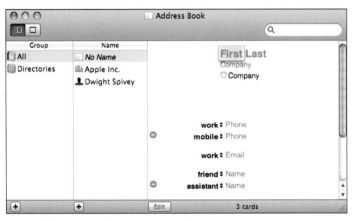

3.8 Creating a new card is really easy to do.

Begin entering information into the card, using the Tab button on your keyboard to move to the next available field. If there is a field that you don't want to use, simply leave it blank and it won't appear on the card once you've saved it. To add new fields, choose Card ⇨ Add Field and select one from the list.

When you are finished adding information to the card, press ⌘+S or click the Edit button below the card's window to save it. You can always edit the information in the card by clicking to highlight it in the Name column of the Address Book window, and then clicking the Edit button beneath the card's window.

Genius

You can also add new cards quite easily when you receive a vCard in an e-mail. A vCard is sort of like a digital business card that someone may attach to their e-mails so that others, such as you, can easily save their contact information. Using Mail, simply double-click the vCard in the e-mail to create a new card in Address Book.

New groups

A great feature that I use quite a bit in Address Book is groups. Using groups, you can create different categories of contacts, such as Family, Work, and Church. As with cards, you have several techniques you can use to create new groups:

- **Press ⌘+Shift+N.**
- **Choose File ➪ New Group from the menu.**
- **Click the + button underneath the Group column in the main Address Book window.**

Be sure to give your group a descriptive name of the items it will contain. To add cards to the groups, just drag-and-drop the desired card from the Name column onto the preferred group in the Group column, as shown in figure 3.9. This action doesn't remove the card from the Name column; it just places a copy of the card in the group.

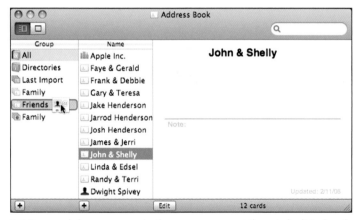

3.9 Drag-and-drop names onto the group you want them to be listed under.

Genius

There's an even faster way to create a group. Select multiple cards from the Name column by holding the ⌘ key while you click the names, and then choose File ➪ New Group from Selection.

How to Use Smart Groups

Smart Groups are groups that cards are automatically added to if they meet certain criteria that you have already specified. For example, if you create a Smart Group that looks
for cards that have certain last names, when a new card is created using that last name,
it is immediately added to the Smart Group. To create a Smart Group:

1. **Press ⌘+Option+N, or choose File ⇨ New Smart Group from the
   menu.**
2. **Give the Smart Group a descriptive name.**
3. **Decide whether the Smart Group will contain cards that match
   any or all of the conditions you are about to set.**
4. **Add or remove conditions by clicking the + or – buttons to the
   right of the first and subsequent conditions.**
5. **Check the "Highlight group when updated" check box to have
   Address Book notify you when a card has been added to the
   Smart Group.**
6. **Click OK to save the new Smart Group, or click Cancel to get rid
   of it.**

You can change a Smart Group's criteria at any time, as shown in Figure 3.10, by
ctrl+clicking its name in the Group column and selecting Edit Smart Group.

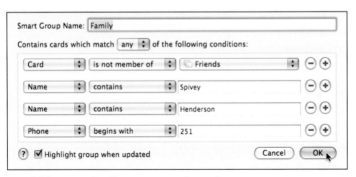

3.10 Adding some intelligence to your Smart Group.

Import and Export Contacts

Address Book works well with other applications that use standard formats for importing and exporting contacts, such as Mail, Thunderbird, Entourage, and Outlook.

Import Contacts

Address Book can import files from other applications when created in the following formats:

- **vCard**
- **LDIF**
- **Tab-delimited**
- **Comma-separated (CSV), which is usually the most compatible with other applications.**

Consult the other application to find out how to export contacts from it in one of the above formats.

To import contacts:

1. **Choose File ⇨ Import, and then select the format of the file you will be importing.**

2. **Browse your Mac for the file you want to import, click to highlight the file, and then click the Open button in the bottom-right corner.**

   - **If importing a tab-delimited or comma-separated file, choose the Text File format.**

   - **If importing a vCard that contains contacts you already have in Address Book, you must choose how to handle the conflict.** As shown in figure 3.11, you can choose to update the old card with the new information, keep the old card, keep only the new card, or keep both cards.

3.11 Decide the ultimate fate of your new vCards.

Caution

When you import an Address Book Archive, your existing Address Book database is replaced, which causes you to lose all the cards that are currently in Address Book. You are prompted by Address Book to be sure that you want to continue this action, so be sure you have a backup archive before continuing (see the upcoming export instructions in this chapter).

Export Contacts

The file format preferred by Address Book for exporting contacts is vCard. vCard is a standard format that's common to most applications that have functionality similar to Address Book.

To export vCards from Address Book:

1. **Select the contacts you want to export from either the Group or the Name column.**

2. **Choose File ⇨ Export, and then select vCard as the format.**

3. **Give the exported vCard a name, browse to the destination on your Mac's hard drive you want to save the exported file to, and then click Save.**

Genius

I'm sure you noticed in the File⇨Export menu that there is another selection called Address Book Archive. Choose this format when you want to make a complete backup file of your Address Book database. I highly recommend performing this kind of export after you've imported a large number of files to make sure you don't lose all the work you've just put in. At the very least, make one of these backups once a month.

Address Book Preferences

As with most other applications, Address Book has many preferences to help you customize your experience. Open the preferences by either choosing Address Book ⇨ Preferences from the menu, or pressing ⌘+,.

General

The General preferences allow you to make several basic appearance and behavior modifications, as shown in figure 3.12.

The Show first name, Sort By, Address Format, and Font Size options are all very self-explanatory, but Table 3.5 gives a brief description of the others.

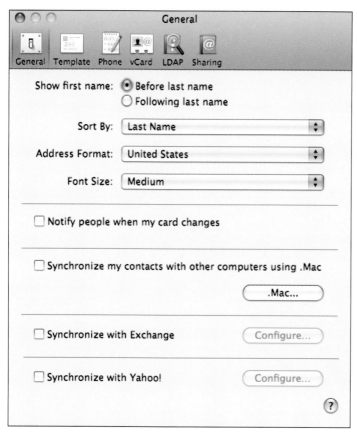

3.12 The General preferences, at your disposal.

Table 3.5 General Preferences Options

Option	Function
Notify people when my card changes	Address Book sends an e-mail to your contacts whenever you make changes to your personal contact information, provided you check this box.
Synchronize my contacts with other computers usingMobileMe	If you have a MobileMe account, you can save your contacts on it so that you can synchronize contacts between Macs.
Synchronize with Exchange	Most corporations use Exchange servers for e-mail, and those servers typically use company-wide address books. Check this box to have Address Book synchronize addresses with your Exchange server. Click Configure to enter your Exchange server account information. See your IT administrator if you have any questions or difficulties with the synchronization.
Synchronize with Yahoo!	You can synchronize Address Book with your Yahoo! address book by checking this box. Click the Configure button to enter your Yahoo! ID (username) and password.

Template

Use the Template preferences, shown in figure 3.13, to modify what fields are automatically displayed when creating new cards. Remove fields by clicking the – buttons to the left of them, and add fields by clicking the + button or by choosing a field type from the Add Field pop-up menu.

Phone

Phone simply allows you to modify the format in which Address Book displays phone numbers. You may want to change this to reflect the country that you or your contact are in. Choose the preferred format from the

3.13 I love the Template preferences for allowing customization of the new card fields!

Formats pop-up menu, or create your own format by clicking the blue triangle next to the Formats pop-up menu, and then clicking the + button in the bottom-left corner of the window.

vCard

The vCard options allow you to change the default vCard format version in Address Book, and to specify just how much information you want to share with others when sending them your vCards. Table 3.6 explains the vCard options.

Table 3.6 vCard Options for Address Book

Option	Function
vCard Format	Choose between versions 3.0 and 2.1. Version 3.0 is the default; choose 2.1 if others have problems importing your vCards.
vCard 2.1 Encoding	Select the appropriate encoding for your language. English-speakers generally want to stick with Western (Mac OS Roman). This is only available if you select 2.1 for the vCard format.
Enable private me card	Lets you choose which items in your personal vCard to share with those you are sending the vCard to. For example, you may not want them to know your personal e-mail or your home address, but you may want them to see other fields in your card. When this box is checked, you can edit your personal vCard and deselect the items you don't want to be exported with your contact information.
Export notes	Check this box to include notes you have entered in your contacts' in vCards information.
Export photos	Checking this box will include any photos that you've associated in vCards with the card or cards being exported.

LDAP

LDAP, or Lightweight Directory Access Protocol, is a common protocol used for address servers, which are used on most corporate networks for storing corporate contact information for their employees. Address Book can access LDAP servers, but you will need to contact your IT department for information on how to log on to the server.

To add an LDAP server to Address Book:

1. **Choose Address Book ➪ Preferences, and then click the LDAP tab.**
2. **Click the + button in the bottom-left corner to add a server.**
3. **Enter the server information as provided by your IT department.**
4. **Click Save to add the LDAP server to the Address Book list.**

Sharing

The Sharing preferences let you share your Address Book contacts through your .Mac account with other users who have .Mac accounts. To share your Address Book:

1. **Choose Address Book ➪ Preferences, and then click the Sharing tab.**
2. **Check the "Share your address book" check box.**
3. **Click the + button in the bottom-left corner to add contacts with whom you want to share your Address Book.** Remember, both you and the contacts you are sharing with must have a .Mac account.
4. **Click the Send Invitation button to have Address Book e-mail them an invitation to access your Address Book.**

See Detailed Maps of Addresses

A great feature included in Address Book is the ability to see maps of the addresses in your cards. This functionality really shines when you need to get to a client's location but aren't sure where to go. Here's how to use this cool feature:

1. **Click the card you need in the Name column so that you can see their contact information.**
2. **Ctrl+click (or right-click if you have a two-button mouse) the address in the contact information window, and then choose Map Of, as shown in figure 3.14.**

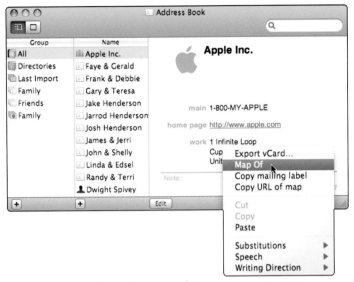

3.14 Choose Map Of from this contextual menu to get a detailed map.

3. **Safari automatically opens to the Google Maps page, displaying a map of the address's location.** From here you can even get directions from your current location to the address. Address Book and Google Maps really work well together to give you accurate information; this feature is a pleasure to use.

Connect a Device to Your Mac

Leopard is quite a friendly operating system, connecting and interacting with tons of different devices right out of the box. You won't even need to download drivers to connect to most devices, such as PDAs and cell phones. Leopard can connect to and synchronize information with these kinds of devices, making it very easy to keep contact information and calendar data consistent across multiple devices. iSync is the synchronization tool of choice for Leopard, and is simplicity incarnate.

In order for your Mac to synchronize with a device, it must first be able to converse with it. Typically, devices connect through a wireless Bluetooth connection or a USB cable.

Supported devices

Leopard has built-in support for so many devices, it's mind numbing. PDAs using the Palm OS, cell phones from all major brands, and Pocket PCs are all supported for use with iSync. To see a list of approved devices, visit www.apple.com/macosx/features/isync/index.html.

Bluetooth

The most common method of connecting a device with iSync is through Bluetooth. Bluetooth is a wireless connection protocol used mainly for small device-to-device connections.

Before you can synchronize your Bluetooth device, you must make sure that Bluetooth is enabled on both the device and your Mac. If your Mac is an older model, you may need to connect a USB Bluetooth adapter in order to use the Bluetooth protocol. Open System Preferences by choosing Apple menu ⇨ System Preferences; if you see a Bluetooth logo in the Hardware section, your Mac is Bluetooth-capable.

Consult your device's documentation for help in enabling Bluetooth.

To enable Bluetooth:

1. **Choose Apple menu ⇨ System Preferences.**

2. **Click the Bluetooth icon in the Hardware section.**

3. **Check the boxes next to On and Discoverable, as shown in figure 3.15, to turn on Bluetooth and to make your Mac visible to other devices running Bluetooth.** Don't close the Bluetooth System Preferences yet!

3.15 The Bluetooth System Preferences window, with no devices configured for Bluetooth communication.

Genius

Make sure that your Bluetooth-enabled device is also set to be discoverable. This allows your Mac to see the Bluetooth device.

Next, configure your Bluetooth device to communicate with Leopard:

1. **If there are no devices set up for Bluetooth communication with your Mac, click the Set Up New Device button.** Otherwise, click the + button in the bottom-left corner of the Bluetooth preferences window.

2. **In the Bluetooth Setup Assistant Introduction window, click Continue.**

3. **Select the type of device you're configuring from the list, and click Continue again.** In this example, I will be using my mobile phone. Bluetooth Setup Assistant scans the area for a Bluetooth-enabled device. As you can see in figure 3.16, it discovered my Z520a cell phone.

4. **Highlight the device's name and click Continue.** Bluetooth Setup Assistant gathers information about your device at this point.

5. **When it is finished, click Continue.** Next, your Mac and phone will pair up. Bluetooth Setup Assistant generates a passcode that you must enter on your phone to complete the process. Once the pairing process is complete, Bluetooth Setup Assistant asks which services you want to use with your device.

6. **The only option necessary for our purposes in this chapter is Set up iSync to transfer contacts and events; make sure that its box is checked, and then click Continue.**

3.16 Bluetooth Setup Assistant has discovered my cell phone.

7. **Click Quit on the next screen to complete the device setup procedures.** You are now ready to use your device with iSync. In some cases, iSync automatically opens and your device is listed in its window. If that's not the case for you, I'll explain how to add a device to iSync in just a bit.

Caution   Apple highly recommends that you only synchronize your device with one computer. This is to avoid the possibility of synchronization problems. Possible issues could be the loss of data, receiving duplicate information, or simply synchronizing the wrong information.

USB

iSync is also able to communicate with devices that connect with USB. To connect a USB device:

1. **With iSync closed, turn on the device.**

2. **Attach one end of the USB cable to the device, and the other to your Mac.**

3. **Open iSync and follow the instructions in the next section of this chapter.**

Use iSync

It's syncing time. Open iSync to get started:

- Choose Go ⇨ Applications.

- Double-click the iSync icon to open the application. The iSync window is quite sparse until you add devices for it to synchronize with, as shown in figure 3.17.

3.17 The iSync main window is a barren landscape when it's without a device to synchronize with.

Add a device to iSync

iSync is now ready to add a new device to its repertoire. To add a new device:

1. **Press ⌘+N, or choose Devices ⇨ Add Device from the menu.** iSync should find any Bluetooth-enabled devices you've set up for use with your Mac, or any USB devices that are attached to your Mac and turned on.

2. **Double-click your device, and it is added to iSync, as shown in figure 3.18.**

3. **Close the Add Device window.**

Sync devices with your Mac

Before you actually begin the synchronization of your device with iSync, you should make sure that all the synchronization options are set to your satisfaction. Table 3.7 lists the available options.

3.18 My cell phone is now added to iSync.

Table 3.7 iSync Synchronization Options

Option	Function
For first sync	This option is only visible prior to the first synchronization of the device. Decide whether to merge information from the device and your Mac or to erase the data on your device before syncing.
Turn on device synchronization	Check this box to allow your Mac to synchronize with the particular device.
Contacts	Check this box to allow iSync to synchronize contact information between the Mac and your device. Choose which contacts to synchronize from the Synchronize pop-up menu.
Calendars	Select this option to allow calendar events to be synchronized between the Mac and your device. Decide which calendars in iCal to synchronize with your device.
Put events created on phone into	Decide which calendar in iCal will store the calendar events you create on your device.

Option	Function
More Options	Click this button to make extra synchronization options available for this device. These extras include synchronizing only contacts that have phone numbers associated with them, synchronizing alarms, synchronizing all-day events, and deciding whether to synchronize events prior to or after a specified period of time. Figure 03.19 shows you the list of extra options.

Once you've got the synchronization preferences set, click the Sync Devices button in the upper-right corner of the iSync window. iSync shows a progress bar of the synchronization process, as shown in figure 3.19.

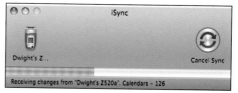

3.19 iSync is working to get your device and your Mac in concert with one another.

If you change your mind, stop the synchronization process by clicking the Cancel Sync button on the right side of the iSync window.

Once synchronization is complete, iSync lets you know. Your contacts and calendar events are now synchronized between your Mac and the device!

The Data Change alert

You will be alerted during the synchronization process when the amount of information that is going to be changed on your Mac and the device it's synchronizing with reaches a certain percentage, which is set by you in the iSync preferences (see the next section), as shown in Figure 3.20. This is simply to inform you what items will be changed or added so that you can decide whether or not to continue with the synchronization.

Syncing a Palm OS Device

Synchronizing information with a Palm OS device requires a bit more than does synchronizing with a cell phone. You must have the Palm Desktop software installed on your Mac and have synchronized your Palm device with the HotSync Manager before using iSync. Consult the iSync Help section for much more information on using your Palm OS device; choose Help ⇨ iSync Help from the menu, and search for Palm OS to find all the relevant topics on setting up the Palm OS device.

3.20 The Data Change Alert window lets you know when a lot of data is about to change on your Mac and the device you're synchronizing it with.

iSync preferences

Figure 3.21 shows the iSync Preferences window. You can modify these settings to make iSync work the way you want it to, and to allow your Mac to synchronize with other devices.

Table 3.8 lists the preferences that are available for iSync.

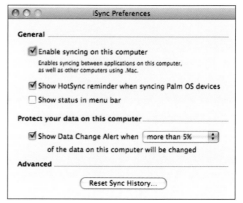

3.21 Make changes to the iSync preferences as needed.

Table 3.8 iSync Preferences Explained

Option	Function
Enable syncing on this computer	This option is pretty much a necessity if you want to synchronize any device with your Mac. The only good reason I've ever encountered for disabling synchronization is if you are running memory-intensive applications and need to temporarily keep your Mac from using up its memory resources unnecessarily.
Show HotSync reminder when syncing Palm OS devices	Reminds you to use the HotSync software that came with your Palm device to sync information, as opposed to using iSync.
Show status in menu bar	Displays an iSync icon in the menu bar so that you can easily monitor or initialize synchronization.
Show Data Change Alert when x of the data on this computer will be changed	Decide at what point iSync will display the Data Change Alert.
Reset Sync History	Clicking this button completely restores the synchronization settings for every application your Mac uses to sync information with, such as Mail, iCal, iSync, and even .Mac. Perform this reset if you are having problems synchronizing with a device.

Caution

When you reset your synchronization history, all the default synchronization settings in Leopard and its applications are restored to their defaults. If you've changed any of the synchronization settings prior to resetting the synchronization history, those changes will need to be made again.

How Do I Master the Web with Safari?

Since the advent of television, nothing has impacted the way humans conduct their daily activities quite like the Internet. For many people, checking e-mail and surfing the Web are as routine as waking up in the morning. Leopard comes loaded with the third version of the Web's best surfboard: Safari. Safari is a lightning-fast and standards-compliant Web browser that will have even the most demanding of browser critics smiling.

Getting Around in Safari **88**

Using Bookmarks **89**

Private Browsing **92**

Viewing Windows Media Files **93**

Finding Text on a Web Site **94**

Setting Safari Preferences **95**

Getting Around in Safari

Let's get started by learning our way around the Safari user interface. Knowing what's what is half the battle when it comes to using any application, and figure 4.1 highlights the major points of interest in Safari's interface.

Browsing basics

Safari is an outstanding browser, but when it comes to simply surfing the Web, it works pretty much like any other browser that you've used before: Type the address of the Web page you want to view in the Address field and press the Return key. Nothing magic about that procedure, is there? Here are a few other basic tips that don't require entire sections of a chapter to be devoted to them:

- **Use the Previous and Next arrow buttons to navigate between pages you've visited.**

- **Click the Refresh button to reload the current Web page if you believe the information it contains has been updated.**

- **Perform a quick search with Google by typing your subject in the Search field and pressing Return.**

- **To block unwanted pop-up windows that plague some sites, choose Safari ⇨ Block Pop-up Windows, or press ⌘+Shift+K.**

- **To open a new window, press ⌘+N.**

- **To close a window, press ⌘+W.**

Tabbed browsing

Tabbed browsing is the most useful feature in Safari, in my humble opinion. Tabs allow you to open multiple Web sites in a single window, and navigate between them by simply clicking the tab of the page you want. This prevents the problem of having a gazillion windows open at one time. Figure 4.1 shows a Safari window with several tabs open.

Try one of these methods to open new tabs:

- **⌘-click a link.**

- **Ctrl-click, or right-click, a link and select Open Link in New Tab from the resulting pop-up menu.**

- **Press ⌘+T.**

To close a tab, simply click the X in its upper-left corner.

Previous/Next page

Refresh page Address field Search

Toolbar Bookmarks bar Tabs

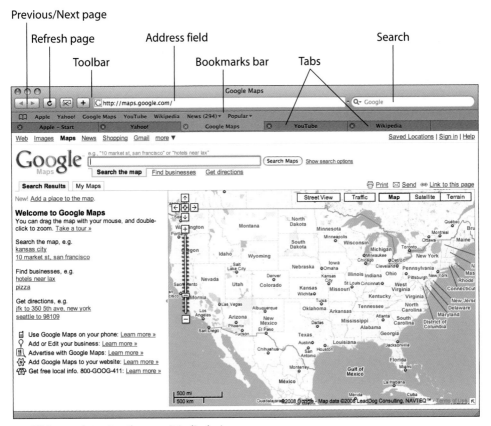

4.1 Click any tab to view the page it is displaying.

Where Does that Link Go?

You never quite know where that link you just clicked will actually take you unless you can see the address it points to. Safari has a great way to know what Web page you are about to be whisked to before you click it: the Status bar. The Status bar resides at the bottom of your Safari window and displays the address of a link when you hold your mouse pointer over it. Unfortunately, it's not there by default; you have to enable it first. To enable the Status bar, choose View ⇨ Show Status Bar, or press ⌘+/.

Using Bookmarks

Bookmarks are links that you create for your favorite Web sites so that you can easily and quickly visit them. To bookmark a Web site:

89

1. **Choose Bookmarks ⇨ Add Bookmark, or press ⌘+D.**

2. **Give the bookmark an appropriate name.**

3. **Select a location for the bookmark to reside.**

4. **Click the Add button, shown in figure 4.2, to create the bookmark.**

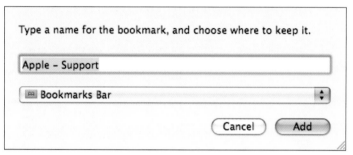

Type a name for the bookmark, and choose where to keep it.

Apple – Support

Bookmarks Bar

Cancel   Add

4.2 Create bookmarks so that you can quickly access your favorite locations on the Web.

Genius

Safari has an even easier way to create a bookmark. Simply click-and-drag the address of the page in the Address field to the Bookmarks bar, give it a name, and then click OK.

Organizing bookmarks

Like toys in a child's room, bookmarks can get quickly out of hand if they aren't organized. To open the Bookmarks window, shown in figure 4.3, choose Bookmarks ⇨ Show All Bookmarks, press ⌘+Option+B, or simply click the icon in the Bookmarks bar that looks like an opened book.

The bookmarks list is on the left side of the window, and houses your bookmark collections. Each collection can contain subfolders as well as bookmarks.

You can organize bookmarks in the Bookmarks window by doing the following:

- **Arrange bookmarks in a collection.** Select the collection you want to organize, and arrange the bookmarks in the order you want them to appear by dragging and dropping them into their preferred position in the list.

- **Arrange bookmark folders in the order you want them to be listed.** Click-and-drag the bookmark folder you want to move to its new position in the bookmarks list.

- **Create new collections.** Click the + button under the left column to create a new bookmark collection, and then give the collection a descriptive name.

- **Create subfolders in collections.** Select the collection you want to add a subfolder to. Click the + button under the right column and give the subfolder a descriptive name.

- **Change the name or address of a bookmark.** Select the collection that contains the bookmark you want to change. Right-click or Ctrl-click the bookmark, and select either Edit Name or Edit Address to make your changes.

- **Delete a bookmark or collection.** Right-click or Ctrl-click the item you want to remove, and select Delete from the list.

Bookmarks list   Bookmark name   Bookmark address   Search for bookmarks

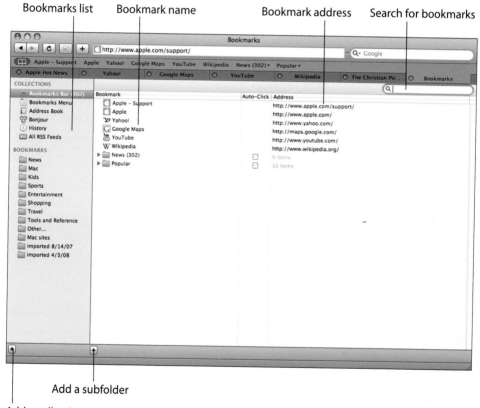

Add a subfolder

Add a collection

4.3 Bookmarks waiting to be whipped into shape!

Genius

You can keep bookmark folders in the Bookmarks bar to provide fast access to multiple sites. Apple has already provided a News folder and a Popular folder in the Bookmarks bar; you can experiment with them to see how beneficial this functionality is.

Importing and exporting bookmarks

Most browsers can export a list of their bookmarks so that you can easily back them up or use them in another browser. To import bookmarks into Safari:

1. **Choose File ⇨ Import Bookmarks.**

2. **Browse your Mac using the Import Bookmarks window, and find the bookmarks file you want to import.**

3. **Highlight the file and click the Import button.**

4. **The Bookmarks window automatically opens and reveals the list of imported bookmarks so that you can organize them.**

To export bookmarks from Safari:

1. **Choose File ⇨ Export Bookmarks.**

2. **Name your bookmarks file in the Export Bookmarks window.**

3. **Browse your Mac for a location to save the bookmarks and click Save.**

Private Browsing

Are you the type who doesn't like the world knowing your business? Do you value your privacy when surfing the Web? Are you a super spy who doesn't want your evil arch nemesis to know what Web sites you've been visiting? You are in luck if you use Safari! Private Browsing is a feature of Safari that prevents anyone else using your Mac from ever knowing what pages you've viewed during your browsing session. To enable Private Browsing:

1. **Choose Safari ⇨ Private Browsing.**

2. **Click OK to enable Private Browsing, as shown in figure 4.4.**

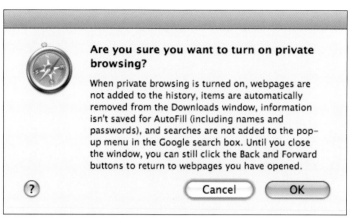

Are you sure you want to turn on private browsing?

When private browsing is turned on, webpages are not added to the history, items are automatically removed from the Downloads window, information isn't saved for AutoFill (including names and passwords), and searches are not added to the pop-up menu in the Google search box. Until you close the window, you can still click the Back and Forward buttons to return to webpages you have opened.

Cancel   OK

4.4 Enable Private Browsing for added privacy.

Note

Private Browsing is only in effect for as long as you are in the current window. When you close the window (not tabs, but the actual window), Private Browsing is disabled.

Viewing Windows Media Files

Watching videos on the Web is becoming more and more common, and two of the most popular formats for viewing video are QuickTime and Windows Media. Leopard has QuickTime built right in, but it has no way for you to view Windows Media files out of the box. Don't worry: The Windows Media Components for QuickTime, by Flip4Mac, make this a non-issue. To get the WMV (Windows Media) components:

1. **Go to this Web site, www.microsoft.com/mac/products/flip4mac.mspx, and click the appropriate links to download the WMV Components disk image.** Safari automatically opens the installer program, as shown in figure 4.5.

2. **Click Continue and accept the license agreements.**

3. **Select your Mac's hard disk as the drive to install the necessary files on, and then click Continue.**

4. **Click the Install button, and enter the username and password of an Administrator account to begin the installation.**

5. **When you see the Install Succeeded prompt, you are finished and can now view Windows Media files on your Mac.**

4.5 You are just a few steps away from viewing Windows Media files in Leopard.

Note The WMV components will work with any browser on your Mac, not just Safari. Nothing further needs to be done in your other browsers to view Windows Media files.

Finding Text on a Web Site

Sometimes you may be only looking for a word or a phrase on a Web page, but it's so packed with information that it would take you half the day to find it. Safari provides a great mechanism for finding text on a Web page that can quickly point you to what you need. To search for text on a Web page:

1. **Press ⌘+F to open the Find field near the upper-right corner of the window (underneath the Bookmarks bar).**

2. **Type the search term or phrase in the Find field, and Safari immediately begins searching as you type.**

3. **Safari displays the number of instances it has found for your search terms on the page next to the left- and right-arrow buttons.** The first instance found on the page is highlighted in yellow, as shown in figure 4.6.

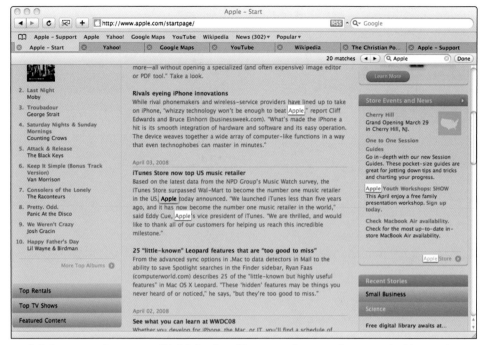

4.6 Safari grays out the page and highlights found instances of my search terms — in this case, the word *Apple*.

4. **Click the left- and right-arrow buttons to cycle through the matches.**

5. **Click the Done button next to the Find field when you are finished.**

Setting Safari Preferences

At the heart of Safari's great features are its preferences. They tell Safari how you want it to behave in both everyday browsing and special circumstances. In this section of the chapter, I discuss the preferences in some detail so that you can take maximum advantage of them to streamline and customize your surfing experience.

General

Table 4.1 gives the scoop on the options available in the General pane of Safari's preferences, which is shown in figure 4.7.

4.7 These are Safari's basic options.

Table 4.1 General Preferences

Option	Description
Default web browser	Choose which Web browser will be the default for your Mac, if you've indeed installed browsers other than Safari, such as Firefox or Opera. Thankfully, there's no longer an Internet Explorer for Mac, so that's one more pat on the back for Leopard!
New windows open with	Select whether new windows should open with your home page, a blank page, your bookmarks, or the same page as the previous window.
Home page	Enter the URL (address) of the Internet site you want to be your home page. Click the Set to Current Page button to make the Web site you are currently viewing your home page.
Remove history items	Delete items from your browsing history after the prescribed length of time.
Save downloaded files to	Select which folder your downloaded files will be saved in.

Option	Description
Remove download list items	Safari keeps a history of files you've downloaded. This option lets you choose how often items on that list should be purged.
Open "safe" files after downloading	Check this option to have Safari automatically open certain types of files, such as disk images and zipped archives, when they are finished downloading.
Open links from applications	Choose to open links from other applications, such as your e-mail program, in either a new window or a new tab in the current window.

Appearance

The Appearance pane lets you choose the fonts that Safari uses to display text in a window. Click the Select buttons to choose a font if the default Times and Courier aren't to your liking.

If you are a speed freak (or conversely, are using a dial-up connection) and don't care about the pictures and graphics that adorn most of today's Web sites, uncheck the Display images when the page opens check box; pages will zip open, displaying their text but no images.

Bookmarks

The selections in the Bookmarks pane allow you to include links that are in your Address Book and home pages of devices running the Bonjour network protocol in your Bookmarks bar, Bookmarks menu, or your Collections.

If you have multiple Macs and a MobileMe account, you can synchronize your Safari bookmarks by selecting the Synchronize bookmarks with other computers using MobileMe check box.

Tabs

The Tabs pane lets you tell Safari how it should handle new tabs when they are opened, as well as whether it can close multiple tabs at once without prompting you.

There are also keyboard shortcuts listed to help you easily open and navigate to new tabs and windows.

RSS

Figure 4.8 shows the options that are available to you in the RSS preferences pane; Table 4.2 describes them for you.

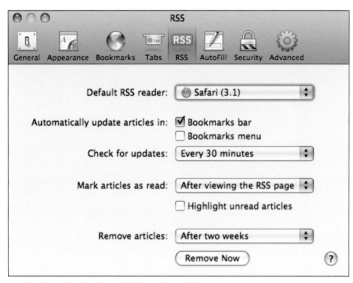

4.8 Options for viewing RSS feeds in Safari.

Table 4.2 RSS Feed Preferences Options

Option	Description
Default RSS reader	If you've downloaded other RSS readers, you can designate one of them to be the default reader for your Mac using this drop-down menu.
Automatically update articles in	Safari can let you know when a site has updated its contents by displaying the number of new articles in the Bookmarks bar, Bookmarks menu, or both.
Check for updates	Determine how often Safari should check your subscribed RSS feeds for updates to their content.
Mark articles as read	Choose whether to mark articles as having been read after you've viewed the page or clicked its link. The "Highlight unread articles" option causes unread feeds to be more visible.
Remove articles	Decide how often to delete old articles. Click the Remove Now button to instantly clear out all of the articles.

AutoFill

Safari uses AutoFill to remember the information you enter into forms on Web sites so that it can automatically enter that information for you in the future. The options available are:

- **Using info from my Address Book card.** This option lets Safari use the information you've entered about yourself in the Address Book application. Click the Edit button to open Address Book and change your information.

- **User names and passwords.** Check this option to have Safari save the usernames and passwords that you use to log on to secure Web sites. I do not recommend this option if security is of any importance to you. Click Edit to see a list of Web sites and the usernames used for them.

- **Other forms.** Safari remembers the information you enter into fields of Web sites, such as online application forms or addresses for driving directions. Clicking Edit allows you to see all the sites you've entered information into in the past.

Security

Table 4.3 lists the options available in the Security pane, as shown in figure 4.9.

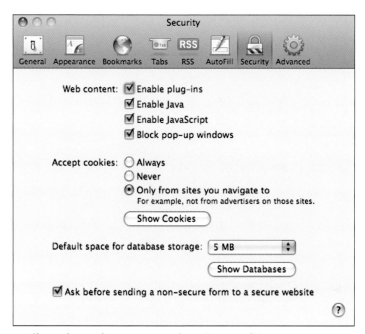

4.9 Choose how to best secure your browsing expeditions.

Table 4.3 Security Options for Safari

Option	Description
Web content	Plug-ins help Safari view or play certain types of content on Web sites, such as movies and sound files. Java and JavaScript are also used for interactive elements on many Web pages. Check the boxes next to these options to enable Safari to use them to enrich your browsing. Check the "Block pop-up windows" option to avoid those pesky ads that infest some Web sites.
Accept cookies	Cookies are text files that some sites use to authenticate you or to track your browsing habits. It's best to select the "Only from sites you navigate to" option. Click the Show Cookies button to view the cookies that Safari is currently storing.
Default space for database storage	Some sites allow you to create and edit documents online, and they use space on your hard drive to store those documents. Use this drop-down menu to allocate the amount of hard disk space you want available for such tasks. Click the Show Databases button to see a list of databases stored by Safari.
Ask before sending a non-secure form to a secure website	When you check this box, Safari prompts you if you are about to send sensitive information to a Web site with little or no security.

Note

One of my few gripes with Safari is the inability to allow some Web sites to open pop-up windows while blocking others. With Safari, it's all or nothing: You either enable pop-up blocking, or you don't. Because some sites have legitimate uses for pop-ups (some folks would argue that all pop-ups are legitimate, but that's not for us to debate here), you have to temporarily turn off pop-up blocking when visiting those sites and turn it back on immediately after leaving them.

Advanced

The Universal Access options in the Advanced pane allow the user to make small text display with a larger font for easier reading, and let them use the Tab key to navigate items on a Web page without using a mouse.

The Style sheet drop-down menu lets you choose a Cascading Style Sheet of your own to use when browsing the Web.

Click the Change Settings button next to the Proxies option to allow your Mac to access the Internet when using a firewall. You may want to ask your IT department what proxy settings to use if you are on a corporate network.

The Show Develop menu in menu bar option displays the Develop menu, which is used mainly by programmers for testing their Web pages.

This Web Site Won't Open in Safari!

Sometimes Web developers put (usually) superficial limitations on which browsers can access their Web sites, for example, if the developer harbors a personal preference for Internet Explorer. Thankfully, this practice is beginning to rapidly decline with the increased use of browsers such as Safari and Firefox, so hopefully you won't often run into this problem. You can bypass their contrived limits, however:

1. **Enable the Develop menu as mentioned in the previous section.**

2. **Choose Develop ⇨ User Agent.**

3. **Select the browser version you want Safari to emulate from the list.** Safari can even pretend it's a browser on a Microsoft Windows PC.

4. **Refresh the offending Web page, and usually you will bypass the bogus limitation.**

How Can I Communicate with Mail and iChat?

Mail is Leopard's easy-to-use e-mail application that is head and shoulders above most e-mail programs that I've used. Mail was already a great e-mail client in its previous incarnation, but with Leopard, it took a big leap forward. The inclusion of RSS and Stationery makes the newest version of Mail an instant hit. Just as there are several e-mail clients to choose from, there are a lot of instant messaging applications available for Mac OS X. However, none work quite as well as the one that comes with Leopard: iChat. iChat not only lets you send text messages, but it also lets you audio and even video chat!

Getting Around in Mail 104

Creating a New Account 106

Composing and Sending New E-mail............................. 110

Receiving, Replying to, and Forwarding E-mail..................... 113

Organizing Mail, Notes, and To Dos 113

Using RSS Feeds... 117

Getting Started with iChat 118

Chat with Friends, Family, and Coworkers 120

Advanced iChat 122

Make Presentations with iChat Theater 124

Getting Around in Mail

Mail is a very straightforward application, and most of its tools are in plain view for easy clicking capability. Figure 5.1 shows Mail's main window so that you can get familiar with its features.

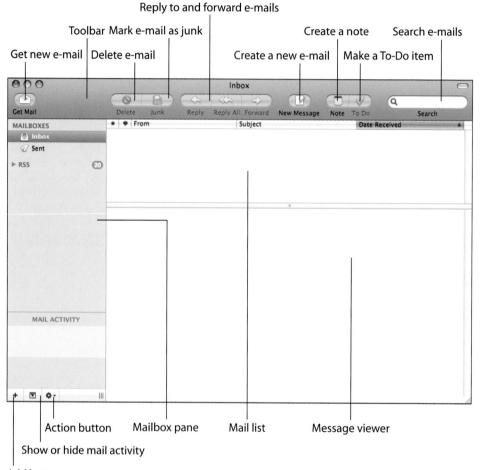

5.1 Mail's main window in its default layout.

Table 5.1 explains a few of the features that are available in the main window. All others are discussed in further detail throughout this chapter.

Table 5.1 Mail's Main Window Features

Feature	Description
Junk	If you use e-mail at all, at some point you will get junk e-mail. Junk e-mail is anything that you simply don't want, whether it is unsolicited advertising or messages from your long-lost cousin who just found out you won the lottery. Highlight the offending message in the Mail list and click the Junk button to permanently mark an e-mail as junk, and to filter future e-mails like it automatically into the Junk folder.
Search	Enter a search term into the Search field, and Mail finds all e-mails that contain the term.
Mailbox pane	Lists all the mailboxes you have created in Mail. Click a mailbox to display its contents.
Add button	Click to quickly create a new mailbox or a new Smart Mailbox, or to add an RSS feed.
Show or hide mail activity	Click to show or hide the Mail activity window, which displays a progress bar when sending or receiving mail.
Action button	Select a mailbox from the Mailbox pane, and then click the Action button (looks like a small gear) to perform the actions in its pop-up list for that mailbox. The Action button also works with RSS feeds.
Mail list	Displays all the e-mails currently in the mailbox that you have selected in the Mailbox pane.
Message viewer	Shows the contents of the e-mail you have selected in the Mail list.

Customize the main toolbar

The toolbar is where Mail's controls reside, but you aren't limited to just the default set of controls. You can modify the controls to your liking quite easily:

1. **Choose View ⇨ Customize Toolbar.**

2. **From the huge list of available controls (shown in figure 5.2), select the ones you want to add to the toolbar.**

3. **Drag the controls you want to add into the toolbar and drop them into the position you like.**

4. **You can arrange the controls in the order you want them to appear by dragging-and-dropping them into the preferred position.** The neat thing is how the other controls move out of the way of the one you are moving.

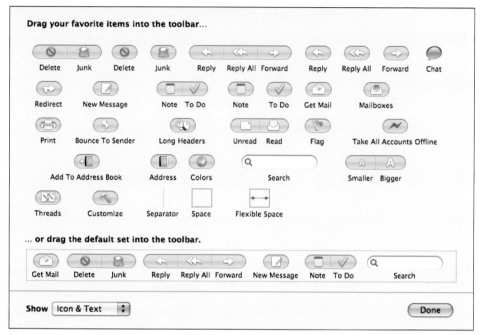

5.2 A plethora of tools for you to use.

5. **Delete controls from the toolbar by dragging them out of the window and dropping them.** They disappear from the toolbar with a puff of smoke!

6. **Click the Done button when you are finished customizing.**

Creating a New Account

Mail won't do much more than take up space on your hard drive if you don't have an e-mail account. When you sign on with an Internet Service Provider (ISP), they should provide you with all the information you need to add an e-mail account to Mail. Be sure to get all the e-mail information from them before you begin to use Mail.

Automatic setup

The first time you start up Mail, you are asked to set up an account in the Welcome to Mail screen, shown in figure 5.3.

Welcome to Mail

Welcome to Mail

You'll be guided through the necessary steps to set up your mail account.

To get started, fill out the following information:

Full Name: Genius

Email Address: portablegenius@comcast.net

Password: ••••••••

☑ Automatically set up account

Cancel   Go Back   Create

5.3 The Welcome to Mail screen.

To set up the account:

1. **Enter a name for the account.**

2. **Type the e-mail address you will use for the account.**

3. **Enter the password for your e-mail account.**

4. **Select the Automatically set up account check box, which should work for most Internet Service Providers.** If this selection doesn't work you will have to manually set up the account, which I discuss in the next section.

5. **Click the Create button, and Mail does the rest of the work for you!**

You can also set up additional accounts automatically:

1. **Choose Mail ⇨ Preferences, or press ⌘+,.**

2. **Select the Accounts tab in the preferences window to open the Accounts pane (see figure 5.4).**

3. **Click the + button in the lower-left corner to add an account.**

4. **Enter the required information in the Add Account window, select the Automatically set up account check box, and then click the Create button.**

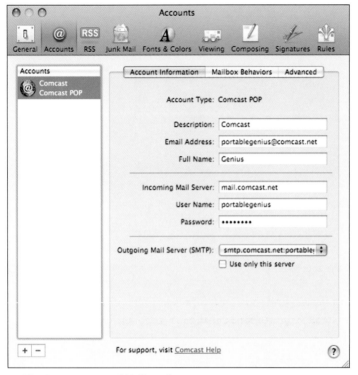

5.4 The Accounts pane of Mail's preferences.

Manual setup

Mail supports POP, IMAP, and Exchange e-mail accounts, and you can add any of these types manually if you prefer this to an automatic setup. Ask your ISP or network administrator what type of account you have and what settings you need to know when setting up your account.

To manually create a new account:

1. **Choose Mail ⇨ Preferences, or press ⌘+,.**

2. **Select the Accounts tab in the preferences window to open the Accounts pane.**

3. **Click the + button in the lower-left corner to add an account.**

4. **Enter the required information in the Add Account window, deselect the Automatically set up account check box, and click Continue.**

5. **In the Incoming Mail Server window (see figure 5.5), choose your Account Type (in my case, POP), and enter the required information as provided by your ISP or network administrator. Click Continue.**

5.5 This information is required to receive e-mail.

6. **In the Outgoing Mail Server window, enter the information for your SMTP server (see figure 5.6), which is required for you to send e-mail to other people.** Click Continue to proceed.

5.6 Enter this information, and you're almost done configuring the account.

7. **Select the Take account online check box to instantly begin using your account, and then click the Create button.**

Composing and Sending New E-mail

Composing your own e-mail and sending it to your intended recipient is a snap with Mail. To begin sending off that world-changing memorandum, do the following:

1. **Click the New Message button in the toolbar.**

2. **In the New Message window, enter the e-mail address of the person you want to receive your message in the To field, as shown in figure 5.7.** To send a copy of the e-mail to other folks, enter their addresses in the Cc field.

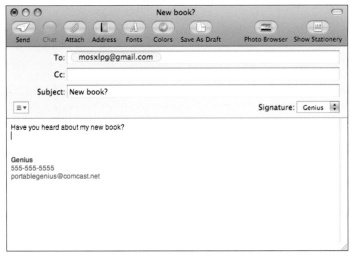

5.7 Putting together that perfect e-mail.

3. **Enter the topic of your e-mail in the Subject field.**

4. **Click the Customize button on the left (represented by a small square containing three horizontal lines and a downward-pointing arrow), and choose whether any other fields, such as Bcc, should appear in the New Message window.**

5. **Type the content of your e-mail and click the Send button in the upper-left corner.**

6. **Congratulate yourself for being a full-blown member of Internet society.**

Using Stationery

One of the coolest new features in Mail for Leopard is the ability to customize e-mails with Stationery. Stationery are preformatted e-mails that Apple provides with Mail, and they can transform an ordinary e-mail into a stunning creation. To use Stationery:

1. **Open a New Message window.**

2. **Click the Show Stationery button in the toolbar.**

3. **Browse the topics listed on the left of the Stationery field (underneath the Subject field and immediately above the e-mail content window), and select the Stationery that is appropriate for your message.**

4. **Customize the contents of your e-mail by dragging-and-dropping your own images into the image placeholders (if any), and enter your own text in the preformatted text fields.**

Adding attachments to e-mails

Sometimes you want to e-mail a picture or send along an accompanying document with your message; these additions are called attachments. To add an attachment to your e-mail:

1. **Open a New Message window and enter the addresses of your recipients.**

2. **Click the Attachment button in the toolbar.**

3. **Browse your trusty Mac for the file you want to attach, select it, and then click the Choose File button.** If sending a picture from your iPhoto or Photo Booth libraries, click the Photo Browser button in the toolbar, drag a picture from the Photo Browser window, and drop it into the body of the e-mail, as shown in figure 5.8.

4. **Send your e-mail on its merry way by clicking the Send button in the toolbar.**

5.8 Drag-and-drop your picture into the e-mail.

Formatting your e-mail's contents

Add a little pizzazz to your message by customizing its fonts and their colors. To format the e-mail:

1. **Open a New Message window.**

2. **Enter the text of your e-mail.**

3. **Highlight the text you want to format.**

4. **Click the Fonts button in the toolbar, and then select the font you want to use.** You can alter the font's typeface and size, underline the text, change the font's color, add a shadow to the text and modify it, and even rotate the text.

Receiving, Replying to, and Forwarding E-mail

Your Inbox typically attempts to receive e-mails automatically every few minutes, but you can also have Mail check the server for new e-mails manually in one of the following ways:

- **Click the Get Mail button in the toolbar.**

- **Press ⌘+Shift+N.**

- **Choose Mailbox ⇨ Get New Mail, and then select the account you want to check.**

Note   You don't have to be working in Mail to see when new e-mail arrives, but Mail does have to be running, of course. The Mail icon in the Dock displays a red circle containing the number of unread e-mails so that you can easily tell when you have a new mail waiting to be read.

When someone sends you an e-mail, it shows up in your Inbox for the account the e-mail was sent to. It appears in the Mail list in bold letters and has a blue dot to the left of the From field. The Inbox also displays a light-blue oval with the number of unread e-mails it contains. Simply click the e-mail in the Mail list to read it in the Message Viewer.

To reply to or forward an e-mail you've received:

1. **Highlight the e-mail you want to respond to in the Mail list.**

2. **Click the Reply button to respond to the person who sent the e-mail to you, the Reply All button to send a message to all recipients of the e-mail, or the Forward button to send the e-mail to other parties.**

3. **Enter text or add attachments to your message.**

4. **Click the Send button in the toolbar.**

Organizing Mail, Notes, and To Dos

In this section, I show you how to use Mailboxes to keep your e-mail organized, Notes to keep your thoughts straight, and To Dos to keep that list of tasks in tip-top shape.

Mailboxes

Mailboxes keep your e-mail organized, and each account can have several mailboxes. Table 5.2 lists some of the types of mailboxes that accounts can have.

Table 5.2 Functions of Standard Mailboxes

Mailbox	Description
Inbox	Incoming messages to your e-mail account are stored here.
Drafts	Sometimes you may want to save an e-mail you've typed so that you can send it at a later time. The Drafts folder is where those saved e-mails reside until you are ready to send them.
Sent	Copies of messages you have sent to people are kept here.
Trash	This is where your deleted messages reside until you are ready to completely erase them from your Mac.
Junk	Messages that are flagged as junk mail are deposited into this mailbox. This way, they don't intrude with your normal activities but can be sifted through later at your convenience.

Create custom and Smart Mailboxes

Mail lets you create your own mailboxes to suit your individual needs. You can make custom mailboxes that are named for different items or topics (such as "Bills"), or you can use Smart Mailboxes. A Smart Mailbox allows you to create rules that the Smart Mailbox follows. For example, you could set up a Smart Mailbox that automatically moves any e-mail that comes from a particular person to itself.

To create a new custom mailbox:

1. **Click the + button in the bottom-left corner of the Mail window, and select New Mailbox.**

2. **In the New Mailbox window, shown in figure 5.9, select a location for the new mailbox to be saved.**

3. **Give the new mailbox a descriptive name and then click OK.** The new mailbox appears in the Mailbox pane on the left side of the Mail window.

To set up a Smart Mailbox (I love these things):

1. **Click the + button in the lower-left corner of the Mail window, and select New Smart Mailbox.**

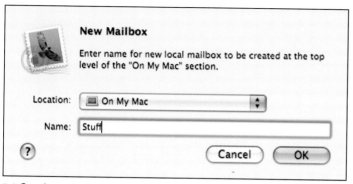

5.9 Creating a new mailbox.

2. **In the sheet that appears (see figure 5.10), give the mailbox a descriptive name.**

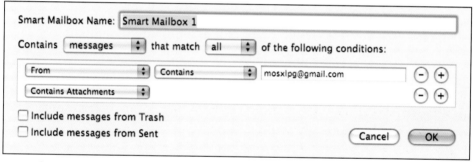

5.10 Make a Smart Mailbox to help you organize and save time finding e-mails.

3. **Select what the mailbox will contain and how the items in it should match the criteria you are about to define.**

4. **Define the criteria for items that the mailbox should or should not contain.** Click the + button to the right to add a new criterion, or the – button to remove it.

5. **Decide whether to include messages that are in the Trash or Sent mailboxes, and check or uncheck the boxes as appropriate.**

6. **Click OK to create the new Smart Mailbox.**

Notes and To Dos

Mail provides the convenience of letting you create Notes, which are ways to jot down ideas when you have them, and save them in Mail or send them to someone via e-mail.

Back Up Those Mailboxes!

It is always a great idea to keep a backup of your e-mails in case something happens to Mail, Leopard, or worse, your Mac. You can restore your lost e-mails to their proper places if you've been making consistent backups of your mailboxes.

To back up a mailbox:

1. **Select the mailbox you want to archive.**
2. **Choose Mailbox ⇨ Archive Mailbox.**
3. **Select the folder you want to save the mailbox archive in, and click the Choose button.**
4. **An archive of the mailbox is created in the appropriate folder using the MBOX format.**

To restore a mailbox:

1. **Choose File ⇨ Import mailboxes.**
2. **Click the radio button next to Mail for Mac OS X and click Continue.**
3. **Browse your Mac to find the archived mailbox you want to restore, select it, and then click Choose.**

To take a note:

1. **Click the Note button in the toolbar.**
2. **Type the contents of the note in the New Note window.**
3. **Click Done to save the note, Send to e-mail the note, Attach to add an item to it (just like with an e-mail), Fonts or Colors to format the text, or To Do to make the note a To Do item.**

To Dos are simply tasks that you need to accomplish. You can keep track of your To Do items with Mail. There are a couple of ways to create a To Do item:

- **Click the To Do button in the toolbar and enter the necessary information, such as the title of the item and the due date.**

- **Highlight text in any message or note that you want to keep track of, such as a part number for an item you need to order or a meeting you need to attend, and click the To Do button in the toolbar.**

Notes and To Dos can easily be accessed from under the Reminders heading in the Mailboxes pane, as shown in figure 5.11.

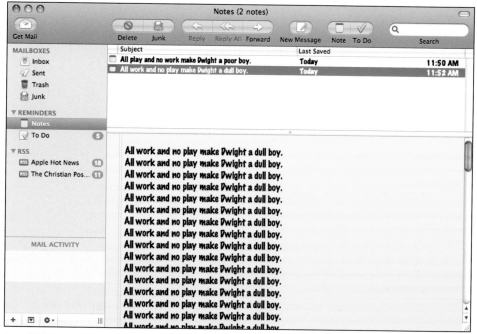

5.11 Click Notes or To Dos to see a list of each.

Using RSS Feeds

RSS (Really Simple Syndication) is used by Web sites that update their information on a frequent basis, such as news sites. The site uses an RSS feed to broadcast when updates to the Web site have been posted. As of Leopard, Mail can now act as an RSS reader, meaning that you can use it to track when new articles are posted to your favorite sites. I love this new feature, and use it now instead of third-party RSS reader applications because I can have one less application open while retaining the functionality.

To use RSS feeds in Mail:

1. **Find out the address of the RSS page for the site you want to track.** When using Safari for your Web browser, it's very easy to detect whether a Web site uses an RSS feed: you see the letters *RSS* to the right of the address in Safari's Address field.

2. **Click the + button in the lower-left corner of Mail's window, and select Add RSS Feeds.**

3. **Select the radio button next to Specify a custom feed URL, as shown in figure 5.12.**

4. **Type the address of the feed (or copy and paste its address from a Web browser Address field) into the text field.**

○ Browse feeds in Safari Bookmarks
⦿ Specify a custom feed URL

feed://www.christianpost.com/rss/feed.xml?category=index

☐ Show in Inbox   (Cancel)   (**Add**)

5.12 Adding an RSS feed to Mail

5. **Click Add.** The feed shows up under the RSS heading in the Mailboxes pane.

6. **Click the feed in the Mailboxes pane to see its latest postings.**

7. **If the article snippet intrigues you, click the Read More link to open the full article in Safari.**

Getting Started with iChat

Instant messaging is one of the most popular forms of communication today. Using the Internet, you can have instant conversations with anyone anywhere in the world. iChat is a great instant messaging client that can do much more than just send text clips back and forth. You can even exchange files with the folks you're chatting with, like sending them pictures, documents, and music. To start using iChat, you need to set up an account and add some contacts to your Buddy List.

Set up an iChat account

iChat can use several different types of instant messaging accounts, which are laid out for you in Table 5.3.

Table 5.3 iChat Account Types

Account type	Description
MobileMe	If you sign up for a MobileMe account, you can use your MobileMe username and password to log into iChat. You can sign up for a free sixty-day trial of MobileMe by choosing Apple menu ⇨ System Preferences, selecting the MobileMe icon, and then clicking the Learn More button.
AIM	AIM stands for AOL Instant Messenger. You can use your existing AIM account, or sign up for a new one at http://dashboard.aim.com/aim.
Jabber	Jabber is an open source implementation of instant messaging. Get a login name by going to www.jabber.org/.
Google Talk	If you have a Google account, you can log in to chat with Google Talk users with iChat. Learn more about Google Talk at www.google.com/talk/.

Genius

You can only chat with people who are using the same account type as you. For example, if you have a .Mac account but your friend is using a Jabber account, you can't instant message them unless one of you signs up for the other's account type. My recommendation would be to go ahead and sign up for all four account types (you must pay for .Mac, however); that way, you've covered your bases!

After you get your account affiliations in order, it's time to start up iChat.

1. **From within the Finder, press ⌘+Shift+A to open the Applications folder.**

2. **Double-click the iChat icon.**

Note

When you open iChat for the first time, you are greeted with a welcome screen. Simply click Continue to move forward and set up an account.

To add your instant messaging account to iChat:

1. **Select iChat and choose Preferences from the menu.**

2. **Click the Accounts tab, and then click the + button in the lower-left corner of the window.**

3. **In the Account Setup window, choose the account type you want to use, enter the information for the account, and click Done.** Your new account is now added to the list.

Add buddies to your Buddy List

After you add an account, you are logged into it automatically, and a Buddy List window appears, as shown in figure 5.13.

You can add some buddies to your list, using the following steps:

1. **Click the + button in the lower-left corner of your Buddy List and choose Add Buddy.**

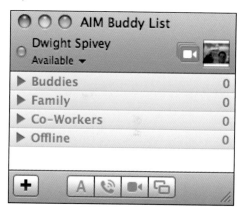

5.13 My list of buddies is pretty short, isn't it?

2. **Enter your buddy's account information in the window, similar to the one
shown in figure 5.14, and click Add.**

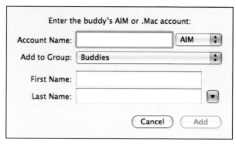

Your newly added buddy should show up in
your Buddy List, ready and waiting to chat
with you.

5.14 Adding a buddy to your Buddy List couldn't
be much easier.

Chat with Friends, Family, and Coworkers

You've got your iChat accounts, and you've added a buddy or two to your Buddy List. The only
thing left to do at this point is to start chatting. As I mentioned earlier, there are three ways in iChat
to converse with someone: using text, audio, and video. I show you how to get started with each
method in the following section.

Text chats

Text chats are the most common method of instant messaging to date, but as more and more people get connected to broadband Internet connections (such as cable and DSL), the trend will most
likely be towards video.

To start a text chat:

1. **Select the buddy you want to chat with from your Buddy List.**

2. **Click the A button in the bottom of the Buddy List window to initiate the chat session.**

Find Out Your Buddy's iChat Capabilities

You may have the ability to do everything with iChat: text, audio, and video. However, if
your buddy is on an older version of iChat, has a slower Internet connection or computer,
or uses a different chat client altogether, they may not be able to join you in one form of
chat or another. You can check their iChat abilities quite easily:

1. **Select your buddy's name in the Buddy List.**

2. **Choose Buddies ⇨ Show Profile from the menu.**

3. **Your buddy's iChat capabilities are listed in the Profile tab of the
Info window.**

---

3. **Start typing away, and soon you'll be chatting like there's no tomorrow.** After you're finished typing a response, press Return to send it.

Audio chats

You may wonder why you would audio chat when you've got a phone, but in some cases, phone conversations may not be free; audio chats are always free.

To begin an audio chat:

1. **Select the buddy you want to chat with from your Buddy List.**

2. **Click the phone button in the bottom of the Buddy List window to initiate the audio chat session.**

3. **Your buddy receives an invitation, just like the one in figure 5.15.** They can choose to send a text reply instead of speaking with you, decline the invitation altogether and bruise your ego, or accept, and you two can begin conversing.

5.15 Accept the invitation to begin audio chatting.

Note You must have a microphone and speakers attached to your Mac to audio chat. Most Macs today have both features built right in.

Video chats

Video chats are where it's at! The ability to see and speak to one another across the miles (for free, no less) is the dream of every displaced parent and grandparent. It was a godsend when I had to be away from my wife and kids for two weeks on business.

To initiate a video chat:

1. **Select the buddy you want to chat with from your Buddy List.**

2. **Click the video button (which looks like a small video camera) in the bottom of the Buddy List window to initiate the video chat.**

3. **Your buddy receives an invitation, just like in the audio chat.** Again, they can choose to send a text reply, decline the invitation, or accept the invitation. It may take a few seconds to connect to one another, depending on the speed of your Internet connections.

4. **Once you establish a connection, you can see one another and talk just like you were there.** You see your buddy in the large window, and yourself in a smaller preview window (so you can see just how goofy you look to your friend). figure 5.16 shows me talking with my daughter.

5.16 Video chatting with my favorite ballerina.

Note

To video chat, you must have a broadband Internet connection — no ifs, ands, or buts about it. Dial-up simply doesn't have the ability to stream video.

Advanced iChat

As if iChat can't do enough already, there's still more neat stuff you can squeeze out of it, like tabbed chatting and the ability to transfer files through a chat session.

Use Special Effects with Video Chats

Spice up your video chats with special effects, exactly like those used in Photo Booth to add some pizzazz to your snapshots. To add special effects:

1. **Click the Effects button in the lower-left corner of the video chat window.**

2. **Choose from any of the effects on the list to make you appear in the video chat window using those effects.** There are filter effects (like Glow), distortion effects (such as Dent), and you can use video backdrops as well.

See Chapter 7 for more information on using backdrops and custom backdrops; they work exactly the same in iChat as they do in Photo Booth (no need to cover the same ground twice in one book).

Tabbed chatting

If you are someone who is constantly chatting with others, and you have multiple chat windows open at one time, your Desktop gets pretty cluttered. You can clean that clutter up by using tabbed chatting, which moves all chats to a single window. Each chat is given a separate tab in that window; simply click the tab to go to the chat you want to engage in. To enable tabbed chatting:

1. **Choose iChat and select Preferences.**

2. **Click the Messages tab.**

3. **Check the box next to Collect chats into a single window.**

Send files to buddies

iChat allows you to send files of all types through a chat session. To send a file to a buddy:

1. **Open a chat session with a buddy, or just highlight their name in the Buddy List.**

2. **Select Buddy from the menu and choose Send File, or press ⌘+Option+F.**

3. **Browse your Mac for the file you want to send, select it, and click the Send button.**

4. **Your buddy is then asked whether they want to receive the file.**

Receive files from your buddy

When a buddy sends you a file, here's how to retrieve it:

- **If you are not already chatting with the buddy, you receive an invitation, like the one in figure 5.17, to save the file or decline it.**

- **If you are already in a chat session with your buddy, the file appears in the chat window when they send it.** Drag the file from the chat window to your Desktop to save it.

5.17 Press Save to save the file to your Mac, or press Decline to break your buddy's heart.

Make Presentations with iChat Theater

iChat Theater lets you make presentations of documents, Keynote slide shows, iPhoto album slide shows, QuickTime movies, and other files. You control the presentation from your Mac while the recipients view it on their computers. To use iChat Theater:

1. **Choose File ⇨ Share a File with iChat Theater from the menu.**

2. **Browse your Mac to find the file you want to share, select it, and click the Share button.**

3. **If you don't already have a video chat opened with the buddies you want to make the presentation to, you are prompted to start one.**

4. **Once the video chat starts, a control window opens.** If you are presenting an iPhoto album, iPhoto opens so you can use its controls. If presenting a Keynote slide show, Keynote opens so that you may use its controls.

5. **Close the control window once the presentation is finished.**

What Are iTunes' Coolest Features?

Gotta have that music! And those movies. Don't forget about the television shows and podcasts, too! In today's world, we want our entertainment now, we want it affordable, portable, and we prefer it digital. Leopard can meet all those needs with a nifty little tool called iTunes. In the few short years it's been around, iTunes has quickly become an integral part of our entertainment arsenal. When you throw an iPod or iPhone into the mix, iTunes becomes an absolute necessity. Thankfully, it's just as intuitive and easy to use as everything else Mac; you'll be addicted to its charms before you know it!

Getting Around in iTunes 128

Organizing Media 130

Using the iTunes Store 134

Setting iTunes Preferences 135

Getting Around in iTunes

iTunes can handle most of your digital entertainment needs, but you need to know how to use its menus, buttons, and features before you can get much use out of it. This section on finding where everything is located, and the next section that describes the iTunes preferences, will make you a near-expert iTunes user in little time at all.

Understanding the iTunes window layout

Figure 6.1 shows the iTunes default interface, and points out the multitude of buttons and menus. Table 6.1 describes what many of these buttons and menus can help you do in iTunes.

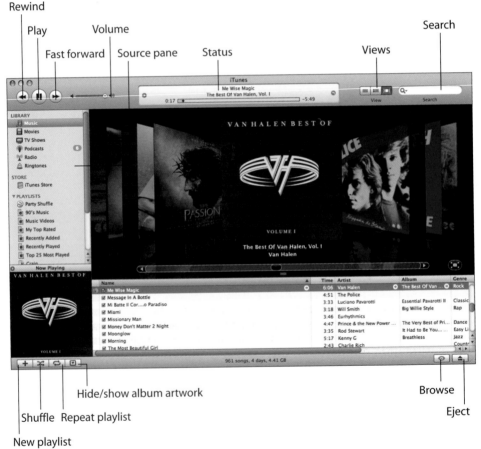

6.1 iTunes is your personal entertainment hub.

Table 6.1 iTunes Functionality

Item	Description
Library	Lists all of the items available for you to use in iTunes.
Store	Click to access the iTunes Store.
Playlists	Lists the playlists and Smart Playlists that you have created.
Album artwork/ Video viewer	See the album artwork for the song you are listening to, or watch videos.
Cover Flow slider	Drag to fly through the album covers when in Cover Flow view.
Eject disc	Click to eject any CDs that are in your Mac.
Full screen	Puts iTunes into Full Screen mode.
Search	Type in text to help you find items in your iTunes Library, such as the name of a song or the artist who sings it.
View	Choose to view items in a list, grouped together by their albums or using Cover Flow.
Status	Shows the status of songs currently being played, CDs being burned, and items being copied.

Full Screen mode

I'm a creature of habit so I still prefer the standard view in iTunes, but I'm beginning to understand why others tend to like Full Screen mode even better. Full Screen mode lets iTunes take over your entire screen, but with a bare minimum of controls at your disposal, as shown in figure 6.2.

Genius

You can add the album cover artwork to your music files in iTunes. Choose the Advanced menu and select Get Album Artwork; iTunes automatically scans your Library and adds artwork to your songs. You must have an iTunes login to perform this action, but it's easy enough to do; iTunes prompts you to create one if you aren't already logged in. An iTunes login performs several functions, including making it easy for Apple to access your billing and shipping information, and to unlock files you've purchased from iTunes.

Play Fast forward   Cover Flow slider   Volume

Rewind   Exit Full Screen mode

6.2 iTunes takes up the entire screen in Full Screen mode.

Organizing Media

iTunes is a pretty useless application without content. It's also a master at helping you organize that content. This section quickly teaches you how to import your own music from CDs or files and how to use the iTunes Store to find and add new content to your collection.

Importing music

Bringing your music into iTunes is the first order of business. Apple makes it ridiculously easy to import your CD collection and music files that you have stored on other computers or discs.

Automatically importing from CDs

When you insert a CD into your Mac, you're asked if you want to import its contents into iTunes, as shown in figure 6.3. Click Yes to automatically import all the content on your CD into iTunes.

Your newly imported content now appears in your Library.

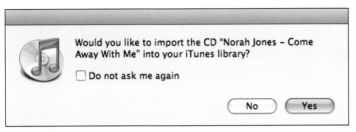

6.3 A confirmation dialog appears when you insert a music CD.

Importing individual music files

iTunes lets you import music files that exist on other media as well, such as a folder on your hard drive or another computer on your network. To import music files:

1. **Press ⌘+O.**

2. **Browse your Mac or your network for the music file or files you want to import from within the Add to Library window.**

3. **Highlight the music files and click Open.**

The new music is now available in your Library.

Creating playlists

You can create playlists using the songs in your Library. Playlists are collections of songs that you arrange in the order that you like them to play. Here's how to make a playlist:

1. **Press ⌘+N.** A playlist called Untitled appears in the Playlists section of the Source pane.

2. **Type a name for your new playlist.** I'm creating a playlist for a compilation of songs by U2 in this tutorial.

3. **Find the items you want to add to your playlist in your Library, and drag-and-drop them onto the name of the new playlist, as shown in figure 6.4.**

6.4 Adding songs to my new playlist.

Using Smart Playlists

Smart Playlists automatically add songs to themselves based on criteria that you set for them. iTunes already comes with a few Smart Playlists, such as Recently Played and Recently Added. To create a new Smart Playlist:

1. **Press ⌘+Option+N.**

2. **Enter the criteria the Smart Playlist should use when adding songs.** In figure 6.5, I'm creating a new Smart Playlist that adds any songs to it that are by Randy Travis (yes, you could say my taste in music is fairly eclectic).

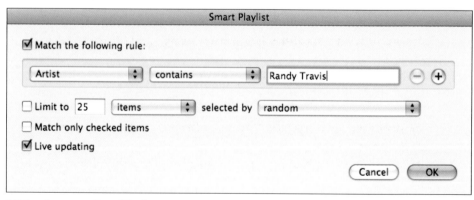

6.5 Creating a new Smart Playlist.

3. **Add more criteria by clicking the + button on the right side of the window, or remove criteria by clicking the – button.** Check the Live updating box to have the Smart Playlist check every time you add an item to your Library to see if it meets the criteria you assigned.

4. **Click OK when you are finished.** Your Smart Playlist automatically populates itself based on the criteria you entered.

Burning CDs

I enjoy a variety of music, and I love having the ability to create my own albums and burn them to CDs. There's nothing to it:

1. **Create a playlist and add the music you want to burn to a CD.**

2. **Right-click, or Ctrl-click, the playlist you want to burn, and select Burn Playlist to Disc, as shown in figure 6.6.**

3. **Insert a blank CD into your Mac, and iTunes takes care of the rest!**

6.6 Burning a playlist to a CD.

Print Your Music

The old days of handwriting the names of your songs onto those boring blank CD labels are over! iTunes lets you create custom CD jewel case inserts, song lists, and album lists in a snap.

1. **Highlight the playlist, artist, or album you want to print information about.**

2. **Press ⌘+P to open a print window.**

3. **Choose whether to print a jewel case insert, a song list, or an album list.**

4. **Select from one of the available themes.**

5. **Click the Print button in the lower-right corner.**

6. **Choose the printer you want to send the job to, and click the Print button.**

The categories of items you can get from the iTunes Store are listed in the iTunes Store section on the left side of the window. Table 6.2 lists the options offered by Apple.

Table 6.2 Items Available for Download or Purchase from the iTunes Store

Item	Description
Music	Download individual songs or entire albums.
Movies	You can rent or buy movies to view.
TV Shows	Watch your television shows on your own time instead of the networks' time.
Music Videos	See previews of and buy videos for your favorite songs.
Audiobooks	Purchase entire audiobooks and listen to them on your Mac, iPod, or iPhone.
Podcasts	Podcasts are radio shows or videos that you can subscribe to and download. I swear by my favorite podcasts!
iPod Games	Buy games that you can play on your iPod.
iTunes Latino	Offers items for Latin music lovers.
iTunes U	Listen to or view lectures from professors at major universities on a huge range of topics. One of my iTunes favorites.

Using the iTunes Store

The iTunes Store is your one-stop shop for content such as music, movies, television shows, and podcasts of all kinds. New items are added to the iTunes Store all the time, and once you've tried it, you'll get hooked just as I have. To access the iTunes Store, simply click the iTunes Store icon in the Source pane, as shown in figure 6.7.

 Note You must have an active Internet connection to use the iTunes Store, and broadband is preferable.

6.7 The iTunes Store is addictive, so be careful!

Setting iTunes Preferences

iTunes preferences are where you tell iTunes how to interact with you, as well as items such as iPods, iPhones, and Apple TV. Let's explore these preferences because they determine how iTunes functions to best suit your needs. Choose iTunes ⇨ Preferences to get started.

General

The General tab lets you choose what items are shown in the Source pane, what to view when browsing your iTunes Library, and whether or not to automatically check for updates. You can also assign a shared name to your Library so others can access your items.

Podcasts

These preferences determine how iTunes handles your podcast subscriptions. You can tell iTunes how often to check for new episodes, what to do when it finds new episodes, and how long it should keep episodes in your Library.

Playback

The Playback preferences, shown in figure 6.8, determine how iTunes plays your music and videos.

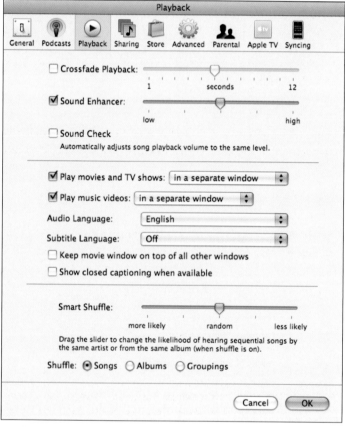

6.8 Listen to music and watch movies and television shows the way you want.

Sharing

The Sharing preferences determine whether you can see other shared iTunes libraries from users on your network, and how you share your libraries with other users, if at all. You can share your iTunes library with up to five other computers on your network, as long as they are in the same network subnet as your Mac. While you can listen to music and watch video shared by other computers on your network, you cannot add them to your iTunes library.

Genius

Selecting the Sound Check option is a good idea. This prevents you from listening to one song that may have a lower volume level and then having your eardrums blown out by another song whose volume level is much higher. Sound Check evens all the volume levels of items in your Library so that there are no "surprise attacks" like the one I described.

Store

You can decide how iTunes handles your purchases. You can choose to download items on the fly with the 1-Click feature, or purchase them the more traditional way, using the shopping cart method.

Advanced

The Advanced preferences are where you make the most useful settings in iTunes, as shown in figure 6.9. Table 6.3 breaks down some of the major features under each tab.

Table 6.3 Major Functions Available in Advanced Preferences

Tab	Function	Description
General	iTunes Music folder location	Lets you choose to keep your imported music in a location other than the default, which is in the Music folder of your user account.
General	Copy files to iTunes to Library	Makes a copy of a music file in your iTunes when adding Music folder. You can uncheck this option if you don't want to have multiple copies of the same file strewn throughout your system, but I personally prefer to make the copy in my iTunes folder and delete the original. It's just easier for me to keep organized that way.
General	Visualizer Size	Sets the default size of your Visualizer. Full screen rocks!
Importing	On CD Insert	Decide how iTunes should react when you insert a CD into your Mac.

continued

Table 6.3 continued

Tab	Function	Description
Importing	Import Using and Setting	Import Using lets you choose which type of encoding to save your imported music in (AAC is the default and retains good sound while maintaining a reasonable file size), and Setting lets you decide the quality of the imported file.
Burning	Preferred Speed	If you are having problems burning a CD, try changing these settings to a slower speed.
Burning	Disc Format	You don't just have to burn music CDs. You can also burn MP3 and data discs.

Parental

Most parents don't like to think of their kids having unfettered access to any and everything on the Internet, so why should items in iTunes be any different? The Parental preferences let Mom and Dad decide what limits to place on iTunes content for their children.

Apple TV

The Apple TV preferences simply help you synchronize with an Apple TV appliance. You can set iTunes to automatically look for Apple TVs when it opens.

Syncing

Syncing preferences simply displays a list of iPods or iPhones that are backed up on your Mac. Check the Disable automatic syncing for all iPhones and iPods check box to prevent your Mac from trying to sync automatically every time one of these devices is connected.

Consult your iPhone or iPod documentation for synchronizing with iTunes and using iTunes to change their settings.

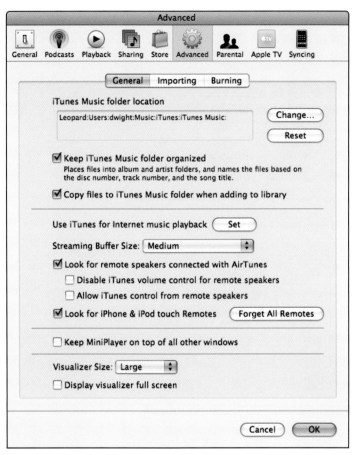

6.9 The General tab of the Advanced preferences.

What Can Leopard Do with Digital Photography?

In today's digital age, you simply can't have a computer, Mac or otherwise, without using it to catalog and share images. Fortunately, Leopard offers you several ways to have fun with digital photography. Photo Booth, while indeed functional, is still all about fun. Besides just making silly pictures, you can use Photo Booth to take video, and you can even use special effects with your pictures and video, including using your own custom backdrops. Since Apple is all about making your digital lifestyle easier, Leopard also works with most digital cameras and scanners right out of the box. Image Capture is the tool Leopard ships with to help you transfer images to and from your digital camera or to import files using your scanner.

Get to Know Photo Booth 142

Take Snapshots 143

Use Special Effects. 144

How to Use Your Pictures and Videos. 147

Working with Image Capture 148

Using a Digital Camera. 150

Using a Scanner 154

Sharing Devices 156

Get to Know Photo Booth

Apple has moved the old-fashioned photo booths that we used to cram ourselves into with our friends on Friday nights from the mall to our Macs. Simple as it is, there are still a few features that could do with explaining. When I get anything new, I'm one of those people who actually likes to read the instructions and know what all the buttons and gadgets are for. Hence my insistence on you learning about the Photo Booth features that I've laid out for you in figure 7.1.

7.1 The Photo Booth main window in Snapshot mode.

Take Snapshots

Any kind of picture you take with Photo Booth is considered a snapshot, whether it's a still picture or a video. You can take three different kinds of snapshots: single still pictures, four quick snapshots (which are much more fun than you might think), and video. Use the snapshot-type buttons under the bottom-left corner of the viewer window to select the kind of snapshot you want to take.

Single snapshots

Single snapshots, or still pictures, are so easy to take it's ridiculous:

1. **Click the Take a still picture button under the bottom-left corner of the viewer window.**

2. **Position yourself in front of your Mac's camera so that your image fits inside the viewer window.**

3. **Click the Camera button.**

4. **Photo Booth begins its countdown from three, flashes, and takes the picture.** That's it!

Take a four-up snapshot

Taking four-up snapshots, or four quick pictures, lets you create different poses in rapid succession. Try it out:

1. **Click the Take four quick pictures button under the bottom-left corner of the viewer window.**

2. **Position yourself in front of your Mac's camera so that your image fits inside the viewer window.**

3. **Click the Camera button to begin the countdown.** Get into your first pose before the first flash goes off!

4. **After the first flash, immediately change to your next pose and continue to do that through all four pictures.** You've only got about a second between snapshots, so you've got to move quickly!

5. **When all four snapshots are taken, you see a preview of your images, similar to figure 7.2.**

7.2 A preview shows in the viewer window so that you can see your four-up handiwork.

Creating video

The ability to make movies is a new feature in Photo Booth. To create that movie magic:

1. **Click the Take a movie clip button under the bottom-left corner of the viewer window.**

2. **Position yourself in front of your Mac's camera so that your image fits inside the viewer window.**

3. **Click the Camera button to begin the countdown.**

4. **Begin your video once the flash goes off.**

5. **When finished with the video, click the Stop button.**

Viewing your snapshots

All of your snapshots are stored in the thumbnail bar at the bottom of the Photo Booth window. You can scroll through the list of snapshots using the right- and left-arrow keys on either side of the bar.

To view a snapshot, simply click it in the thumbnail bar. It displays in the viewer window.

To find a snapshot on your Mac, click the snapshot in the thumbnail bar, and then press ⌘+R to open a Finder window displaying its exact location on the hard drive.

Genius

You can access your snapshots without having to open Photo Booth every time you need them. Photo Booth stores snapshots in the Photo Booth folder, which resides in the Pictures folder of your Home folder (Hard drive/Users/*your account name*/Pictures/Photo Booth).

Use Special Effects

You've only just seen the tip of the Photo Booth iceberg. Photo Booth can do something the old photo booths at the mall could only dream of: add awesome special effects and backdrops!

Snapshot effects

To use visual effects like filters or distortions for your snapshots:

1. **Position yourself in front of your Mac's camera so that your image fits inside the viewer window.**

2. **Click the Effects button to see the cool filter effects shown in figure 7.3.**

7.3 These are the filter effects available in Photo Booth. You gotta love X-Ray!

3. **Click the right arrow next to the Effects button to see the distortion effects, like those shown in figure 7.4.**

4. **Select the effect you want to use by clicking it, and then click the Camera button to take the picture.**

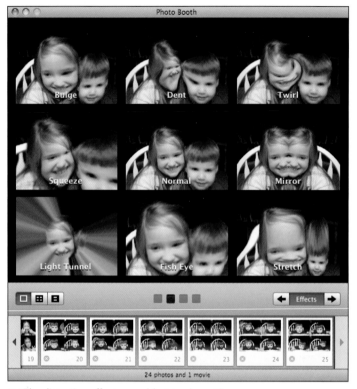

7.4 The distortion effects are a blast to play with.

Video backdrops

Video backdrops are really neat to use. They place a moving video of some exotic location behind you so that it appears like you're really there. Impress family and friends by creating a video of yourself in front of the Eiffel Tower, swimming with the fishes, or flying through the clouds!

1. **Position yourself in front of your Mac's camera so that your image fits inside the viewer window.**

2. **Click the Effects button.**

3. **Click the right arrow next to the Effects button twice until it brings you to the video backdrops.**

4. **Select the backdrop you want to use.**

5. **Step out of the frame when prompted until you see the backdrop you chose in the viewer window.**

6. **Move into the frame of the viewer window and click the Camera button to make your video, as shown in figure 7.5.**

Adding custom backdrops

My favorite feature of Photo Booth is the ability to use my own photos and videos as backdrops. To create a custom backdrop:

7.5 She's not even getting her hair wet!

1. **Click the Effects button and then click the right arrow next to it three times to see the custom backdrop window.**

2. **Drag-and-drop a picture or video from the Finder, iPhoto, or iMovie into one of the Drag Backdrop Here windows.**

3. **Select the new backdrop to use it for your picture or video.**

How to Use Your Pictures and Videos

What to do with all these great snapshots you've been taking? You can save your snapshots in iPhoto if you like, e-mail them to family and friends, or use them to represent you in an online chat session.

Click a snapshot in the thumbnail bar that you would like to work with. Notice in figure 7.6 that when you open the snapshot in preview mode, you now have several new icons underneath the viewer window. Table 7.1 explains what clicking each icon does for you.

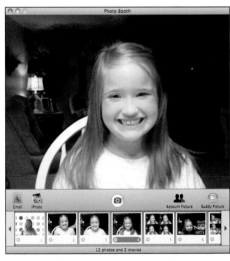

7.6 Icons to help you use your snapshots appear when you click a snapshot in the thumbnail bar.

Table 7.1 Using Your Photo Booth Snapshots

Icon	Action
e-mail	Opens the Mail application and automatically creates a new e-mail containing the snapshot. Enter the e-mail address of your intended recipient and send it right along.
iPhoto	Launches iPhoto (if you have it installed; iPhoto is not part of Leopard, but is part of the Apple iLife application suite) and automatically imports the picture from Photo Booth.
Account Picture	Automatically opens the Accounts pane of System Preferences, selects your user account, and changes your account picture to the one you selected in Photo Booth.
Buddy Picture	Opens iChat and changes the picture that people you chat with will see.

Working with Image Capture

Image Capture is a great tool that may surprise you with its versatility. You can use it to do any of the following:

- **Transfer images from or to your digital camera.**
- **Delete images from your digital camera.**
- **Scan and import images with your scanner.**
- **Create slide shows or Web sites with your images.**
- **Share your digital camera or scanner with other users on your network.**
- **Find shared devices on your network.**

Printing Your Snapshots

You can print your snapshots from Photo Booth just as you can from any other application. To print your snapshots:

1. **Choose File ⇨ Print from the menu, or press ⌘+P.**

2. **When the print dialog opens, choose one of the options in the Photo Booth pane.** You can print the picture normally, or you can print proof sheets (either several different sizes of the same picture on the same page, or eight pictures of the same size).

To open Image Capture, press ⌘+Shift+A from within the Finder, find Image Capture in the resulting Finder window, and then double-click its icon. If you don't have a digital camera or scanner attached to your Mac when you start Image Capture, you are notified in a dialog box that no device is connected. If this is the case for you when you open Image Capture, read on to discover how to connect your device.

Note

You may wonder why iPhoto, Apple's amazing photo-organizing and -editing program, isn't covered in this book. iPhoto is actually part of the iLife application suite, which Apple sells separately from Leopard. Because I'm concentrating on Leopard in this book, Image Capture gets all the glory.

Set Image Capture preferences

Image Capture's preferences aren't nearly as daunting as those in other applications, but they are very important to Image Capture's behavior. To see the preferences, shown in figure 7.7, click the Image Capture menu and select Preferences, or simply press ⌘+,.

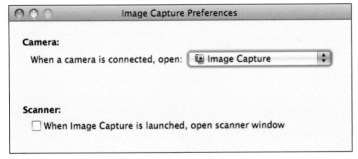

7.7 Determine how Image Capture reacts when a device is attached to your Mac.

In the Camera section, you can choose what application (if any) your Mac should automatically open when you connect your camera to it.

The Scanner section offers you the option of having Image Capture automatically open a scanner window when it is launched. I don't recommend checking this option unless you use Image Capture exclusively with your scanner and no other device, simply because of the annoyance factor.

Connect your device

If you haven't done so already, attach your device to the Mac with whatever connection its manu-facturer recommends (most use USB). If Image Capture is already open, it should automatically dis-play a window when you attach a camera or scanner.

If you have multiple devices attached to your Mac, you can choose the device you want to use by selecting it in the Devices menu.

Genius

Image Capture is versatile enough to import movies and MP3 files, as well as your pictures, assuming your camera has the ability to record such files.

Using a Digital Camera

A digital camera is your window to the world around you, and allows you to keep your memories for a lifetime. However, the memory cards the camera uses to store your precious keepsakes have a finite amount of space, and therefore need to be emptied of their contents every now and again. On the flip side, sometimes you may want to transfer images to your memory card. This is where Image Capture makes its entrance.

Transfer images to and from your camera

As stated earlier in this chapter, when you connect your camera to your Mac with Image Capture already up and running, a window opens (like the one in figure 7.8) that gives you access to and a measure of control over your camera.

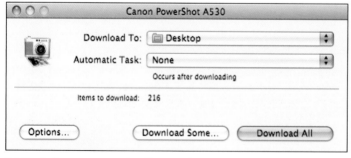

7.8 Control your camera using these options.

The Download To drop-down menu lets you select what folder you want your pictures saved to when importing them.

The Automatic Task drop-down menu allows you to choose what action to take once your picture transfers are complete. You can:

- **Automatically open each image in the Preview application.**

- **Build a slide show or Web page from the downloaded pictures (more on that later in this chapter).**

- **Format the picture to fit a certain standard picture size, such as 5x7 or 8x10.**

Options

Click the Options button in the lower-left corner to further customize how Image Capture transfers your images. These options are discussed individually in Table 7.2.

Table 7.2 Image Download Options

Option	Description
Delete items from camera after downloading	Removes all the pictures that you just imported from your camera once the transfer process is completed. Do not select this option if you want to transfer your pictures to multiple computers.
Create custom icons	Uses the picture itself to make an icon for the file, instead of using the generic icon for that file type.
Add item info to Finder file comments	Information your camera saves in your image file is added to the file comments that you see when you select Get Info for the file while in the Finder.
Embed ColorSync profile	Automatically assigns a color profile to your images. If you don't already know what a color profile is, you probably don't need to check this option.
Automatically download all items	Causes all items on the camera to be downloaded the instant it is turned on and connected to your Mac (with Image Capture already running, of course).

The Information tab in the Options window is pretty much useless except for the geekiest of the Geek Nation. Because you and I are so much cooler than that, I'll skip the details. Suffice it to say that this information may be helpful when troubleshooting issues or helping programmers, but it won't mean anything to 99.99 percent of the rest of us.

Download Some and Download All

Click the Download All button to do just that: download all the pictures and files from your camera. However, if you only want to download a few files, the Download Some button is your best option. Click it now to see a window similar to that shown in figure 7.9.

To import only certain files from your camera:

1. **Click the Download Some button.**

2. **Select the file or files you want to import.** To choose multiple files, hold down the ⌘ key while making your selections.

3. **Make your choices using the Automatic Task and Download Folder drop-down menus in the upper-right corner.**

4. **Click the Download button to proceed with the transfer.**

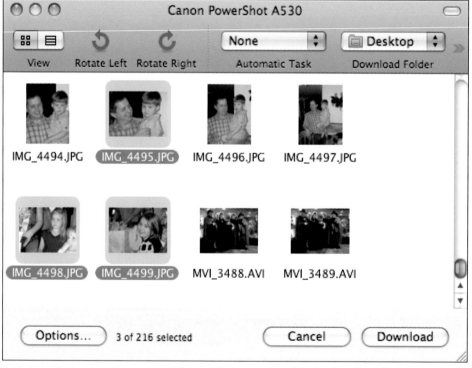

7.9 Select only the pictures you want to download, as opposed to downloading them all at once.

Transfer Images to Your Camera

A really cool feature in Image Capture is the ability to transfer files to your camera, not just from it. To transfer files to your camera:

1. **Click the Download Some button in the device window.**

2. **Drag-and-drop the files you want to move to the camera into the window.** If you cannot drop files into the window, your camera doesn't support this functionality.

3. **When the list of files you are transferring appears, click the Upload button, as shown in figure 7.10.**

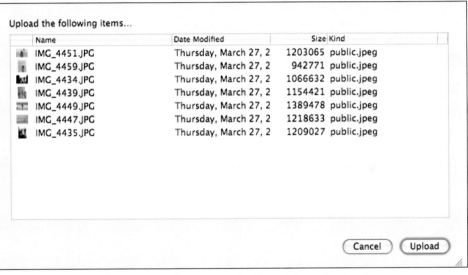

7.10 Won't your camera be surprised when you transfer files to it instead of from it!

Delete images from your camera

Sometimes you may only want to delete some of the images on your digital camera as opposed to all, but deleting individual images can be a chore. Image Capture sure comes in handy in this situation! To delete individual files from your camera:

1. **Click the Download Some button in the device window.**

2. **Select the files you want to remove from your camera.** Hold down the ⌘ key while clicking to choose multiple files.

Getting the Red Out

Image Capture is a great application for what it does, but if you need to touch up photos, such as removing the red in your subject's eyes or cropping part of the image, you need other software. iPhoto is the perfect application for such common tasks (and it is also great at organizing and sharing images); you can purchase it from Apple as part of the iLife suite of applications.

3. **Choose Edit ➪ Delete.**

4. **Click OK to confirm the deletion, or click Cancel to stop it.**

Using a Scanner

Your Mac can happily use Image Capture to import images and documents using a scanner. Simply connect your scanner to get started.

Note You need to install your scanner's software before connecting the scanner to your Mac. The software probably came on a CD with the scanner, but it's always a good idea to visit the manufacturer's Web site for any updated drivers they may have released.

Scanning images

Once you connect your scanner, the scan window should open automatically. If not, click the Devices menu and choose the scanner from the list. Place the item you want to scan onto the glass of the scanner if it is a flatbed scanner, or into the feeder if it is a document-feeding scanner. This is where the fun begins!

Using the Image Capture options

The default scan window that opens offers a lot of options for scanning your documents into your Mac, as shown in figure 7.11.

To scan an item using these options:

1. **Select the type of scanner you are using from the Scan Mode drop-down menu.**

2. **Choose what type of image you are scanning from the Document drop-down menu.**

3. **Select the Resolution you want to use from its drop-down menu.** Resolution plays a major role in the quality of the image. The higher the better, but your file sizes will also be much larger.

4. **Choose a location on your Mac to save the scanned images to by using the Scan To Folder drop-down menu.**

5. **Name the file and select the format you want to use for the scanned image.**

6. **If you are using a document-feeding scanner, simply click the Scan button to begin scanning the pages and skip the rest of the steps.** If using a flatbed or transparency scanner, continue to step 7.

7. **Click the Overview button to see a preview of the item on the glass.**

8. **Click-and-drag your mouse over the portion of the preview that you want to scan, and then click the Scan button.**

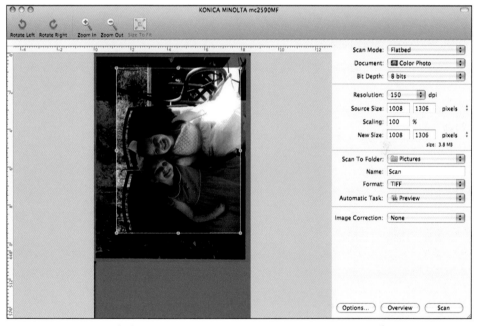

7.11 Image Capture's default scan window and its options.

Using your scanner's software options

Your scanner's software may offer many options that are not available in Image Capture's standard scan window. To access those features:

1. **Choose Devices ⇨ Browse Devices, or press ⌘+B.**

2. **Click the Use TWAIN UI button next to your scanner's name in the devices list to open the device window, as shown in figure 7.12.**

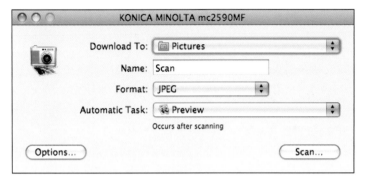

7.12 The TWAIN UI device options window.

3. **Select where to download the images, what to name them, what format to save them in, and what task to automatically perform once the download is complete.**

4. **Click the Scan button to use your scanner's features to scan your images and documents.** Consult your scanner's documentation for instructions on using its features.

Sharing Devices

You can share devices that you attach to your Mac through Image Capture. Other Macs can access your shared devices from their Image Capture application, as long as they are on the same network subnet as your Mac and are running Mac OS X 10.3 or higher.

To share devices:

1. **Open the Image Capture Device Browser by clicking the Devices menu and selecting Browse Devices, or by pressing ⌘+B.**

2. **Click the Sharing button in the lower-left corner.**

3. **Check the Share my devices check box to turn on sharing.**

4. **Enter a name for your shared devices.**

5. **If you want to restrict access to your devices, click the Password check box and enter the desired password in the text field.**

6. **Click OK to enable sharing.**

To access devices shared from other Macs:

1. **Press ⌘+B to open the Device Browser.**

2. **Click the arrow next to Remote Image Capture devices.**

3. **Select the device you want to use from the list.**

How Do I Work with PDFs and Images?

PDFs, or Portable Document Format files, are the *de facto* standard for disseminating documents over the Internet and throughout many corporations due largely to their portability across multiple operating systems, their relatively small file sizes, and availability of security options for sensitive information. Leopard includes an application called Preview that has the ability to open, edit, and save PDFs built right into it, because most of the graphics that you see on your screen are created by virtue of PDF technology anyway. I'll show you how to work with PDF files using Preview in this chapter. Preview isn't limited to handling just PDFs, however; it's also quite a handy way to open, and even edit, image (picture) files. Apple does provide a fantastic program called iPhoto for editing and organizing pictures, but it is part of their iLife suite of applications, not Leopard. Because not every person who buys Leopard has iLife, I'll concentrate on using Preview for your digital picture needs in *Mac OS X Leopard Portable Genius*.

File Types Supported by Preview 160

Open and Save Files in Preview 160

Set Preview's Preferences 162

View and Edit PDFs 165

View and Edit Images 167

File Types Supported by Preview

Preview is sort of a Swiss army knife application, meaning that it can handle many different file types and various tasks. Table 8.1 lists the file types supported by Preview.

Table 8.1 Supported File Types

File extension	File type/Description
PDF	Portable Document Format. A widely used cross-platform document format.
JPG	Joint Photographic Experts Group. A popular image file format used by most digital cameras. Also known as JPEG.
GIF	Graphics Interchange Format. An image file format mainly used on the Internet for small animations.
HDR	High Dynamic Range. An image file format associated with high-end digital cameras.
TIFF	Tagged Image File Format. A popular image file format used primarily by graphic artists.
PSD	Photoshop Document. Adobe Photoshop's default image file format.
PNG	Portable Network Graphics. An image file format.
BMP	Bitmap. An image file format.
RAW	A file format for an image that has not been processed in any way. This format is mostly used by digital cameras and scanners.
SGI	Silicon Graphics Image. The native raster graphics file format of Silicon Graphics workstations.

Open and Save Files in Preview

Preview can open any of the file types mentioned in the previous section. To open a file in Preview, do the following:

1. **From within Finder, choose Go ⇨ Applications, and then double-click the Preview icon to open the application.**

2. **Choose File ⇨ Open, or press ⌘+O, to bring up the Open dialog.**

3. **Browse your Mac for the file you want to open, click the file's icon once to highlight it, and then click the Open button, as shown in figure 8.1.**

Genius

If Preview's icon is in your Dock, whether due to it already being open or because you keep an alias for it there, you can simply drag-and-drop a file onto the Preview icon in the Dock to open it.

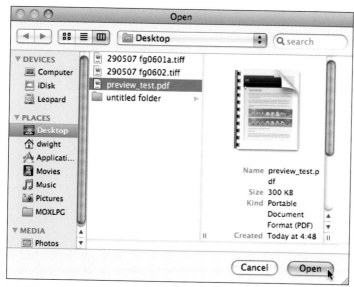

8.1 Choose the file you want to open in Preview.

If you've made changes to a file you've opened in Preview, and you want to save those changes, press ⌘+S; you can also choose File ⇨ Save. If you've made changes to a file, but you want to save the changed file under a different name, press ⌘+Shift+S to open the Save As dialog, as shown in figure 8.2. Enter a new name for the file, choose a location to save the file on your Mac, and then click Save.

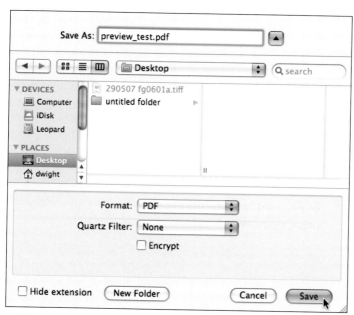

8.2 Name your file, choose a location to save it to, and then click Save.

Link File Types to Applications

If you've ever double-clicked a file to open it, only to have it open in an application you didn't expect, you'll love this little nugget. To make a certain file type open in only the application you designate for it, do the following:

1. **Click the file one time to highlight it, and then press ⌘+I to open the file's Info window, as shown in Figure 8.3.** You could also ctrl-click, or right-click, the file and select Get Info from the pop-up list to open the Info window.

2. **If the gray triangle to the left of the Open with section is point-ing to the right, click it to expand the section.**

3. **Click the pop-up menu to choose the application you want to set as the default for opening this file.**

4. **To make the selected application the system-wide default for opening all files of this type, click the Change All button.**

5. **Close the Info window by clicking the red button in the upper-left corner.**

Set Preview's Preferences

The way you set the preferences for Preview affects how you use the application. I'm a big advocate for making Leopard and all of its applications work the way you want them to. It's very important to set any application's preferences to fit your work style.

Preview's preferences are divided into four cat-egories: General, Images, PDF, and Bookmarks.

8.3 Get Info on any file by highlighting it and pressing ⌘+I.

Open Preview, and then press ⌘+; to open the Preview Preferences window.

General

Table 8.2 breaks down the settings in the General tab of Preview's Preferences window.

Table 8.2 General Preferences

Preference	Function
User name	Enter the name of the person (usually yourself) that will be used to tag images and PDFs that you create or change.
Add name to annotations	Associates your username to any annotations you make in files.
Window background	Change the default background color of the windows you open in Preview by clicking the color box, and then choosing a new color from the color palette window.

Images

Table 8.3 explains the options that are available in the Images tab of the Preview Preferences window.

Table 8.3 Image Preferences

Preference	Function
When opening images	Lets you choose whether to open all images in one window, groups of images in the same window, or each image in its own window.
Default image size	Opens images at their actual size, or scales them to fit your window.
Respect image and screen DPI for scale	Displays images at their actual sizes.

PDF

The PDF tab's options are explained in Table 8.4.

Bookmarks

Preview allows you to bookmark images and PDFs so that you can zip right to them when needed; this is very much like using bookmarks in a Web browser. To add a bookmark, open the file you want and press ⌘+D, or choose Bookmarks ⇨ Add Bookmark from the menu.

Table 8.4 PDF Preferences

Preference	Function
Default document scale	Allows Preview to automatically scale the PDF, or set it to open at the scale you desire.
Respect screen DPI for scale	Displays a PDF at its actual size.
Greeking threshold	Greeking renders smaller fonts as a blur so that they display faster. You can set the threshold to a higher number if PDFs take a long time to render text.
Anti-alias text and line art	Check this box to smooth lines in text and line art. Unchecking this box may produce jagged line art and text.
Open sidebar only for Table of Contents	Check this box to open the window's sidebar only when a PDF contains a table of contents.
Remember last page viewed	Causes Preview to open a PDF on the page you were last viewing when you closed it.
Use logical page numbers	Makes the Go to Page command correlate with the actual physical pages in the PDF. If the first few pages of a PDF aren't numbered (a cover page, for example), then the Go to command may not bring you to the page you expect it to. Checking this box rectifies that problem.

The Bookmarks tab, shown in figure 8.4, lists all the bookmarks you've created. You can rename them, or delete them from the list by clicking the Remove button.

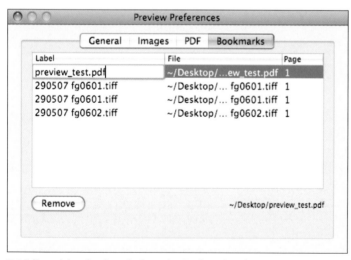

8.4 Edit or delete bookmarks from the Bookmarks tab.

View and Edit PDFs

Leopard is a whiz at opening, viewing, editing, and creating PDF files. I've already covered opening files; I'll concentrate on viewing and editing them in this section, while Chapter 9 expounds on the creation of PDFs.

To get started, you need to open a PDF, as described earlier in this chapter.

Mark up and annotate PDFs

To mark up a PDF is to highlight, strike through, or underline text that needs to be edited or removed; to annotate means to add notes or links, or to spotlight an area of the page with an oval or rectangle. Figure 8.5 shows an example of markups and annotations.

To mark up a PDF, do the following:

1. **Click and drag the mouse cursor over the text you want to mark up to highlight it.**

2. **Choose Tools ⇨ Mark Up.**

3. **Select which type of markup to use:**

   - Highlight Text (⌘+Ctrl+H).

   - Strike Through Text (⌘+Ctrl+S).

   - Underline Text (⌘+Ctrl+U).

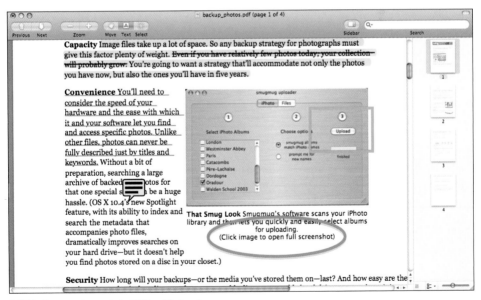

8.5 Mark up and annotate PDFs with Preview.

To make annotations, do the following:

1. **Choose Tools ⇨ Annotate.**

2. **Select which type of annotation you want to use:**

   - Add Oval (⌘+Ctrl+O).

   - Add Rectangle (⌘+Ctrl+R).

   - Add Note (⌘+Ctrl+N).

   - Add Link (⌘+Ctrl+L).

Genius

If marking up and annotating PDFs is something you do often, memorize the keyboard shortcuts for them. Keyboard shortcuts can save you much more time than you may realize. It's well worth taking the time to learn them if you work in a fast-paced environment.

Delete pages from a PDF

Just a couple of years ago, the only way to delete or rearrange pages was to pay through the nose for a third-party program that could accomplish these tasks. Thanks to Apple, Preview now has that ability, providing a professional level of service without having to shell out a professional level of money.

To delete a page from a multi-page document, do the following:

1. **If the sidebar is not visible on the right side of the window, choose View ⇨ Sidebar, or press ⌘+Shift+D.**

2. **Find the page you want to delete in the sidebar, and click to select it.** The sidebar must be displaying thumbnails, not Table of Contents or Annotations. To set the sidebar to display thumbnails, click the pop-up menu at the bottom of the sidebar and choose Thumbnails.

3. **Choose Edit ⇨ Delete Selected Page (⌘+Delete) to remove the page from your PDF.** Preview automatically renumbers your pages for you.

4. **Save your PDF (⌘+S) to keep the changes, or press ⌘+Z to undo a change.**

Rearrange pages in a PDF

As mentioned in the previous section, rearranging pages in a PDF is a treat for anyone who doesn't have an expensive third-party application. To shuffle your PDF's pages, do the following:

1. **Make the sidebar visible by pressing ⌘+Shift+D.**

2. **Search the sidebar for the page you want to move.** The sidebar must be displaying thumbnails, not Table of Contents or Annotations. To set the sidebar to display thumbnails, click the pop-up menu at the bottom of the sidebar and choose Thumbnails.

3. **Click-and-drag the page to the location in the sidebar you prefer, and then drop it in place (figure 8.6).**

4. **Save the changes by pressing ⌘+S, or undo them by pressing ⌘+Z.**

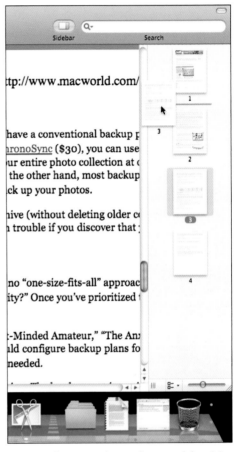

8.6 Move the page to its new home and drop it in.

View and Edit Images

Preview is more than happy to fill the role of basic image editor if you don't already have one with more frills, like iPhoto or Adobe Photoshop. While not able to manipulate photos and add effects to them like the two applications I just mentioned, it can handle standard resizing, rotating, and a few other nifty tricks.

Open an image in Preview, and we'll get started.

Get the Inside Scoop on Images

Most people simply want to open, view, and perhaps minimally edit their pictures, but others (and you know who you are!) want the lowdown on every element of the picture. You like to know information such as the camera used to take the image, the compression type, the aperture, the Photometric Interpretation (a fancy name for color model), and other geeky information that only a professional photographer could appreciate.

Preview can get all that stuff for you if you simply select Tools ⇨ Inspector, or press ⌘+I, when your image is open. The Inspector lays it all out for you, as you can see in figure 8.7.

Resizing and rotating images

If a photo or image is just too big dimension-ally, Preview can easily squeeze it until it fits the spot where you want to place it.

To adjust the size of your image, choose Tools ⇨ Adjust Size. You are presented with the dia-log shown in figure 8.8.

Make changes to these settings if you need to adjust your image, and click OK when you are finished. Table 8.5 explains the options and how they affect the image.

Preview also lets you rotate images to change their orientation. If you've got a picture that was taken by holding the camera sideways (to take a full-length shot of someone), you can rotate that image so that the subject is standing upright instead of on their side when you open the image in Preview.

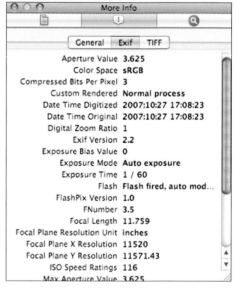

8.7 Your images can't hide from the Inspector!

Table 8.5 Size Adjustments

Option	Function
Fit into	Lets you choose automatic size settings from the pop-up menu. Use Other to make a custom size.
Width and Height	Changes the physical size of the image.
Resolution	Changes the quality of the image. Increasing this number may have adverse affects on the image.
Scale proportionally	Keeps the dimensions of the image intact when checked. For instance, if you change the width, the height changes proportionally.
Resample image	Uncheck this box if you want to reduce the dimensions of a file without losing image details.

To rotate an image to the left, press ⌘+L, and to rotate it to the right, press ⌘+R.

You can also flip an image to make the subject face a different direction, as I've done in figure 8.9. I flipped my image both vertically and horizontally to give you a better idea of what these functions do.

To flip your image horizontally, choose Tools ➪ Flip Horizontal; to go vertical, choose Tools ➪ Flip Vertical.

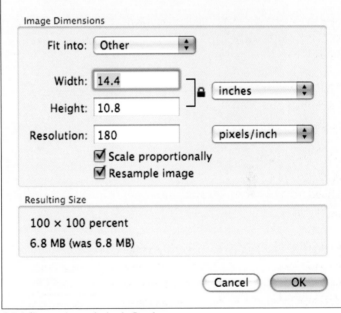

8.8 Adjust an image's size in Preview.

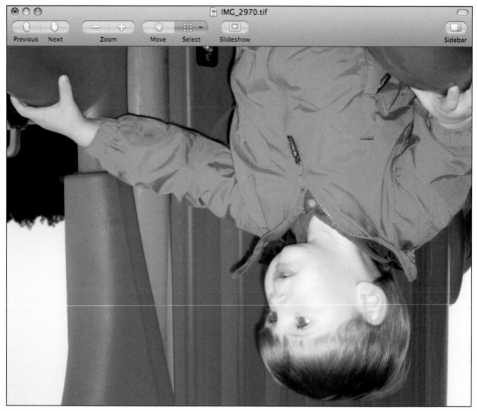

8.9 My son is flipping out in this picture!

Adjusting color in images

Sometimes the colors in your pictures just don't look quite right. What is someone who isn't a color specialist to do? Preview has the answers! Preview can handle basic color adjustments very well, indeed.

To make color corrections in Preview, choose Tools ⇨ Adjust Color, or press ⌘+Option+C. The color adjustment sliders in the Adjust Color window, shown in figure 8.10, can work wonders on your images.

You can also crop an image in Preview. Notice that the mouse cursor changes to a crosshair when you move it over your image; use this crosshair to select an area on your image that you want to crop, or extract, from the rest of the image. Place the crosshair underneath or over the area you want to crop, and then click-and-drag to draw a box around the area. Once the area is selected, press ⌘+K, and then save your new image (⌘+S).

When you move the sliders, your image is automatically updated to reflect the adjustments that you made.

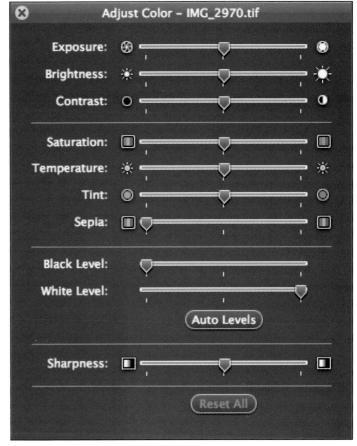

8.10 Move the sliders to make the necessary adjustments to your image's colors.

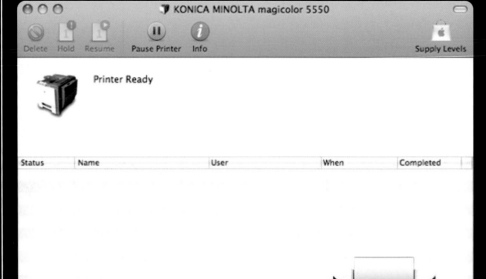

Like surfing the Web and accessing e-mail, printing is one of the basic functions of life for your Mac. The Mac OS has always been known for its printing prowess, but Leopard ups the ante quite a bit from previous versions of Mac OS X in terms of ease of installation and managing jobs. Because the Mac has been the publishing industry's best buddy for more than two decades, Apple has made sure that printing a document from Mac OS X is just what it should be — simple and intuitive — which is exactly how I like it, thank you very much.

Set Up a Printer 174

Print Documents 183

Set Up a Printer

Installing a printer in Mac OS X is a snap, provided that everything the Mac needs to communicate with the printer is installed (software and drivers) and the necessary hardware (devices and cables) is functioning up to par.

There are three main steps that you must take before you can use your printer with your Mac:

1. **Install the software that came with your printer.**

2. **Connect your printer to your Mac or your network.**

   - If your printer has a USB connection, connect one end of the USB cable to the printer, and the other end to your Mac.

   - If your printer has a network, or Ethernet, interface, use an Ethernet (or RJ-45) cable to connect it to your network's router or switch.

Caution Before you purchase a printer, make absolutely certain that the printer is Mac-compatible (most are compatible with your Mac, but it's best to be sure). Don't just trust the well-meaning employees at the electronics superstore; check it out for yourself by going to the printer manufacturer's Web page and checking the specifications for the printer, or look for familiar Mac logos on the printer's box. Logos to look for would be the large X logo with the "Made for Mac OS X" tagline, and the happy Mac, which is the same as the Finder icon on the left side of your Dock (see figure 9.1). If you buy your printer directly from Apple it's a safe bet the printer is Mac compatible.

3. **Use the Print & Fax System Preferences pane to create a print queue for the printer (in other words, install the printer).**

Install your printer's software

Mac OS X needs special software, called a driver, to be able to communicate effectively with your printer, just as it does to speak to any other device you may connect to it, such as a scanner or input device (such as a mouse or trackball). Mac OS X comes preloaded with tons of printer drivers from several of the most popular printer manufacturers,

9.1 This is one of the familiar Mac logos to look for on the box of the printer you want to purchase.

and so chances are pretty good that you won't need to install any additional software. However, the safest way to go is to install the software the manufacturer provides in the box, typically on a CD; if no CD is in the box, you can download the latest software from the manufacturer's support Web site.

Genius I think it's always a good idea to just go to the manufacturer's Web site and download the drivers right from the beginning. This ensures that you have the latest and greatest software for your printer.

Caution Be sure the driver files you download are for the version of Mac OS X you are using; if you're reading this book, the automatic assumption is that you're running Leopard, or Mac OS X 10.5.

Unfortunately, there's not one right way to install drivers. Printer manufacturers provide drivers and software in a number of ways using different installer applications, so the way you installed your HP printer's software may be different than it was when you installed your Konica Minolta, Brother, Xerox, or Epson software.

Some printer manufacturers may install other software in addition to the printer driver, such as utilities that allow you to monitor the printer's consumables (such as toners, ink cartridges, and drums), perform maintenance tasks, and run diagnostics for troubleshooting. These utilities are typically installed in the Hard Drive ➪ Applications folder. Consult your printer manufacturer if you're not sure about what software should be installed to maximize your use of the printer (other than the driver, of course).

Generally, you should follow the installation instructions included in the printer box, but here is the typical process used to install printer drivers and software:

1. **Insert the CD that came with your printer, or download the software from the printer manufacturer's Web site.**

2. **Double-click the CD's icon to open a window to see its contents (if one doesn't open automatically), and then double-click the software installer icon.**

3. **Drivers downloaded from the Web are usually in the form of a disk image, which is a virtual disk.** When you download the driver using Safari, Safari automatically opens and mounts the disk image, and displays a window showing the disk image's contents. Double-click the installer icon in the disk image's window.

4. **Enter your user account's login password when prompted during installation.**

5. **When the software installation is complete, you see a prompt similar to figure 9.2.** Click Close to complete the process.

9.2 Click Close to finish the driver software installation process.

Your Mac should now have the necessary drivers and utilities to communicate with your printer. You can now move on to the second major step in your printer setup, connecting your printer.

Connect your printer

How you connect your printer is just as important as having the correct driver software installed. Some printers come with only one connection type, which is usually USB, but others may have multiple connection options, the most common being an Ethernet interface for directly connecting the printer to your network.

USB

Connecting with USB is certainly the easiest way for your Mac to get its print on, and USB is reasonably fast for most printing needs. There's not much to it, really:

1. **Connect one end of the USB cable to the printer.**

2. **Connect the other end of the USB cable to the Mac.**

Voila! The printer is connected!

Note

Most printers don't ship with a USB cable in the box, so be sure to pick one up before you leave the store where you purchase it. If the store employees don't know what kind of cable you need, tell them it is a "USB device cable." A USB device cable has a standard A plug on one end (the flat, rectangular USB connector most of us are familiar with), and a standard B plug on the other end (a smaller, almost completely square connector). The standard B plug is the end that you connect to your printer.

Network

Connect your printer to your network if you want multiple Macs to be able to print to it. Typically, connecting to a network involves hooking up your printer to a router or network switch through an Ethernet cable. There are other methods of using your printer with a network, such as sharing the printer from a Mac, using print servers (devices designed to connect a printer that doesn't have an Ethernet port to an Ethernet router), or using a wireless network adapter. Sharing a printer is covered later in this chapter and also in Chapter 13.

Using print servers and wireless network adapters to connect your printer to a network achieves the same goals as using an Ethernet cable, which is to assign a network, or IP (Internet Protocol), address to the printer. Because Ethernet cable is the most common method, I will stick with it as the default network connection to concentrate on.

Here are general instructions for connecting your printer to a network:

1. **With the printer off, insert one end of the Ethernet cable into the Ethernet port on your printer.**

2. **Insert the other end of the Ethernet cable into an available Ethernet port on your network router or switch.**

3. **Turn on the printer.** Consult your printer's documentation to find out how to determine what IP address was assigned to your printer by your network router.

Network printers can communicate with your Mac using one of three protocols: AppleTalk, Bonjour (known as Rendezvous in an earlier incarnation), and IP Printing.

- **AppleTalk is an older protocol developed by Apple in the late '80s and early '90s, and some newer printers are no longer using it**. As a matter of fact, Apple has been trying to steer Mac users away from it since Mac OS X 10.2. However, it requires no configuration at all; your Mac just sees it on the network when you are creating a print queue, and you can easily install it.

- **Bonjour is the newest no-configuration-needed protocol from Apple.** Like AppleTalk before it, your Mac simply sees a printer running the Bonjour protocol, and printer queue installation is a snap. Older printers most likely won't have Bonjour, so AppleTalk will have to suffice.

- **IP (Internet Protocol) Printing is the most difficult to set up because you must know the IP address of the printer being installed.** I say it's the most difficult, but the only real difficulty with IP Printing is that it is more time-consuming to set up than the other two competing protocols.

If you're on a small network, AppleTalk or Bonjour are the best bet because of their extreme simplicity. Consult with your IT administrator if you are on a larger corporate network to find out how they prefer you to install the printer. I would only use IP Printing if your IT department preferred it.

Genius

You are going to have to make a decision in the next section if you are installing a network printer. There are three main protocols you can use to install a network printer: AppleTalk, Bonjour, or IP Printing. You need to choose one of them as the method you use to communicate with your printer over the network. See the sidebar entitled "Which Network Protocol Should I Use?" for more information.

Create a print queue

The next step on your printer installation odyssey is to create a print queue. Creating a print queue allows you to print to the printer from your Mac, as well as manage print jobs. I'm going to show you how to set up a print queue for your printer, regardless of the connection type it uses.

Note If you connect with USB after installing the printer's software, your Mac sometimes automatically creates a print queue; you don't have to lift a finger! To see whether this is the case, click Apple menu ➪ System Preferences ➪ Print & Fax. Now, get to printing!

Now that you have the printer connected, let's get your printer rolling:

1. **Choose Apple menu ➪ System Preferences, or click the System Preferences icon in the Dock.**

2. **Click the Print & Fax icon in the Hardware section of the System Preferences to open the Print & Fax preferences pane (see figure 9.3).**

3. **Select the + button in the lower-left corner of the pane (see figure 9.4) to add a printer to the list.** In order to delete a printer from the printer list, you would highlight the printer in the list and select the – button.

9.3 Click the Print & Fax icon to open its preferences pane.

179

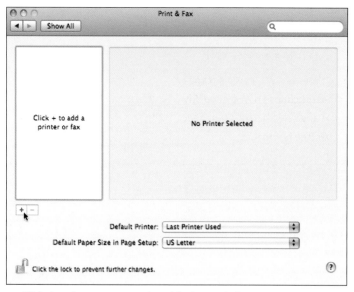

9.4 Click the + button to open the add printer window.

4. **The add printer window opens. Use one of the following methods to create a print queue for your printer:**

   ● If you are installing the printer through USB, AppleTalk, or Bonjour, do the following:

   a. Click the Default button in the upper-left corner of the window's toolbar.

   b. Click the name of the printer in the window.

   c. The Print Using pop-up menu should automatically show the name of the printer you are setting up. If not, click the pop-up menu, choose the Select a driver to use option, browse the list of installed printer drivers and select the one you need, and then click the Add button in the bottom-right corner (see figure 9.5).

   ● If you are using IP Printing as your protocol of choice, do the following:

   a. Click the IP button in the toolbar.

   b. Select the correct protocol from the Protocol pop-up menu. Consult your printer manufacturer's documentation, Web site, or technical support department for more information on which protocol to choose.

   c. Type the printer's IP address into the Address field.

   d. Type the printer's queue name into the Queue field. Again, consult your printer manufacturer's documentation for the proper setting.

   e. Edit the Name and Location fields to your liking.

   f. The Print Using pop-up menu may show the name of the printer you are setting up. If not, click the pop-up menu, choose the Select a driver to use option, browse the list of installed printer drivers and select the one you need, and then click the Add button in the bottom-right corner (see figure 9.5).

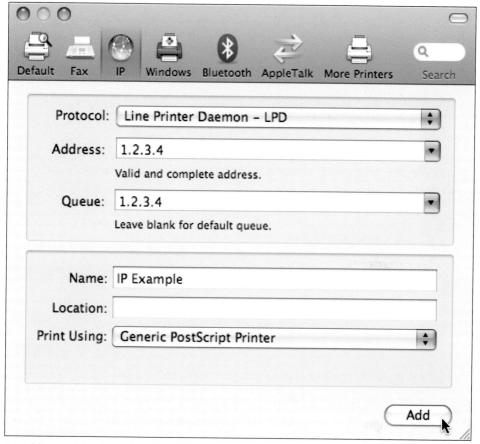

9.5 Adding a printer through USB, AppleTalk, or Bonjour is so simple to do. Be sure to enter the correct Address and Queue information when using IP Printing.

Your newly installed printer queue is now visible in the printer list of the Print & Fax pane, similar to the one shown in figure 9.6.

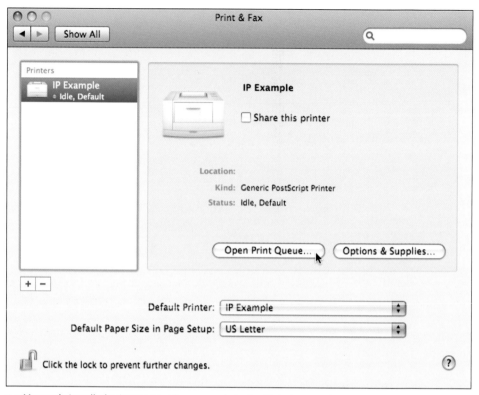

9.6 My newly installed printer queue is now ready to feed jobs to my printer.

To make certain you can now enjoy the fruits of your labor, you need to try a test print. Follow these steps to do so:

1. **Highlight the printer in the printer list by clicking its name.**

2. **Click the Open Print Queue button.**

3. **In the print queue's menu (upper-left corner of your screen, next to the Apple menu), choose Printer ⇨ Print Test Page, as shown in figure 9.7.**

9.7 Print a test page to make sure everything is working properly with your printer.

CUPS

At some point during your printing experience with Leopard, you may run across the term *CUPS*. CUPS is an acronym that stands for Common UNIX Printing System, which is the print system utilized by Mac OS X; it has no relation to the containers that hold our liquid refreshment, nor is it referring to protective athletic wear. CUPS controls all aspects of printing in Mac OS X, such as creating print queues, creating print jobs using the information provided to it by the printer's driver software, and managing jobs in the print queue.

Print Documents

Now that you've got a printer installed, you can get busy printing those pressing sales figures, your family's vacation photos, or that map showing how to get to Aunt Linda's house.

TextEdit is the application I will use to show you how to print documents in Leopard. From within the Finder menus, choose Go ⇨ Applications (or ⌘+Shift+A), and then double-click the TextEdit icon.

TextEdit automatically opens a new blank document when it first starts up. Type something interesting in the document, and let's print it out.

To print from just about any application in Mac OS X, do the following:

1. **Choose File ⇨ Page Setup:**

   a. Select the printer you will be printing to in the Format for pop-up menu (see figure 9.8).

   b. Choose the paper size you want to print on in the Paper Size pop-up menu (also figure 9.8).

   c. Make adjustments to the Orientation and Scale as you see fit.

   d. Click OK.

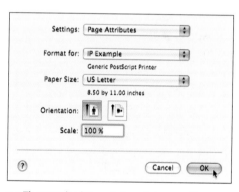

9.8 The standard Page Setup dialog used in most Mac OS X applications.

2. Choose File ⇨ Print, or ⌘+P:

    a. Change any print options, if necessary. See the next section for a description of the key options that are available.

    b. Click the Print button (see figure 9.9) to send your print job to the printer queue, where it is passed on to the printer.

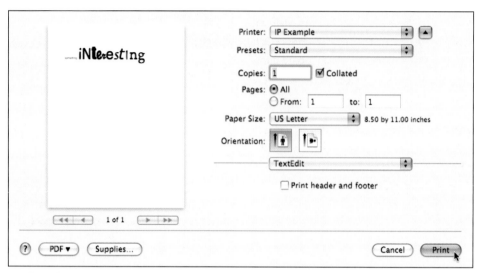

9.9 This is the standard Mac OS X print dialog used by most applications.

Genius

Some printers (typically PostScript-capable laser printers) are able to directly print documents, such as PDFs, or images, such as JPEGs and TIFFs, by simply dragging-and-dropping the file into the print queue for the printer; you don't even have to open the file in an application. Check with your printer manufacturer to see whether your printer can handle such a cool task.

Discover Leopard's print options

Leopard has many built-in print options that allow you to configure your print jobs in so many ways that your head will spin. I cover the most often-used options in this section.

Caution Some applications, such as QuarkXPress and Adobe InDesign, use their own print dialogs, which can really throw you for a loop if you're used to the standard Mac OS X way of doing things. Peruse the application's documentation to learn how to navigate the myriad options they provide.

The main sheet of the standard print dialog offers some bare-bones basics, as well as application-specific print settings. Figure 9.9 illustrates the main sheet of the standard print dialog when using TextEdit, and Table 9.1 breaks down the options.

To access the other printing options that Mac OS X Leopard provides, click the options pop-up menu, as shown in figure 9.10. Tables 9.1 to 9.7 list the options and their functions.

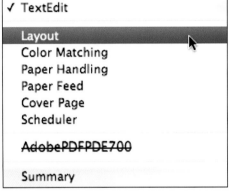

9.10 Choose from several option sheets to customize your Leopard printing experience to the max.

Table 9.1 Basic Print Options

Option	Function
Printer	Select a printer from the pop-up menu.
Presets	Choose a preconfigured set of options.
Copies	Enter the number of copies you want to print.
Collated	Check this box to print all pages of the document sequentially before printing the next copy.
Pages	Specify the page range you want to print.
Paper Size	Select the size of the media you are printing on.
Orientation	You can select Portrait or Landscape.
Options menu	This is a pop-up menu that allows you to select from several option sheets (see figure 9.10). This menu is typically set to the application-specific settings in the main sheet of the Print dialog; For example, figure 9.9 shows TextEdit.

185

Table 9.2 Layout Options

Option	Function
Pages per Sheet	Use this option to print multiple pages of your document on a single side of your paper.
Layout Direction	Choose how the pages are laid out on the page when printing multiple pages per sheet.
Border	Place a border around the individual pages when printing multiple pages per sheet.
Two-Sided	This option is only available if your printer supports a duplexer option, which allows the printer to print on both sides of the sheet.
Reverse Page Orientation	This option causes the job to print out upside down. This is useful if you have media, such as letterhead that needs to be printed in a certain direction but you can't place it in the printer in that direction.

Table 9.3 Color Matching Options

Option	Function
ColorSync/In Printer	Choosing ColorSync allows Leopard to handle color matching, while choosing In Printer lets the printer do all the grunt work.
Profile	This option allows you to associate a color profile with this print job.

Table 9.4 Paper Handling Options

Option	Function
Pages to Print	Print all pages, or just the odd- or even-numbered pages.
Destination Paper Size	Allows the document to be printed on a different paper size than specified in the Page Setup dialog. This option is only available if the Scale to fit paper size box is checked.
Scale to fit paper size	Check this box to scale the page's contents to fit the size selected in the Destination Paper Size pop-up menu.
Scale down only	Check this box to prevent the items on the page from being scaled larger than they presently are.
Page Order	Choose from Automatic, Normal, or Reverse page order.

Table 9.5 Paper Feed Options

Option	Function
All pages from	Select a paper tray to print the job from. This option is only useful if your printer supports multiple paper trays.
First page from	Print the first page of a document using a particular paper tray. For example, use this option if you want to print the first page of a job on your company's letterhead, which is in one tray on your printer.
Remaining from	Print the remainder of the print job from the paper tray you select. This option is only available when selecting the "First page from" option. Continuing the example from the First page from option, select the paper tray on your printer that contains plain paper to finish the rest of your job, as opposed to wasting letterhead.

Table 9.6 Cover Page Options

Option	Function
Print Cover Page	Select either Before document or After document if you want to print a cover page that differentiates your jobs from those of other people using the printer.
Cover Page Type	Select the type of cover page to print. This option is only available if Before document or After document is selected in the Print Cover Page options.
Billing Info	This information is used to identify you if you are being billed for each job you print.

Table 9.7 Scheduler Options

Option	Function
Print Document	Specify a time for Leopard to send this document from the printer's queue to the printer.
Priority	Set the level of this document's priority so that it prints ahead of or behind other jobs as necessary.

Create your own PDFs

PDF files have become a standard document format that almost anyone who has used a computer has seen at some point. Most documents on the Internet are PDF files. Anyone on any computer can open PDFs, whether they are running Mac OS X, Windows, or Linux, as long as they have a PDF reader application installed, such as Preview or Adobe Reader.

Once upon a time, PDFs could only be generated by expensive software. Mac OS X has changed that due to its extensive use of the PDF file format throughout the operating system. Leopard affords you the ability to create PDFs from any document you please, for free!

Let's use the trusty TextEdit document you created earlier in this chapter to illustrate creating a PDF.

To create a PDF using Leopard, do the following:

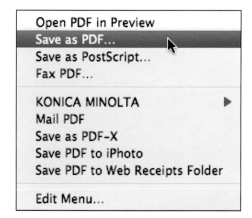

1. **Open a document in an application.** In this case, the interesting TextEdit document.

2. **Choose File ⇨ Print.**

3. **Click the PDF button in the lower-left corner of the window to see the PDF options you have at your beck and call (see figure 9.11).**

4. **Select Save As PDF from the menu to open the Save dialog, as shown in Figure 9.12.**

9.11 Leopard gives you several options for creating PDF files from any document you want.

5. **Give the PDF an appropriate name, decide where on your Mac to save it (it defaults to your user account's Documents folder), and click Save.** I'll describe some of the other items in this Save dialog in the next section.

Security options

The ability to create PDFs with any document on your Mac without expensive third-party software is a huge boon, no doubt about it. However, that third-party software (specifically Adobe Acrobat) has always had the ability to make PDF files secure from prying eyes that shouldn't be seeing their contents. This is a great feature and is required in some corporations when disseminating sensitive information. Previous versions of Mac OS X were lacking in this department, but Leopard has come to the rescue of the security-obsessed among us.

To secure your PDFs, look back at step 5 of the previous section, prior to clicking Save. Click the Security Options button to see the PDF Security Options window (see figure 9.13). Table 9.8 spells out the available options. Click the OK button to assign the security options you have chosen for this file.

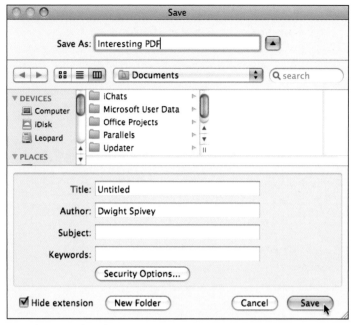

9.12 There are a lot of options available in the PDF Save dialog.

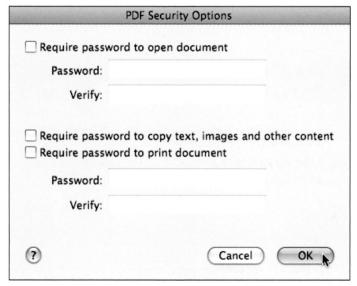

9.13 Secure your PDFs from anyone not authorized to view them.

Table 9.8 PDF Security Options

Option	Function
Require password to open document	Check this box to enable the password feature. Type a secure password in the Password field, and then retype it in the Verify field.
Require password to copy text, images and other content	Check this box to prevent someone from copying elements of the PDF and pasting them into an unsecured document without knowing the password to do so. Type a secure password in the Password field, and then retype it in the Verify field.
Require password to print document	If this box is checked, a user must know the password in order to print this document. Type a secure password in the Password field, and then retype it in the Verify field.

Can I Customize Leopard?

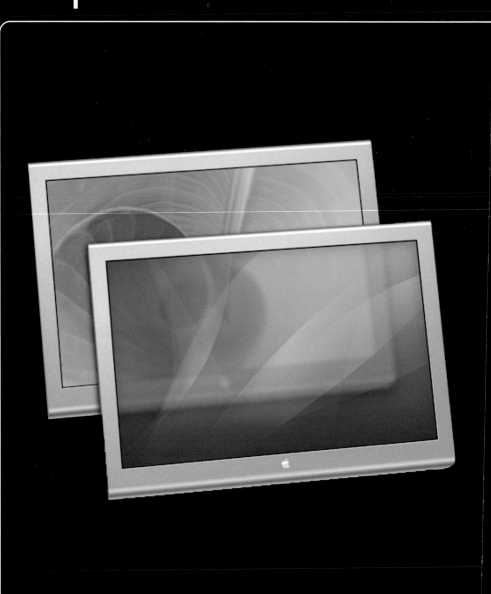

As attractive as Leopard's spots already are, it's always fun to customize the appearance and functionality of your Mac to match your personality and preferences. Customizing your Mac makes for a more enjoyable work and play environment, just as you get more enjoyment from your home once you've decorated it to your tastes. One of the slickest ways that Leopard lets you customize your Mac experience is Dashboard and its Widgets. These miniature applications are designed for your convenience and can do a multitude of things, like keep you up to speed with the weather or flight information. This chapter explores the numerous ways you can tweak Leopard so that you feel as comfortable in front of your computer as you do when sitting in your living room.

The Appearance Preferences Pane **194**

Desktop Pictures and Screen Savers **197**

Customize the Finder **201**

Open and Close Widgets **209**

Widgets Supplied with Leopard **210**

Advanced Dashboard **212**

Where to Find More Cool Widgets **214**

Create Your Own Widgets Using Web Clips **215**

The Appearance Preferences Pane

The Appearance preferences pane, shown in figure 10.1, is your first stop on the Mac customization tour. This Appearance pane allows you to modify basic color and textual elements of your Finder windows. To open this pane, click the System Preferences icon in the Dock, or choose Apple menu ➪ System Preferences. Then click the Appearance icon in the Personal category of the System Preferences window.

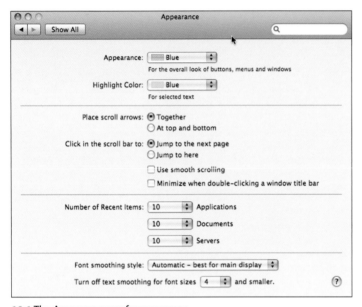

10.1 The Appearance preferences pane.

Color modifications

The Appearance menu lets you choose the color you prefer for your system-wide menus and buttons. I hope either blue or graphite suits your taste because those are your only options.

You can change the default color used to highlight text with the Highlight Color menu. Thankfully there's a lengthy list of color choices that are available to you here.

Genius

You can switch between the "Jump to the next page" and "Jump to here" options by holding down the Option key while clicking in the scroll bar.

Table 10.1 Scrolling Options

Option	Description
Place scroll arrows	Scroll arrows, like those in figure 10.2, can be placed together at the bottom of the scroll bar, or separately, with an arrow on each end of the scroll bar.
	My personal preference is to keep them together because this placement keeps me from having to move my mouse very much.
Click in the scroll bar to	This lets your Mac know how it should behave when you click inside the scroll bar.
	"Jump to the next page" causes each click in the scroll bar to advance you one page-length in the document.
	The "Jump to here" option moves you to the spot in the document that you are clicking; if you click the top of the scroll bar, then you jump to the first page of the document.
Use smooth scrolling	Scroll through your documents or Web pages smoothly instead of jumping from page to page.
Minimize when double-clicking a window title bar	Check this box to cause windows to minimize to the Dock when you double-click their title bar.

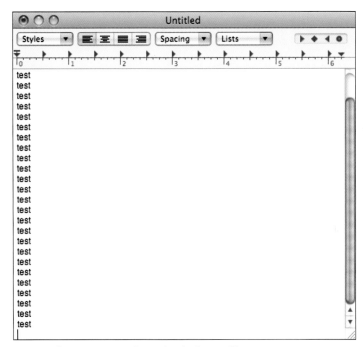

10.2 Scroll arrows grouped together in the scroll bar.

Scrolling options

These options allow you to control how your Mac scrolls through documents or Web pages that are too large to fit onto the screen in their entirety.

Accessing recently used items

A very handy way to see and quickly access applications, documents, and servers that you've used in the recent past is by clicking the Apple menu and holding your mouse over Recent Items, as shown in figure 10.3. The Number of Recent Items pop-up menus in the Appearance preferences pane let you choose how many of each item type you want to list.

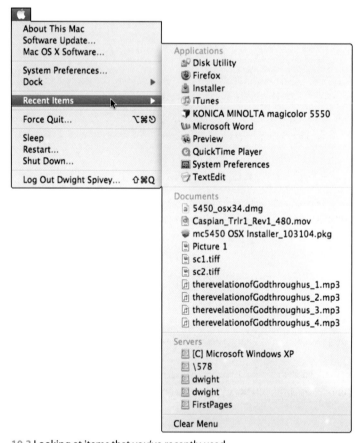

10.3 Looking at items that you've recently used.

Viewing fonts

Mac OS X uses a technique called anti-aliasing, or font smoothing, to help fonts appear without jagged edges.

There are several font-smoothing methods employed by Mac OS X; each one is designed to improve how fonts look on different display types. Select the style that you prefer from the Font smoothing style pop-up menu.

The only possible downside to font smoothing is that some fonts may appear fuzzy. Smaller font sizes can be almost impossible to read, and so the Appearance pane offers the option to turn off font smoothing for fonts smaller than the size you choose at the bottom of the pane.

Desktop Pictures and Screen Savers

No two things personalize your Mac quite like great desktop pictures and really cool screen savers. From photos of the kids to fantastic paintings of faraway space battles, or from extreme close-ups of beautiful flowers to a constant streaming news feed, desktop pictures and screen savers can be very personal displays of individual tastes and styles.

Choose a desktop picture

Open System Preferences by clicking its icon in the Dock or by choosing Apple menu ⇨ System Preferences. Click the Desktop & Screen Saver icon in the Personal category, and then choose the Desktop tab at the top of the pane.

Genius

A speedy way to open the Desktop preferences pane is to right-click or ctrl-click your current desktop picture and select Change Desktop Background from the list.

The left side of the Desktop tab, shown in figure 10.4, lists the desktop pictures available on your system. Apple has taken the liberty of supplying you with a lot of different pictures and has even arranged them into subject folders.

10.4 The Desktop tab of the Desktop & Screen Saver preferences pane.

You can also add your personal collection of desktop pictures to this list by following these steps:

1. **Click the + button below the list.**

2. **Browse your Mac's hard drive for the folder that contains the desktop pictures you want to use.**

3. **Click the Choose button.**

To remove folders from the list, simply highlight the folder to be removed, and then select the – button below the list.

Browse the list for the desktop picture you want to use, and just click it once to set it as your Mac's default desktop picture.

Should you get quickly bored with your choice of desktop picture or if it's just too hard to decide which one you like best, check the Change picture check box at the bottom of the pane. Use the pop-up menu next to this check box to determine how often your Mac should change its desktop background. To add even more spice to your desktop selection, check the Random order check box, which allows your Mac to use its own discretion when choosing a desktop picture.

Select a screen saver

Screen savers look really great on your Mac's screen and they are somewhat useful for security purposes, but if not for these factors, screen savers would be obsolete in today's computing world. At one time, screen savers were a necessary tool that prevented burn-in from occurring on CRT-based monitors. New monitors are typically LCD or plasma, and burn-in just isn't a concern any longer.

Note

Mac OS X comes loaded with several really neat screen savers, but because there are plenty of screen savers that can be downloaded from the Web, you can personalize to your heart's content. Open Safari and search for "Mac OS X screen savers" on Google to find more screen savers than you can shake a stick at.

To choose a screen saver that meets your personal standards of coolness, do the following:

1. **Open the Desktop & Screen Saver pane in System Preferences (Apple menu ⇨ System Preferences ⇨ Desktop & Screen Saver), and click the Screen Saver tab.**

2. **Browse the list of screen savers on the left side of the pane and find the one that grabs your attention.**

3. **Click the Test button to see the screen saver as it will look when engaged during normal use.** Move the mouse or press any key on your keyboard to exit the test.

4. **To let Mac OS X choose the screen saver it uses, check the Use random screen saver check box.**

5. **Check the Show with clock check box if you would like a digital clock to be displayed onscreen with the screen saver.**

6. **Use the Start screen saver slider to set the amount of time that your Mac is idle before the screen saver starts.**

7. **Close the System Preferences once you've finalized your selection.**

Set the screen saver's options

Some screen savers allow you to change the way they behave by supplying an Options button underneath the Preview window, as shown in figure 10.5. Click the Options button to make adjustments to the look and feel of the chosen screen saver.

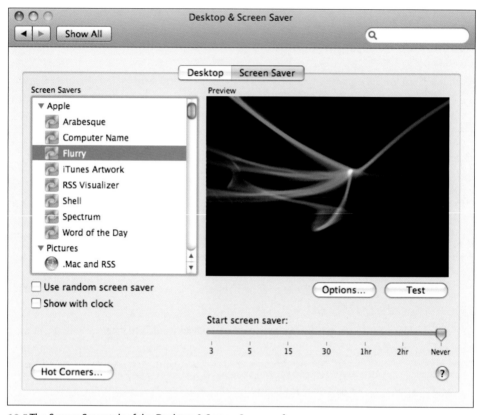

10.5 The Screen Saver tab of the Desktop & Screen Saver preferences pane.

Take the Flurry screen saver as an example; select it from the screen saver list on the left of the pane. Click the Options button to see the options that are specific to your selected screen saver.

Usually options for screen savers are very straightforward. Choose an option from the Color pop-up menu to change the color of the streams and move the sliders to change the number of streams, the thickness of the streams, and the speed at which the streams move.

Using hot corners

Have you noticed the Hot Corners button in the bottom-left corner of the pane? Click that button to see the Hot Corners preferences sheet, similar to the one in figure 10.6. Hot corners allow you to set actions for your Mac to take when you move the mouse pointer to one of the four corners of your screen.

Click one of the four pop-up menus to select an action for the corresponding screen corner. Table 10.2 lists actions that you can use for hot corners.

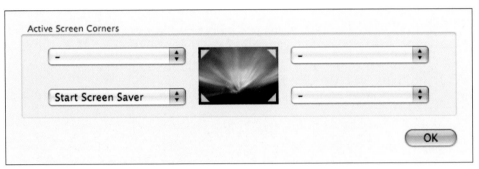

Active Screen Corners

Start Screen Saver

OK

10.6 The Hot Corners preferences sheet, also known as Active Screen Corners.

Table 10.2 Hot Corner Actions

Action	Result
Start Screen Saver and Disable Screen Saver	These two options speak quite clearly for themselves.
All Windows	All open windows are arranged in the screen so that they can all be seen. This is the same function that Exposé performs with the F9 key, as described in Chapter 1.
Application Windows	All open windows for the currently active application are neatly arranged so that each of their contents can be displayed at once. This is also achieved with the F10 key and Exposé, as discussed in Chapter 1.
Desktop	This is yet another feature of Exposé (using the F11 key), which causes all open windows to zoom off the screen so the desktop can be clearly seen.
Dashboard	Dashboard opens when the mouse is moved to the hot corner. See sections later in this chapter for more information on Dashboard.
Spaces	Opens the Spaces application, displaying all the spaces at once on the screen. Spaces is covered in detail in Chapter 1.
Sleep Display	Causes the Mac's monitor to go into sleep mode.
- (minus sign)	Disables the hot corner.

Customize the Finder

The Finder is the application you will use most often on your Mac, and so you may as well customize it to fit your needs and likes. Mac OS X gives you a lot of latitude when it comes to customizing the Finder, and I'll show you a few of my favorite tweaks to this quintessential Mac OS standby in this section. While Chapter 1 covers the ins and outs of using the Finder, in this chapter you can discover how to give the Finder that personal touch.

Finder windows

The Finder is a great tool for navigating your Mac, but I like to take full advantage of the customization available so that I can make the Finder work for me.

Figure 10.7 is an example of the Finder modified to my specs. The biggest differences between my customized Finder window and the default window configuration are that the toolbar and sidebar have been changed significantly to give me quick access to the tools and folders that I frequent the most in my daily activities, and that I've changed my view from Icons to Columns. There's also a new addition to the bottom of the window, known as the path bar.

10.7 The Finder done my way.

In the rest of this section, I will show you how I got from A to Z. Of course, you don't have to make the same changes to your Finder that I have made to mine; in fact, I encourage you to experiment with all the options the Finder affords, even those I may not touch on, so that you can find what combination works the best for you.

Note

The path bar is an easy way to see where you've been and to be able to quickly get back there. Enable the path bar by opening a new Finder window, and then select View ⇨ Show Path Bar; the path bar shows up in the bottom of the Finder window, exactly as shown in Figure 10.7. The folders in the path bar change as you browse your Mac's hard drive. Click one of the folders in the path bar to zoom back to one of the previous folders in your path. It's sort of like taking a tiny step back in time!

Modify the toolbar

The toolbar gives you fast access to common tasks and actions, and helps you to navigate your Mac more efficiently. You can change the default set of tools in the toolbar to add items that you use more than others, and remove those items that you don't need, by using the Customize Toolbar sheet (see figure 10.8).

Follow these steps to customize your Finder's toolbar:

1. **Activate the Finder by clicking its icon on the left side of the Dock.**

2. **Open a new Finder window by pressing ⌘+N.**

3. **Choose View ⇨ Customize Toolbar to open the Customize Toolbar sheet.**

4. **To add an item to the toolbar, drag-and-drop the item from the sheet to the position in the toolbar you desire.**

5. **To remove an item from the toolbar, simply drag-and-drop its icon anywhere outside of the Finder window, and it disappears in a puff of smoke!**

6. **If the arrangement of the icons in the toolbar doesn't suit you, just click-and-drag them to the spot where they work best.** As you drag an icon, the other icons move automatically to make room for it.

7. **Once you've got everything just right, click the Done button to close the sheet.**

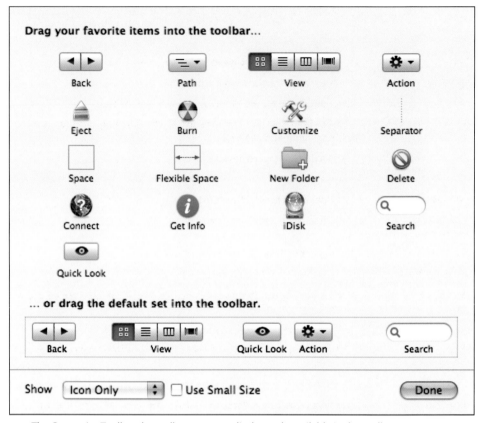

10.8 The Customize Toolbar sheet allows you to edit the tools available in the toolbar.

Table 10.3 gives an overview of each item's function to help you make an informed decision about which ones you'd like to include.

Genius

The fastest way to alter items already on the toolbar, or even the toolbar itself, without using the Customize Toolbar sheet, is by using the trusty ⌘ key. To quickly rearrange items on the toolbar, hold down the ⌘ key and click-and-drag the item to its new location. To remove an item, simply ⌘-click-and-drag it out of the toolbar, and then drop it. Cycle through the toolbar's Show options by holding down the ⌘ key and clicking the oval button in the upper-right corner of the Finder window. Continue clicking the oval button to see the various options. You can also hide the toolbar completely by simply clicking the oval button, without using the ⌘ key.

Table 10.3 Customize Toolbar Sheet Items

Item	Description/Action
Back	Navigate forward or backward in the folder path.
Path	Click to see the current folder path.
View	Quickly change the view for the current Finder window.
Action	Choose from a list of common actions, such as creating a new folder or getting information on an item.
Eject	Eject a disc or other removable media.
Burn	Burn a CD or DVD.
Customize	Provides quick access to the Customize Toolbar sheet.
Separator, Space, and Flexible Space	Use to separate items and groups of items.
New Folder	Creates a new folder in the current folder.
Delete	Moves the selected file or folder to the Trash.
Connect	Opens the Connect to Server window, allowing you to quickly connect to other computers.
Get Info	Shows all information relative to the selected file or folder.
iDisk	Connects to your iDisk (a subscription to Apple's .MobileMe service is required).
Search	Enter the names of items you need to find on your Mac's hard drive.
Quick Look	Provides a glance at the contents of a file, without having to open the application that created it.
Show	Choose how to display the items in the toolbar using the pop-up menu and the Use Small Size check box.

Change the sidebar

The sidebar contains links, or shortcuts, to folders, discs, and servers that you often need to access. You can modify the sidebar's contents in a number of ways:

- To remove an item you don't use, click-and-drag the item out of the sidebar, and then drop it.

- Add your favorite folders by dragging their icons into the sidebar under the Places section (see figure 10.9). The other items in the sidebar shift as necessary to make room for their new neighbor.

- Adjust the size of the sidebar by clicking-and-dragging the divider bar (see figure 10.9).

● Hide the sidebar from view altogether by clicking the oval button in the upper-right corner of the window.

● Rearrange items in the sidebar by clicking-and-dragging them to their new location.

Genius

See the Set Finder's preferences section of Chapter 1 to discover how to choose which Devices, Shared, Places, and Search For items are displayed by default in your sidebar.

Divider bar

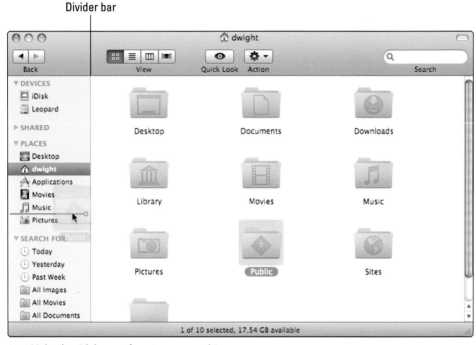

10.9 Make the sidebar conform to your needs!

Add a background image or color

One trick that adds a touch of class and functionality to your Finder windows is to add a background picture or color to them. The background pictures or colors can be used for simple decoration, or to differentiate the contents of each folder. For example, if you keep records of your children's homework on your Mac, you could assign a picture of each individual child to the particular folder containing their homework. When you open each child's folder in a Finder window, a

light background picture of your little darling instantly identifies whose homework you're checking; this is especially helpful if you have multiple windows open at once. To add a background
image or color to your Finder windows, do the following:

1. **Open the folder that you'd like to add the image or color to.**

2. **Choose View ⇨ Show View Options, or press ⌘+J.**

3. **Select the Color option in the Background section to add a color to the window, or select the Picture option to place an image in the background (see figure 10.10).**

   - If you chose to use a color, click inside the white square to the right of the radio button to open the Colors palette. Select the color that you want to use for the background and click OK.

   - If you went with a picture, click the Select button to the right of the radio button, browse your Mac for the image you need, highlight it, and click Select to apply the image to the window.

Changing icons

A very popular method for redecorating your Mac is by using custom icons for applications, folders, and files. You could change a plain folder icon to something more suitable to its contents, such as using an icon of a football for the folder that you use to keep your son's practice and game schedules. I've seen many a Mac whose icons had been changed system-wide, from top to bottom; every default Mac OS X folder had been modified!

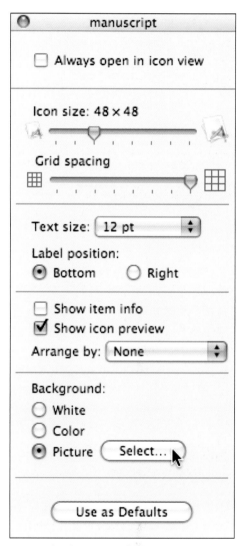

10.10 Make changes to a folder's window background by using the Background section of the View Options window.

Caution A potential "oops" when using an image is that if the image is too large to fit in the window, you only see the part of it that does fit. The Preview application that is loaded with Mac OS X Leopard is a great tool for easily resizing images. See Chapter 8 for step-by-step instructions.

Here's how to change any item's icon in Mac OS X:

1. **Highlight the icon you want to use and click ⌘+I (Get Info) to open its Info window.**

2. **Click the icon picture in the upper-left corner of the Info window (see figure 10.11), and then copy the icon by using ⌘+C or choosing Edit ⇨ Copy.**

3. **Close the Info window.**

4. **Highlight the item whose icon you want to change, and open its Info window by using ⌘+I.**

5. **Click the icon picture in the upper-left corner of the Info window and paste the new icon there by using ⌘+V or choosing Edit ⇨ Paste.**

6. **Close the changed item's Info window.**

10.11 Change an item's icon from within its Info window.

Open and Close Widgets

Leopard includes an application called Dashboard that affords you another fun way to customize your Mac. Dashboard lets you access and manage a multitude of widgets that you can use for tracking packages, getting driving directions, browsing the Yellow Pages, checking your stocks, seeing the latest weather forecasts, finding out what movies are playing at your local multiplex, playing Sudoku, and the list goes on and on. Widgets are one of those rare things that make your life easier and are really, really cool to use at the same time! In the next few sections, I will show you how to access, use, customize, and even create your own widgets.

To open Dashboard and see the default set of running widgets, do one of the following:

- **Click the Dashboard icon in your Dock**
- **Press the F12 key**

In the main body of the screen, you see the four widgets that Leopard is running out of the gate: Calculator, iCal, Weather, and World Clock. These are very basic widgets that you can use to get your feet wet in the world of widgetry (yes, I just coined that term!). To get a quick feel for using a widget, click the Calculator to bring it to the forefront, and then use your mouse to perform calculations on the widget's virtual keypad, or use your keyboard to enter information.

Take notice of the + within the small circle that appears in the lower-left corner of the screen when you activate Dashboard. Click the + to open the widget bar, which grants access to all the widgets that Leopard so graciously includes as well as allows you to change the widgets you have running.

Peruse the Widget bar until you see a widget that strikes your fancy, and then click to open it. When you click the widget you want to open, Dashboard drops the widget on your screen, which causes an amazing ripple effect to occur, similar to that of dropping a rock in a still pond. That little trick, shown in figure 10.12, will enthrall even the most steadfast Mac skeptic!

To close any widget, click the X located in its upper-left corner. Dashboard even has a neat effect for this action: The widget is sucked into the X until it disappears! If that's not neat enough for you, hold down the Shift key while clicking the X to see it disappear in slow motion.

10.12 The ripple effect caused by opening a new widget has only one use: to look very, very cool!

Widgets Supplied with Leopard

Because there are quite a few widgets that come preinstalled in Leopard, I thought it would be a good idea to give you a quick synopsis of what's available and what it can do. Table 10.4 spells out the details of these widgets.

Table 10.4 Leopard Widgets

Widget	Functions
Widgets	Opens the Widget Manager.
Address Book	Lets you quickly search your address book and displays information for the contact.
Business	Searches your local Yellow Pages for business listings.
Calculator	Performs basic mathematical computations.
Dictionary	A fast way to access the meanings of words. Also doubles as a thesaurus.
ESPN	Finds all the latest scores and sports news.
Flight Tracker	When you enter a flight number, Flight Tracker details its status. This little Widget does some really cool stuff. Check it out, whether you have a flight to track or not!
Google	Supplies you with a Google search window at a press of the F12 key.
iCal	Displays your schedule for the day selected.
iTunes	Provides a tiny remote control for using iTunes. iTunes must be open for this one to work.
Movies	Gives you the show times for the movies currently playing in local theaters. You can also view the trailer for the film, as well as buy tickets online.
People	Finds people by their name and city.
Ski Report	You can enter your favorite ski resort to get the latest information on skiing conditions.
Stickies	You can use them just like you would the real thing: to keep little notes all over your Mac!
Stocks	Keeps up with all the latest Wall Street comings and goings for stocks that you specify.
Tile Game	Keeps a really, really bored person occupied for a while.
Translation	Instantly translates words or phrases from one language to another.
Unit Converter	Converts units for several different measurements, such as time, length, currency, and pressure.
Weather	Provides the latest weather prognostications for your neck of the woods. Covered in detail in the "Advanced Dashboard" section of this chapter.
Web Clip	Lets you create your own Widgets. More on this feature in the "Advanced Dashboard" section.
World Clock	Displays an analog clock, which can give you the time of day for hundreds of locations around the world.

Advanced Dashboard

Dashboard is certainly a basic application, but it does afford you the opportunity to do a little fine-tuning — to tinker with it a bit, if you will. In this section, I will show you how to manage the widgets you have installed, how to set preferences for your widgets, and how to create your own widget using a Web page.

Managing widgets

Leopard comes fully stocked with a great set of widgets, but there are a lot of them, and the ones you never use just seem to be taking up real estate on your screen unnecessarily. If you install other widgets, as discussed later in this chapter, there will be still more widget icons to browse through in the Widget bar. Dashboard provides a handy way to disable the widgets that you hardly ever use, without actually uninstalling them; this comes in handy should you decide to try one of them in the future.

To disable, or enable, widgets, do the following:

1. **Press F12 to open Dashboard.**

2. **Click the + in the lower-left corner of your screen to open the Widget bar.**

3. **Click the Manage Widgets button to open the Widget manager, as shown in figure 10.13.**

4. **Uncheck boxes next to widgets that you want to disable, and check the boxes for those you want to enable.**

5. **Close the Widget manager window when finished.**

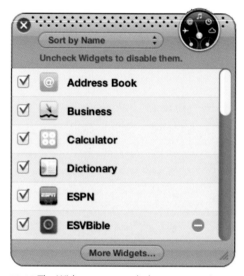

10.13 The Widget manager helps you organize your Widget bar.

How to Uninstall Widgets

You can easily uninstall widgets that you have added to Dashboard by opening the Widget manager and clicking the remove symbol (which looks like a red circle with a horizontal white line in the middle of it) to the right of the widget's name.

But what if you want to uninstall a widget that came with Leopard? There are no red uninstall symbols next to their names, so what is one to do? Leopard's default widgets are located in Hard Drive ⇨ Library ⇨ Widgets. To remove one of these widgets, drag it to the Trash and enter your Administrator password.

Setting preferences in widgets

Many widgets require a bit of customization to utilize them effectively. For instance, Movies doesn't do you much good if it's giving you show times and theaters in Cupertino, California, but you live in Sevierville, Tennessee. As another example, Stocks won't be of much assistance if you want to see what the hot new stock you just bought into is doing, but all you see are the default stocks that are set up in the widget.

Let's use Weather to illustrate how to edit the preferences of a Widget:

1. **Press F12 to open Dashboard.**

2. **Position your mouse pointer over the lower-right corner of the Weather Widget to see the Information button, which looks like a small "i" (see figure 10.14).**

3. **Click the Information button to flip over the widget so that you can see its available preferences.** Make the preference changes you desire, and then click the Done button.

10.14 Click the Information button to open a widget's preferences, if available.

4. **The widget should now reflect the changes you made to its preferences.**

Note

Not all widgets give you the option of adjusting their preferences; don't beat yourself up if you can't seem to find the elusive Information button in a given widget.

Where to Find More Cool Widgets

So far, the only widgets you've been privy to were those that came with Leopard, but I'm about to change that. There are hundreds of widgets that have been developed, and some of them are just exactly what you're looking for.

The best place to find new widgets is Apple's own Web site (more on that in a moment), but you can also find a lot of other widgets by simply performing a search on Google for "Mac OS X Widgets."

To get new widgets the quick and easy way, do the following:

1. **Press F12 to open Dashboard.**

2. **Click the + in the lower-left corner of your screen to open the Widget bar.**

3. **Click the Manage Widgets button to open the Widget manager, and then click the More Widgets button at the bottom of the window.** Safari automatically whisks you away to Apple's Dashboard Widgets Web site, shown in figure 10.15, where you can browse the massive amounts of available widgets that have been created by developers and regular users alike.

4. **Find a Widget that you want to try by using the Widget Browser.**

5. **Click the Download link to have Safari download the Widget.**

6. **Click the Install button when prompted to open your new Widget in Dashboard.** If you like what you see, click the Keep button; if not, click Delete.

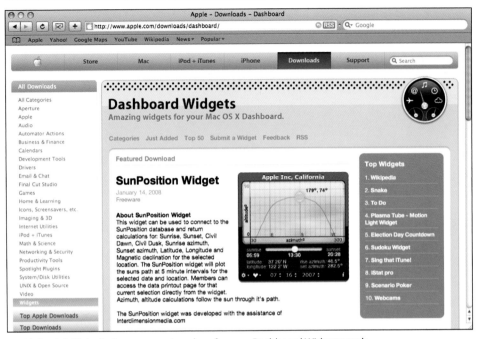

10.15 Apple's Web site is your one-stop shop for your Dashboard Widget needs.

Create Your Own Widgets Using Web Clips

A neat feature that is new to Dashboard in Leopard is the ability to create your own widgets using clips of Web pages. This is a great feature for tracking information from a certain Web site without having to constantly navigate to that Web site to check its status. I'll use the Top Widgets list on Apple's Dashboard Widgets Web site for this example, which allows me to see the most popular widgets available without having to open Safari and browse to the site; I can simply view the list in Dashboard by pressing F12 (see figure 10.16).

To create a Widget using Web Clips, do the following:

1. **Press F12 to open Dashboard.**

2. **Click the + in the lower-left corner of the screen, and select the Web Clip icon in the Widget bar.**

3. **Click the Safari icon in the Web Clip Widget window to open Safari.**

4. **Enter the address of the site you want to use to create your widget.** In this case, I'm using www.apple.com/downloads/dashboard/.

5. **Choose File ➪ Open in Dashboard.** The Web page darkens and you are presented with a selection box, as shown in figure 10.16.

6. **Position the selection box over the section of the Web page you want to use for your Widget, and then click to select the area.** You can drag the handles that appear around the selection box to adjust the area that is selected.

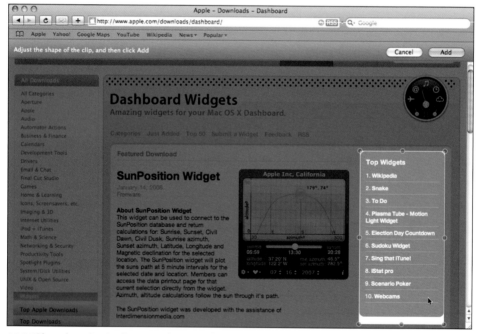

10.16 Place the selection box over the part of the Web page that you want to use for your widget.

7. **Click the Add button in the upper-right corner of Safari's window (in the purple bar).**

8. Safari passes the selection on to Dashboard, where your new widget is created.

How Do I Change Leopard's System Preferences?

y this point you are familiar with my affinity for making your Mac behave

ke you want it to. No other place in Leopard gives you more control over

our Mac than System Preferences. This is where you get to assert yourself as

he alpha user, firmly establishing yourself as the ruler of your personal com-

uting domain. System Preferences is the central location in Mac OS X for

naking both local and system-wide changes networking, security, software

nd hardware, sound, and Leopard's appearance. This chapter shows you

now to tame Leopard by explaining what preferences are available and how

ou can change them if you need to, or just simply want to.

Personal 220

Hardware 225

nternet & Network 229

System 232

Other System Preferences 236

Personal

As its name indicates, the Personal section of the System Preferences is where you can customize the way your Mac looks and behaves, suiting it to your tastes. I cover the International and Security preferences here, because the others are already covered in detail in other chapters of this book. Table 11.4 at the end of this chapter lists the preferences that I discuss in other chapters, gives a very brief description of their functions, and points you to those relevant chapters.

Open the System Preferences before reading any further in this chapter by choosing Apple menu ➪ System Preferences; you are rewarded with the System Preferences window, as shown in figure 11.1.

11.1 Click the preference you want to view or change from within the System Preferences window.

International

Leopard is quite the international sensation and can speak more languages than I ever knew existed! The International preferences pane helps your Mac flex its multilingual muscles.

Language

The Language tab (see figure 11.2) of the International preferences pane allows you to decide the order in which languages are used for application menus, for sorting items, and for dialog windows.

11.2 Your Mac can be very cosmopolitan using the International preferences pane.

Formats

You can decide how items such as dates, time, monetary increments, and measurements display on your Mac by default, using the Formats tab. figure 11.3 shows the options that are available for localizing Leopard.

Click the Customize buttons in the Dates and Times sections to further customize their layouts.

Genius

Leopard is fluent in more than 110 languages, so the list of available languages is quite lengthy. To save yourself from having to hunt for the languages you find useful in the future, click the Edit List button and uncheck the languages you don't need.

221

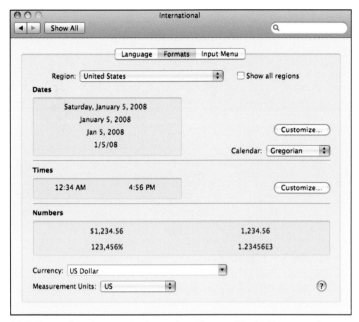

11.3 Choose how best to display regional items with the Formats tab.

Input Menu

Some languages use more characters than there are keys on your keyboard; in these cases, input methods provide a way for you to access those characters. The Input Menu tab allows you to choose from among the multitude of input methods that ship with Leopard.

For more information on this topic, click the Help button (?) in the lower-right corner of this tab.

Security

Even a Mac needs to be secured from outside troublemakers, so Leopard comes packaged with some very nice security features, which you can access through the Security preferences pane.

General

Figure 11.4 shows the options available under the General tab. These are fairly self-explanatory, but some aren't quite as intuitive as others. The General tab options are as follows:

- **Require password to wake this computer from sleep or screen saver:** Check this box to lock your Mac from any user who doesn't know your account password once it has gone to sleep or a screen saver has been activated.

- **Disable automatic login:** If this box is unchecked, your Mac simply boots up into the default account, without any prompt for a password.

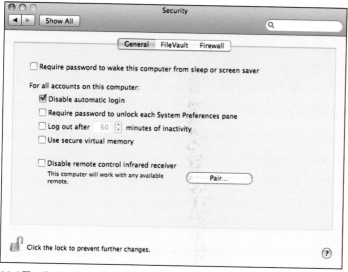

11.4 The General tab of the Security preferences.

Caution

I highly recommend that you use both the *Require password to wake this computer from sleep or screen saver* and *Disable automatic login* options. Not checking these options allows unfettered access to anyone who turns on, restarts, or wakes up your Mac. At this point, the fate of your Mac and all the files it holds is entirely in the hands of the trespasser.

- **Require password to unlock each System Preferences pane:** There is a lock icon in the bottom-left corner of each preferences pane. If you check this box, the icon will be in the locked position for every pane in System Preferences, and will only unlock with an administrator password.

- **Log out after x minutes of inactivity:** Select this option to have your Mac automatically log out of your account after the specified time of inactivity.

- **Use secure virtual memory:** Your Mac uses portions of your hard drive like RAM (memory) to store information. Select this option to have Leopard erase this information from your hard drive to prevent others from accessing it if they get hold of your drive.

- **Disable remote control infrared receiver:** Some Macs have infrared receivers that they use to receive commands from an Apple remote control for viewing movies, listening to music, and other activities. Check this box if you want to disable your infrared receiver so that other Mac owners can't control your Mac using their remote.

FileVault

FileVault lets you enable the Leopard FileVault feature, which I must not recommend unless you are a very savvy and security-minded computer user. FileVault encrypts your entire home folder, which prevents anyone else from seeing its contents. Although this sounds great, the big downfall for someone who is not used to such high security is that if they forget their user account password (or if they don't remember or failed to even set the master password), then their home folder contents are lost. Yikes!

If you want to turn on FileVault protection for your account, click the Turn On FileVault button in the lower-right corner. Your Mac must have enough space available on its hard drive to store an encrypted version.

Caution If you enable a master password, anyone who knows that password can decrypt the contents of any FileVault-protected accounts on the entire Mac. This endangers every account on the computer, so I highly recommend not setting a master password.

Firewall

A firewall prevents unauthorized users from accessing your Mac through the Internet. These bothersome folks are up to no good, but a firewall may keep them at bay. Choose one of these three options:

- **Allow all incoming connections:** Provides no protection at all.

- **Allow only essential services:** According to Apple, essential services are sets of applications that allow your Mac to discover services (such as shared files and printers) provided by other computers on your network. Using this setting keeps services other than these from connecting to your Mac.

- **Set access for specific services and applications:** Select this option to manually pick and choose which applications and services you want to allow access to on your Mac. Click the + button in the lower-left corner of the window to browse your computer for those applications and services; to remove them from the list, click the - button.

Genius If you are connecting to the Internet through a router, you probably won't need to enable the Leopard firewall because the router will most likely be running one. Check your router's documentation to be certain of its firewall settings.

Hardware

The Hardware section of System Preferences lets Leopard know how you want it to interact with various hardware components of your Mac.

CDs & DVDs

When you insert a CD or DVD into your Mac's disc drive, something's going to happen; however, what happens is up to you entirely. The CDs & DVDs preferences pane lets you tell Leopard how it should behave when you insert a disc, as shown in figure 11.5.

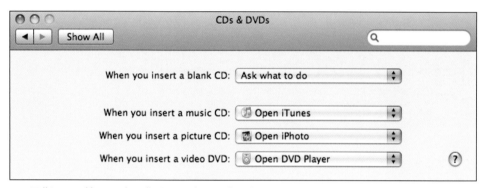

11.5 Tell Leopard how to handle CDs and DVDs from here.

Displays

Displays preferences help you to set the resolution of your Mac's monitor or screen. The options in both tabs of the pane, Display and Color, are standard on any computer.

The Display tab allows you to change these settings:

- **Colors:** Lets you select the number of colors to use. Millions is the no-brainer choice for almost any user.

- **Refresh Rate:** Determines how often the display is redrawn. If you aren't using a Mac with a built-in display, such as a laptop or an iMac, consult the documentation that came with your monitor for appropriate refresh rates.

● **Resolutions:** Lets you choose the amount of detail your screen shows. The higher the resolution, the smaller the items are on your screen; the lower the resolution, the larger the items are.

● **Detect Displays:** Click this button to have Leopard automatically discover newly connected displays and to choose the settings to use with them.

Genius

Sometimes the best color is what suits your eye the best, not what Leopard automatically chooses for your monitor. You can create a custom profile for your monitor to use by clicking the Calibrate button and following the instructions. If color matching is old hat to you, check the Expert Mode check box in the Display Calibrator Assistant's Introduction screen to gain access to a more finely-tuned process.

The Color tab is where you can set your display to use color profiles so that it can represent colors more accurately. Uncheck the Show profiles for this display only check box to see all profiles installed on your Mac.

Energy Saver

Everyone's trying to be a bit greener these days, and Leopard is no exception. The Energy Saver preferences provide settings for your computer, hard disk, and your display to sleep when they are inactive for the period of time that you set by dragging the sliders, as shown in figure 11.6.

Click the Options tab in the Energy Saver preferences pane to set these options:

● **Wake for Ethernet network administrator access:** Lets your Mac wake up when a network administrator is trying to access it through the network.

● **Automatically reduce the brightness of the display before display sleep:** The brightness on your display decreases a couple of minutes before it goes to sleep when it is not in use.

● **Restart automatically after a power failure:** If power is interrupted, your Mac automatically restarts itself once the power is restored.

● **Show battery status in the menu bar:** Places a battery icon in the menu bar that allows you to easily monitor the amount of charge still remaining in the battery for a Mac laptop.

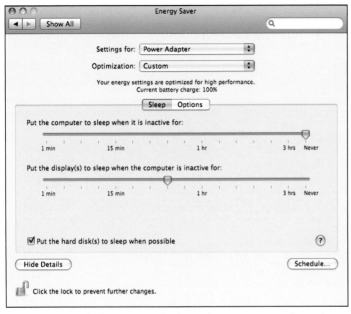

11.6 Save energy by having your display and computer go to sleep when not in use.

Keyboard & Mouse

The Keyboard & Mouse preferences pane gives you the ability to configure how your mouse, keyboard, or trackpad (for laptops), interacts with Leopard. You can also set up a wireless mouse and keyboard using Bluetooth, and even create your own keyboard shortcuts.

Select the Keyboard, Trackpad, or Mouse tabs to modify their behaviors, such as how quickly the keyboard responds to a key press, or how fast your double-click speed is set. The items under each tab are self-explanatory, but if you need further help, click the Help button in the lower-right corner of the window.

The Bluetooth tab is only available on Macs that have Bluetooth installed. Check the battery status of wireless keyboards and mice from here, as well as install new devices by clicking the Set Up New Device button in the lower-right corner.

I love the fact that Apple gives you the opportunity to make your own keyboard shortcuts with the Keyboard Shortcuts tab (shown in figure 11.7). Uncheck the shortcuts you want to disable, click the + button in the lower-left corner to create a new shortcut, or highlight a shortcut in the list and click the – button to delete it.

Genius

I've gotten myself in trouble before by accidentally deleting keyboard shortcuts that I used often. I was able to retrieve those lost shortcuts by clicking the Restore Defaults button in the lower-right corner, but be warned that if you try this, you lose any custom shortcuts you've created. You can't say I didn't warn you!

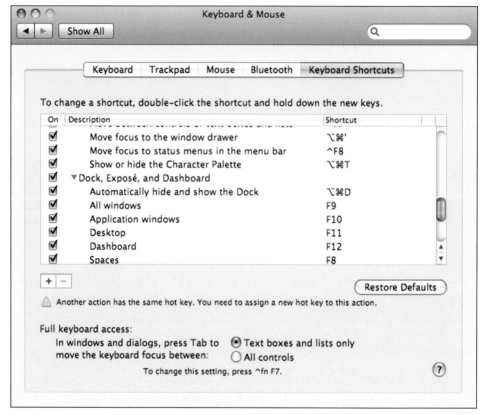

11.7 Create and modify your own keyboard shortcuts.

Sound

Configure your Mac's sound using these preferences. Table 11.1 gives a brief overview of each tab in the pane.

Table 11.1 Sound Preference Pane Options

Tab	Options available
Sound Effects	Select what sounds to use for system alerts, adjust the volume of these alerts, and set the system-wide output volume.
Output	Choose output devices, such as external speakers, to broadcast your Mac's sounds, as well as adjust its sound balance.
Input	Select a sound input device, such as an external microphone. You can adjust devices' input volume and filter unwanted background noise (check the box next to Use ambient noise reduction) as well.

Internet & Network

These preferences are where you tell your Mac how to communicate with the rest of the world through its network connections.

MobileMe

For $99 per year, Apple offers MobileMe, a service that extends your Mac experience to the Internet. The MobileMe service offers the following features:

- **Synchronize calendars, contacts, data, and more.**
- **Access your MobileMe e-mail account through any Web browser on any computer.**
- **Use an iDisk to store files and synchronize folders.**
- **Create your own Web site.**
- **Use Back to My Mac to access your home or office Mac from a remote location using any computer connected to the Internet.**
- **Organize your family's activities, team meetings, church events, and more using Groups.**
- **Share photos and movies with incredible ease using Web Gallery.**

The MobileMe preferences pane is where you can log in to your MobileMe account and set up how your Mac interacts with the MobileMe services. For more information on MobileMe, visit www.apple.com/mobileme/.

Network

The Network preferences pane, shown in figure 11.8, is where you configure settings for your various network connection types.

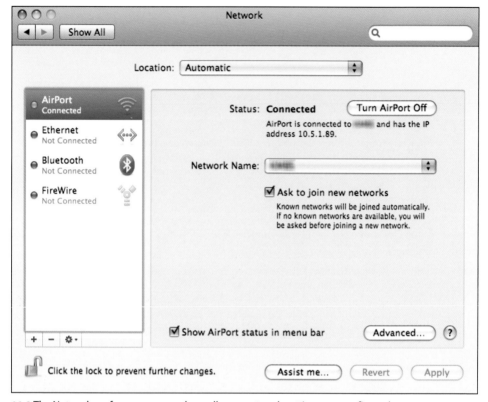

11.8 The Network preferences pane, where all your network settings are configured.

The list on the left side of the pane shows the network connections that your Mac supports. The contents of this list vary, depending on the network hardware that is available on your Mac.

- **Airport:** Settings for using your Mac's built-in Airport card or a third-party wireless adapter to access the network wirelessly.

- **Ethernet:** Connection settings for attaching to a network using your Mac's built-in Ethernet port.

- **Bluetooth:** Your Mac can use its Bluetooth adapter to share your cellular phone's Internet access, assuming the phone has a Bluetooth adapter as well.

- **FireWire:** Leopard also allows you to connect two Macs together with a FireWire cable, so that you can share files or Internet connections between them.

Click one of the network connections to gain access to its innermost workings. The Advanced button in the lower-right corner of each tab's pane is used to inspect or manually set the network connections for that particular connection method, as shown for the Airport connection type in figure 11.9.

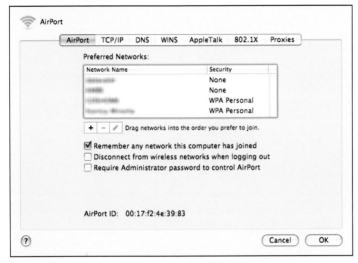

11.9 Advanced settings let you fine-tune the network options.

Detailed information on the options that are available for each of the connection types can be found by clicking the Help button in their respective panes.

QuickTime

QuickTime is the multimedia technology that Apple embeds in Mac OS X. Use the QuickTime settings in this preferences pane (see figure 11.10) to determine how QuickTime works with the rest of the operating system and to register the Pro version of QuickTime. Table 11.2 lists the tabs in this pane, and what functions are available in each.

11.10 Set QuickTime to work well with the rest of Leopard.

Table 11.2 QuickTime Preferences

Tab	Functions
Register	Enter your registration code if you have upgraded to QuickTime Pro to enable the advanced features of QuickTime, such as the ability to edit video and convert files to different formats.
Browser	Decide how QuickTime will work with your Internet browsers, such as Safari.
Update	Click the Install button to download and install third-party software that extends the capabilities of QuickTime.
Streaming	Change the streaming speed option if you are having difficulties playing movies over the Internet.
Advanced	Select a music synthesizer for playing MIDI files, manually select the protocol that QuickTime uses for your network connection, turn on kiosk mode, export files using older codecs, and set up MIME settings and Media Keys.

System

The System section of the System Preferences contains panes for configuring the accounts on your Mac, updating your Mac's software, choosing a startup disk, and many more system-wide options.

Date & Time

Adjust your Mac's time settings with this preferences pane, shown in figure 11.11. The tabs provide the following options:

- **Date & Time:** Check the Set date & time automatically check box to have your Mac do just that, and then select a time server from the list provided. You can choose to make manual settings by unchecking this box and adjusting the date and time to your preference.

- **Time Zone:** Select the time zone you are in by choosing an area on the map.

- **Clock:** Decide whether and how to display the date and time in the menu bar, and allow your Mac to speak the time to you at the specified intervals.

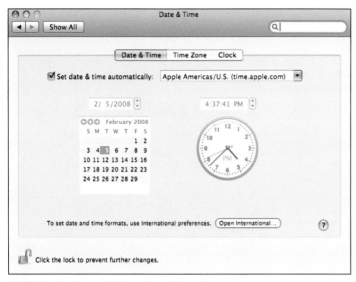

11.11 Set the date and time using this preferences pane.

Software Update

Leopard uses the Software Update application to check for updates to the operating system and compatible applications.

The Scheduled Check tab lets you instantly check the Apple servers for new updates by clicking the Check Now button. You can also schedule update checks using the "Check for updates" option and selecting how often Software Update should check for updates.

The Installed Updates tab lists all the updates that have been downloaded and installed on your Mac.

Genius

There are several different schools of thought when it comes to upgrading to the latest and greatest software. In my opinion, if there's an update available for your operating system or an application installed on your system, go ahead and get it. The vast majority of the time, updates don't cause any problems; on the contrary, they usually end up fixing or preventing them.

Speech

Leopard is so intelligent that it can talk to you, and even respond to spoken commands! Here are the options that are available to you.

Speech Recognition

The Settings section of the Speech Recognition tab, shown in figure 11.12, lets you turn Speakable Items on or off, as well as select the microphone for your Mac to listen to your commands with. You can also select a listening key, which is the key you press to make your Mac listen for your spoken commands.

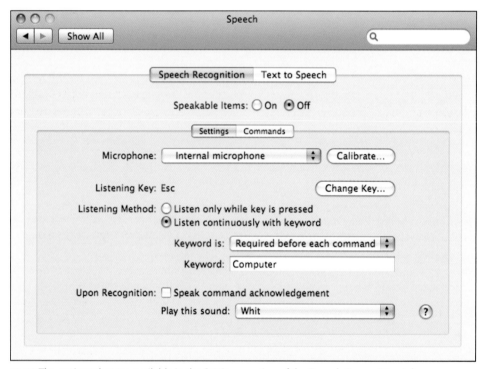

11.12 The options that are available in the Settings section of the Speech Recognition tab.

The Commands section allows you to customize which spoken commands your Mac responds to. Click the Open Speakable Items Folder button to see a list of the preconfigured commands your Mac understands. Click the Helpful Tips button to get great advice on how to successfully use the Speakable Items options and commands.

Text to Speech

This section of the Speech preferences lets you choose which voice your Mac uses when it speaks to you. Select from several preinstalled voices and modify the rate at which your Mac says the words. You can also have Leopard announce system alerts, announce when an application needs to be looked after, and speak text that you've highlighted in a document.

Startup Disk

This preference pane allows you choose to start your Mac from any drive that contains a valid Mac OS X installation. When you first open these preferences, you are presented with a list of disks that are considered to be valid startup devices. Select the disk you want to boot up with, and then click the Restart button.

Universal Access

Leopard implements the Universal Access preferences so that those who may have physical difficulties, such as loss of eyesight, can use a Mac with little to no problem. Table 11.3 lists the tabs and options that are available for eachpreference.

Table 11.3 Universal Access Preferences

Tab	Options
Seeing	VoiceOver tells your Mac to read all text the mouse moves over.
	Zoom turns on the zoom function, which is activated by the keyboard shortcuts listed in the preferences pane.
	Display provides great options for those Mac users whose eyesight isn't what it once was.
Hearing	These options are for Mac users who have difficulty hearing at normal levels. Adjust the volume from here if you like, and have the Mac flash its screen to alert you of incoming information.
Keyboard	This tab provides options for helping Mac users who may have difficulty using the traditional keyboard.
Mouse & Trackpad	Should you have problems using the mouse, you can use Mouse Keys, which causes the numeric keypad (available on most Mac keyboards) to act as a temporary mouse.

Other System Preferences

Table 11.4 lists the "celebrity" preferences that I have discussed in other chapters of this fine book.

Table 11.4 More Personal Preferences

Section	Preferences	Functions	Relevant Chapter
Personal	Appearance	Change the overall look of the Leopard menus, scroll bars, and other screen elements.	10
Personal	Desktop & Screen Saver	Select a desktop picture for your user account, as well as a screen saver.	10
Personal	Dock	Make adjustments to your Dock, such as magnification and hiding settings.	1
Personal	Exposé & Spaces	Manipulate how Exposé organizes items, and set up how Spaces works within Leopard.	1
Personal	Spotlight	Choose which categories of files Spotlight will search on your Mac.	1
Hardware	Print & Fax	Install and set up printers.	9
Hardware	Bluetooth	Set up connections with other Bluetooth-enabled devices.	13
Internet & Network	Sharing	Determine how your Mac shares files, drives, and printers with other computers.	13
System	Accounts	Create accounts for multiple users on your Mac.	12
System	Parental Controls	Set Internet and other boundaries for your children or other users.	12
System	Time Machine	Back up your Mac automatically.	14

How Can I Configure User Accounts?

User accounts are the perfect way to make sure that multiple people can use your Mac without the risk of them completely goofing up the whole thing. I'll show you in this chapter how to create multiple user accounts and what type of accounts you can select. Individual user accounts allow each user to configure their account to their liking, while protecting the other accounts on the Mac. Leopard also provides Parental Controls to help concerned moms and dads keep tabs on their prodigy's computer usage. The Parental Controls in Leopard easily allow parents to configure their child's computing experience to protect both them and the Mac.

Types of Accounts 240

Creating New User Accounts 241

Logging Into Accounts 246

Enable Parental Controls 249

Simple Finder 250

Limit Access to Specific Applications and Functions 252

Restrict Internet and E-mail Access 244

Set Time Limits 257

Keep Account Activity Logs 258

Types of Accounts

Let's face it: Some users can be trusted more than others. Factors useful for assessing a user's trust-worthiness may be their age, maturity, responsibility, or their prowess with a computer. Leopard allows you to create user accounts that have nearly complete access to every component of the operating system, those that have strictly limited access, and anything in between.

Administrator

Administrator accounts are the big dogs of the user accounts world. The default account that is created when you first install Leopard is an administrator account. Administrators can handle almost any task on your Mac, including the following:

- **Create and remove (delete) user accounts.**
- **Change settings for other user accounts.**
- **Change all system settings, including those that are locked in System Preferences.**
- **Install software and drivers that any user on the system can utilize (if you want them to, of course).**
- **Decide whether to rule your Mac kingdom with an iron fist, or be a benevolent ruler, loved and adored by all of your minions.**

Standard

A standard account is adequate for most users. Standard accounts allow the user enough freedom to customize their own account without having the power to alter others. Standard accounts:

- **Can install software, but only they have access to the software.**
- **Can customize their working environment with System Preferences; however, they cannot alter System Preferences that are locked.**
- **Cannot modify, add, or delete other user accounts.**

Managed with Parental Controls

Parental Controls are used to manage, or limit, these accounts and the privileges they have. I discuss Parental Controls in greater detail later in this chapter, so I won't deal with the particulars here.

Sharing Only

A Sharing Only account restricts the user to accessing the computer only through the network, as he would a server. Sharing Only accounts are useful for sharing documents with others in your home or office without giving them access to the rest of your home folder or Mac. The user cannot log onto the Mac with a Sharing Only account name.

Creating New User Accounts

Now that I've covered the different account types, you can start to create some. To make a new user account:

1. **Choose Apple menu ⇨ System Preferences, and click the Accounts icon in the System section to open the Accounts preferences window, as shown in figure 12.1.**

2. **If the lock icon in the bottom-left corner is in the locked position, click the icon to unlock it.** Enter an administrator account name and password when prompted.

12.1 The Accounts preferences window is at your disposal.

3. **Once you have unlocked the Accounts preferences, click the + button in the lower-left corner of the Accounts window to add a new account.**

4. **The new accounts window, shown in figure 12.2, helps you to set up the account.** Table 12.1 lists the new account fields and options, and explains how to configure them.

5. **Once you have the account settings in order, click the Create Account button.**

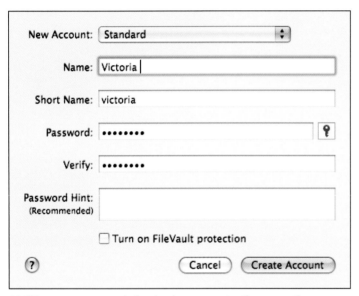

12.2 The new accounts window is where you enter the account's username and password information.

Table 12.1 New Account Settings

Option	Function
New Account	Select the type of account you want to create.
Name	Enter the name of the user to whom the account belongs.
Short Name	Leopard automatically trims the Name to provide a Short Name for the account, but you can edit it if you prefer.
Password	Create a password to allow access to the account.
Verify	Reenter the password you created in the Password field.
Password Hint	Type a hint that will help you to remember the password if you are unable to successfully enter it.
Turn on FileVault protection	Enable this check box if you want to use FileVault for this account. For more on FileVault, see Chapter 11.

Password assistance

If you're having difficulty coming up with a secure password, you can always ask Leopard for a little help. In the new account window, note the icon of the key next to the Password field; click this key icon to open the Password Assistant window, shown in figure 12.3.

12.3 The Password Assistant can help you out of the password selection rut.

Choose the password type you want to use from these options: Manual, Memorable, Letters & Numbers, Numbers Only, Random, and FIPS-181 compliant. Manual allows you to create your own password, while the other options let Leopard choose a password for you, based on the type you select.

Modify account settings

Your new account is in the account list on the left side of the Accounts window, just like in figure 12.4.

There are a handful of modifications you can make to the newly created account at this point:

- **Reset Password.** Click this button to reset the account's password. Only an administrator account can perform this action. You would typically only want to use this feature if the user of the account has forgotten his password, but it can obviously be abused by anyone that also has access to an administrator password.

- **.MobileMe User Name.** If the user of the account has a .MobileMe username, enter it here.

12.4 The new account is ready for use.

- **Allow user to administer this computer.** Check this box if you want to convert a stan-dard account to one with full administrator rights.

- **Enable Parental Controls.** Change the account so that it is managed with Parental Controls by checking this box. See later in this chapter for more on Parental Controls.

The Root Account

Up until now, you thought that administrator accounts were the ultimate power trip, but now meet the real king of the accounts jungle: the root account! The root account is the only account in a UNIX-based operating system (which includes Mac OS X Leopard) that truly has full access to any and every file, visible or invisible, on the computer. Administrator accounts are limited in their ability to browse folders on other accounts, even though they could delete the other accounts entirely. The root account isn't hindered from doing or accessing anything on the entire system, and that's why it's disabled in

Leopard by default: If you are logged in as the root user, one mistake could bring down the entire computer. I do not recommend enabling the root account for any reason; however, if you would like to, here's how (consider yourself duly warned):

1. **Choose Go ⇨ Utilities, and then double-click the Directory Utility icon.**

2. **Click the lock in the lower-left corner of the Directory Utility window, and then enter an administrator username and password when prompted.**

3. **Choose Edit ⇨ Enable Root User from the menu.** The root account is turned on at this point.

4. **The root account doesn't have a password assigned to it until you choose Edit ⇨ Change Root Password, and then enter a password.** You certainly want to create a password; otherwise, your system will be under an enormous security threat.

● **Delete the account.** You can remove the account completely (if you are an administrator) by clicking the account to highlight it, and then clicking the – button in the bottom-left corner of the Accounts window.

● **Change the user account picture.** Click the user account picture to change it to a different picture. Choose a picture from the list, or select Edit Picture to use a different picture that you have stored on your Mac, as shown in figure 12.5. Click the Set button when you are finished in the Edit Picture window.

  ○ **Click the Choose button to browse your Mac for a picture.**

12.5 Edit the picture used for the account to match your preferences.

- **Drag the slider to alter the picture's size, and click-and-drag the picture to center it.**

- **If your Mac has a camera attached or built in, click the Take a video snapshot button to create a picture using this feature.**

Logging Into Accounts

When you first start up your Mac in the morning, or if you have to restart it at some point during the day, you most likely need to log in to the system using your account name and password. You can also log into other accounts at the same time that yours is logged in, without having to restart the Mac or shut down your running applications (now that's cool!).

Login Options

Click the Login Options button in the lower-left corner of the Accounts window to see what options you have (see figure 12.6). Table 12.2 lists and explains each of the available options.

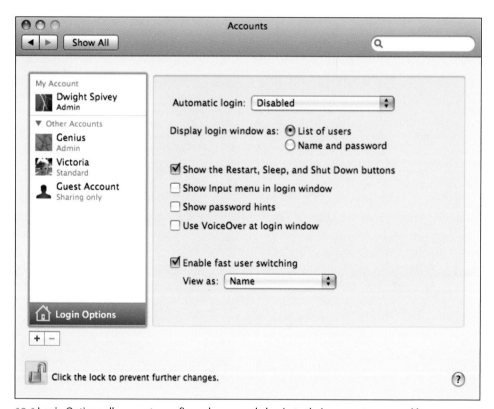

12.6 Login Options allow you to configure how people log in to their accounts on your Mac.

Table 12.2 Login Options

Option	Function
Automatic login	I recommend that you always set this option to Disabled. If you enable this option, your Mac logs in to the default administrator account without prompting you for a password, which is most certainly not a good security decision.
Display login window as	Determine whether the login window at startup should show a list of all the user accounts on the Mac, or whether it should simply prompt for a username and password. Simply prompting for a username and password may be the best idea if security is a concern.
Show the Restart, Sleep, and Shut Down buttons	Select this option to have these buttons appear in the login window.
Show Input menu in login window	This option causes the Input menu, discussed in Chapter 11, to be displayed in the upper part of the login window.
Show password hints	This option allows the password hints that you entered when creating the account to appear in the login window.
Use VoiceOver at login window	Select this option to have the contents of the login window spoken to you by the Mac.
Enable fast user switching	This is the best Login Option of them all. This option allows multiple users to be logged into the Mac at the same time. Each application that is open in an account remains open, even when someone else is logged into their account. This makes it incredibly convenient for you to allow others temporary access to the Mac while not having to start all of your work over again when they're done. The name of the account that the user is currently logged into is shown in the upper-right corner of the screen; click that name to access other accounts, and then enter their name and password to have Leopard switch over to them.
View as	This drop-down menu determines how the user accounts display in the menu.

Genius When utilizing fast user switching, you can quickly access the preferences for your account by clicking the name of the account in the upper-right corner of the screen and selecting Account Preferences from the menu.

Login Items

Login Items are applications or utilities that you have slated to automatically start when you log in to your account. You must be logged into an account to see its Login Items window, shown in figure 12.7.

To change the Login Items for an account:

1. **Click the account you want to alter in the accounts list.**

2. **Select the Login Items tab near the top of the Accounts window.**

3. **To add items to the login list, click the + button under the lower-left corner of the list, and then browse your Mac for the items.**

4. **Remove items from the list by highlighting them and clicking the – button under the lower-left corner of the list.**

5. **Click the Hide check box next to any item you want to be automatically hidden after login.** This prevents windows from the open applications cluttering your Finder window when you first log in.

6. **Close System Preferences.**

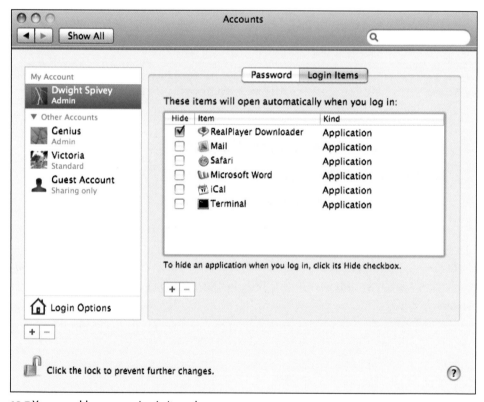

12.7 You can add or remove Login Items here.

Caution Some applications or utilities may add items to your Login Items list that they need to be running to perform tasks in the background. Be careful before removing Login Items for antivirus software and other utilities that constantly monitor your Mac's activities.

Enable Parental Controls

As a parent, I completely understand the desire to protect your children from things that may be beyond their level of maturity and understanding. Parental Controls is just as effective with adults as it is with children, so don't be afraid to manage the accounts of those users who aren't very experienced with computers or perhaps haven't quite grown up in other ways. Sometimes you have to do what is best for Little Leslie, or even Big Bob, whether they like it or not!

To use Parental Controls, you must first create a Managed by Parental Controls account, or enable Parental Controls for an existing account. Follow the instructions in earlier sections of this chapter for creating a new user account or follow these steps to enable Parental Controls on a current account:

1. **Choose Apple menu ⇨ System Preferences and then click the Accounts icon in the System section.**

2. **Click the lock icon in the lower-left corner if it is locked and then enter an administrator username and password to unlock the Accounts preferences.**

3. **Select the account you want to enable Parental Controls for in the accounts list.**

4. **Click the Enable Parental Controls check box.**

5. **Click the Show All button in the upper-left corner of the System Preferences window and then select the Parental Controls icon in the System section.**

6. **Choose the Managed with Parental Controls account in the account list on the left side of the Parental Controls window, as shown in figure 12.8. The account is ready for you to take control.**

12.8 The default Parental Controls window with an account ready to be modified.

Simple Finder

Simple Finder is a Finder without the frills but with basic functionality for a managed user. Simple Finder only allows the user to access three folders in the Dock: My Applications, Documents, and Shared. Simple Finder doesn't allow access to the remainder of the Mac's hard drive or System Preferences.

To use a Simple Finder:

1. **Open the Parental Controls preferences by choosing Apple menu ⇨ System Preferences, and then clicking the Parental Controls icon in the System section.** Because all actions in this chapter are initiated from the Parental Controls preferences window, I won't mention that they need to be open when I give future instructions.

2. **Choose the account you want to modify in the accounts list.**

3. **Check the Use Simple Finder check box in the System tab. The next time you log into the account, it will use a Simple Finder.**

Figure 12.9 shows a typical Simple Finder desktop. The three folders in the Dock give the user access to the applications they have permission to use, as well as their Documents folder and the Shared folder.

To use the account with a full Finder, just uncheck the Use Simple Finder box.

12.9 An account running a Simple Finder.

Changing Finder Preferences in Simple Finder

Simple Finder doesn't allow a user to change many settings. This means that if you do need to change settings, you have to use an administrator account. In previous versions of Mac OS X, you would have to log out of the account using the Simple Finder, log into an administrator account, disable Simple Finder in the managed account, and finally log back into the managed account to change Finder settings. Whew! Thankfully, Leopard changes all that. To change Finder settings while in Simple Finder:

1. **Choose Finder ⇨ Run Full Finder, and then enter an administrator's username and password.**

2. **Choose Finder ⇨ Preferences to make the necessary changes.**

3. **Choose Finder ⇨ Return to Simple Finder when finished; the Simple Finder window returns to normal.**

Limit Access to Specific Applications and Functions

An alternative to Simple Finder is to run a full Finder but with limitations. Parental Controls lets an administrator choose exactly what applications and utilities the managed account can use, and what functions it can perform. To set these kinds of limitations:

1. **In the System tab of the Parental Controls window, check the Only allow selected applications check box.**

2. **In the Check the applications to allow window, browse through the list of available applications and utilities; click the arrows on the left side of the list to expand a category.** When you find an application or utility you want the user of the account to be able to access, check the box to its immediate left.

3. **Check the box next to the functions you want the user to be able to use, as in figure 12.10. Table 12.3 further explains each option.**

Table 12.3 Functional Limitations

Option	Function
Can administer printers	Select this option if you want the user to be able to add or remove printers, and to be able to manage jobs in the printer queues.
Can burn CDs and DVDs	This option allows the user to burn music and data to CDs and DVDs.
Can change password	Select this option so the user of the account can change the account password for themselves.
Can modify the Dock	The user can add, remove, and reposition items in the Dock when you select this option.

12.10 Select the applications and functions that the managed account can access or use.

253

Restrict Internet and E-mail Access

Three of the most powerful societal influences on your youngster are the Internet, e-mail, and instant messaging. For all the wonderful content that's available on the Internet, there's an equal amount of horrifying content just waiting for young eyes to come across it. The Parental Controls I am about to discuss can help protect our most easily impressionable citizens from some of the worst the world has to offer. Take the time to investigate each of these settings to the fullest extent if you have children that will be using your computer to surf the Internet, receive e-mail, or send instant messages.

Web site restrictions

One of the neat features in Parental Controls is the ability to control (for the most part) the Web sites that are accessible while logged into a managed account. To start putting your foot down, click the Content tab in the Parental Controls window and decide whether to allow unfettered access to the Internet, to filter Web sites based on their content, or to restrict access only to certain Web sites.

Allow unrestricted access to Web sites

This works as advertised. If you don't want to restrict the Internet content that can be accessed through this managed account, select this option.

Try to limit access to adult Web sites automatically

This option enables Web site filtering, which scours the contents of a Web site for buzzwords that might tip the filter off that the site is inappropriate for young and curious eyes. Click the Customize button to modify how the filter works, as shown in figure 12.11.

The Web site filter isn't perfect, so sometimes it may filter content that you consider safe for your children and may let other sites through that you would normally curtail.

Click the + button under the Always allow these sites section to enter the addresses of sites you want the filter to allow through, regardless of whether the site's content conflicts with the filter or not.

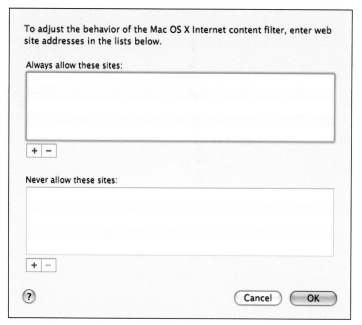

To adjust the behavior of the Mac OS X Internet content filter, enter web site addresses in the lists below.

Always allow these sites:

+ −

Never allow these sites:

+ −

?   Cancel   OK

12.11 Allow or restrict certain Web sites by customizing the Web site filter.

Click the + button under the Never allow these sites section to block access to Web sites that the filter might miss, and which you do not want your children to have the ability to see.

Allow access to only these Web sites

Choose this option to allow access to only the specific sites you enter into the approved list, shown in figure 12.12.

Profanity in the Dictionary

You're probably wondering why I skipped the first item in the Content pane of the Parental Controls window: Hide profanity in Dictionary. This option obviously has its merit, so please check the box if you prefer to hide profane words from prying eyes when your youngster uses the Dictionary application that is part of Leopard. This option just seems an odd fit among the Internet filtering and e-mail discussions, so I gave it its own special mention here.

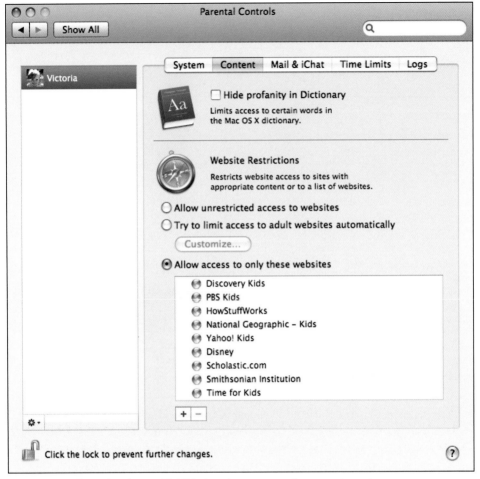

12.12 You can determine the specific Web sites that you want the account user to access.

Click the + button beneath the list of approved sites to add sites (choose Add bookmark), or highlight sites you don't want on the list and click the – button to remove them.

Mail and iChat limitations

Just as important as filtering Web site content is the ability to control whom your kids converse with over the Internet. If you choose to allow the user of the managed account access to e-mail and instant messaging, the Mail & iChat tab of the Parental Controls preferences is right where you want to be (figure 12.13).

12.13 The Mail & iChat tab is where you can control e-mails and instant messages for your managed accounts.

To place restrictions on e-mail and instant messaging, check the boxes next to Limit Mail and Limit iChat. Doing so allows you to add contacts to the Only allow emailing and instant messaging with list. Click the + button underneath the list to add new names, or highlight names and then click the – button to remove them from the list.

One of my favorite features in Parental Controls is the ability to have an e-mail sent to the address of your choice that asks for your permission before allowing someone who's not in the approved list to send e-mails or instant messages to the user of the managed account. Select the Send permission requests to option, and then enter the preferred e-mail address for these requests to be sent.

Set Time Limits

Another great tool in Parental Controls allows you to set limits on the amount of time the user of the managed account can access the Mac. This is one that kids hate and parents love! Table 12.4 describes the options that are available in the Time Limits tab of the Parental Controls window.

Table 12.4 Time Limit Settings

Setting	Operation
Weekday time limits	Check the Limit computer use to check box, and then drag the slider to set the total amount of time the user of the managed account can be logged in for a single weekday (Monday through Friday).
Weekend time limits	Again, check the Limit computer use to check box, and then drag the slider to set the total amount of time the user of the managed account can be logged in for a single weekend day (Saturday and Sunday).
Bedtime	Set the times of day for both school days (Sunday through Thursday) and weekend days (Friday and Saturday) that the user of the managed account cannot have access to it. This prevents them from sneaking up in the middle of the night to check out those Web sites that you may have forgotten to restrict.

Keep Account Activity Logs

When all is said and done, there is simply no way for you to monitor your kid every second of every day. Apple thought of that when they designed Parental Controls. Who better than Leopard to keep track of what Web sites your kids have checked out, which Web sites they are blocked from seeing, the applications they use while logged in, and with whom they are chatting during their session? The Logs tab of Parental Controls, shown in figure 12.14, keeps tabs on all of the account's activity, and so you will be informed of what happened, even if you weren't there to see it.

Select the amount of time to show account activity in the Show activity for pop-up menu. Determine how the logs should be ordered by choosing either Contact or Date from the Group by pop-up menu. If you find an objectionable site, application, or iChat message, click the Restrict button at the bottom of the window to block access to it.

Being diligent in browsing these logs will do nothing but further protect your child from things they may not be ready to deal with just yet.

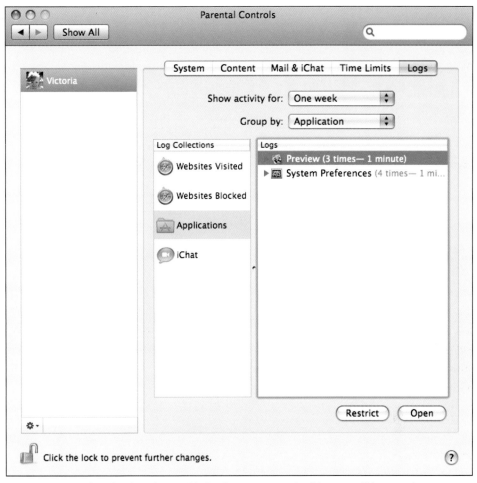

12.14 Some may describe these logs as Big Brother gone awry; I call it responsible parenting.

and Other Items?

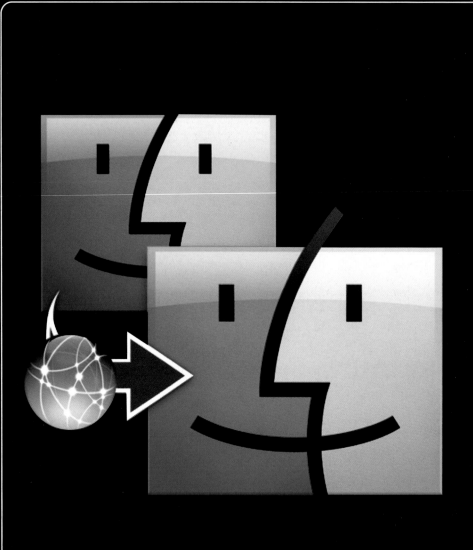

Apple taught Leopard to share with others, and it does its job better than any other operating system around. As a matter of fact, no other operating system is as friendly with its competitors as Leopard. Whether your network consists of mostly Windows PCs or Linux computers, or is an all-Mac configuration, Leopard happily shakes hands and exchanges greetings with its neighbors. You can share files, folders, printers, and even your Internet connection, using a variety of network protocols.

Using the Sharing System Preferences 262

File Sharing 264

Printer Sharing 267

Remote Management 269

Sharing through Bluetooth 270

Using the Sharing System Preferences

The Sharing System Preferences is where all the action begins. That's where you go to enable and configure sharing of all types. Choose Apple menu ⇨ System Preferences and then click the Sharing icon to open the Sharing preferences window, shown in figure 13.1.

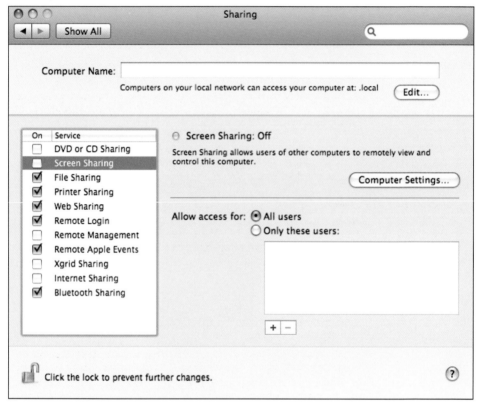

13.1 This is where you tell Leopard how to share with friends.

First things first: If the Computer Name field is blank at the top of the Sharing pane, type a name for your computer. Other users can see your computer on the network using this name.

Sharing preferences at a glance

Your Mac can share many different items, but some don't demand the same amount of coverage as others. For that reason, Table 13.1 gives a brief overview of each sharing option, and the rest of this chapter is devoted to the areas of sharing that need a bit more attention.

Table 13.1 Sharing Preferences

Sharing type	Description
DVD or CD Sharing	Enable this option to allow other computers to remotely connect to and use your Mac's optical drive. This option is helpful if you have a computer that doesn't have an optical drive built in, like the MacBook Air; you can share the optical drive from one of your other Macs so that the computer can utilize it.
Screen Sharing	Use this feature to allow a user of another computer to remotely access your Mac. They can move and open items, such as folders and applications, on your computer. They can see your screen and interact with it.
File Sharing	Turn this option on to let other users access folders that you are sharing from your Mac. There's much more about this later on in this chapter.
Printer Sharing	To share printers that you have created a queue for in your Print & Fax preferences, check the Printer Sharing check box. See more on this feature later in this chapter.
Web Sharing	You can create and store Web pages on your Mac. Check the Web Sharing check box to allow others on your network to access those Web pages from a Web browser on any computer. Your computer's Web site addresses are displayed once you enable Web Sharing.
Remote Login	Enable this option to let users on other computers remotely access your Mac through a Secure Shell (SSH) in Terminal. Even though you can restrict which users have access, I would not recommend using this option due to security reasons, unless you are otherwise directed by someone in your company's IT department. See Chapter 15 for more information on using Terminal.
Remote Management	If you or your network administrators use Apple Remote Desktop to access your computer remotely, you must enable Remote Management. I'll discuss its options later in this chapter.
Remote Apple Events	Turn this option on to allow applications and users on other computers to send Apple Events to your Mac. Apple Events are commands that cause your Mac to perform an action, such as printing or deleting files. I don't recommend using this option unless you know what you're doing and trust other users on your network.
Xgrid Sharing	Check this option if you want to allow an Xgrid server on your network to remotely use your Mac's processing power. Large computing labs use this kind of setup to process gigantic tasks; using the processing power of other computers on the network can greatly help speed up those tasks. Basically, if you don't know what an Xgrid server is, you don't need to enable this option unless told to do so by your IT department.
Internet Sharing	You can share your Mac's Internet connection with other computers through Ethernet, AirPort, or FireWire. This comes in handy if only one Mac has access to the physical Internet connection in your home or office. If you enable this option, you must check which of the aforementioned connection types you are using to share.
Bluetooth Sharing	Use your Mac's Bluetooth connection to communicate with other devices, and then check this box to share files. See the section "Sharing through Bluetooth," later in this chapter.

Use Bonjour with Windows and Leopard

Leopard uses a network protocol called Bonjour that allows almost effortless networking between devices that are running it. Bonjour requires no configuration of any kind; devices that are using Bonjour simply see one another on the network. While Bonjour is built into Leopard, you might be pleased to know that Apple has developed Bonjour for Windows as well. See how simple networking can really be between Mac OS X and Windows by downloading and installing Bonjour for Windows from www.apple.com/support/downloads/bonjourforwindows.html.

File Sharing

File sharing is what most people think of when you mention sharing on a computer. Leopard lets you decide which folders and volumes to share from your Mac, and you have control over who can access those shared items. Check the File Sharing check box to enable it on your Mac, just as I've done in figure 13.2.

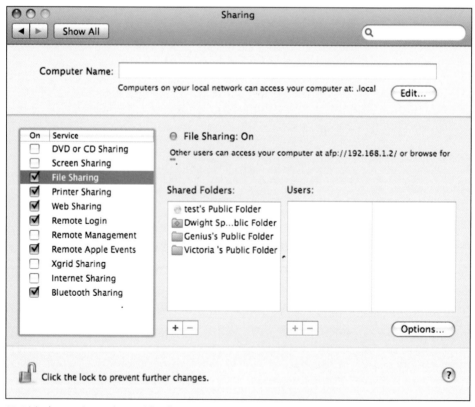

13.2 It's always nice to share with others.

Add shared folders and users

The Shared Folders window lists the folders on your hard drive that are set up for sharing files. To add folders to this list:

1. **Click the + button beneath the Shared Folders window.**
2. **Browse your Mac and select the folder you want to share.**
3. **Click the Add button to begin sharing items in this folder.**

Next, you need to specify which users can access the folders you are sharing:

1. **Click the + button under the Users window.**
2. **Select a group of users from the list on the left and then choose the user you want to share the specified folder with, as shown in figure 13.3.**

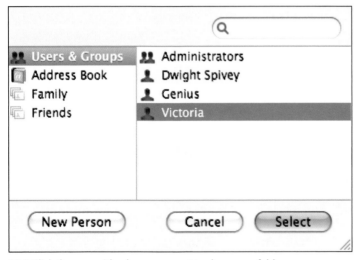

13.3 Click the user with whom you want to share your folder.

3. **Click the Select button to add the user to the list of authorized users.**
4. **Choose the user's name in the list and assign permissions to them by clicking the pop-up arrows, as shown in figure 13.4.**
   - **Read & Write:** This allows the user to modify and delete the files in the shared folder, as well as copy new files into it.

- **Read Only:** This means the user can only see and open the files being shared in the folder.

- **Write Only (Drop Box):** This only allows the user to copy files into the folder; they can't see or open its contents.

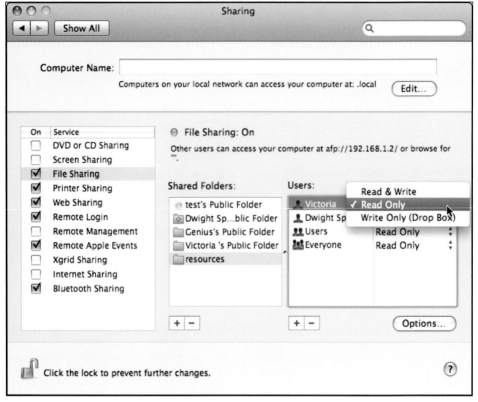

13.4 Assigning file-sharing permissions for a user.

You can remove folders or users by highlighting them and clicking the – button under the appropriate window.

Enabling file-sharing protocols

Leopard is very advanced in its sharing capabilities, and can share using multiple protocols. Click the Options button in the lower-right corner of the File Sharing pane to see which protocols are available, as shown in figure 13.5. Table 13.2 briefly explains the protocols.

Checking the box next to the protocols you want to use enables them, allowing you to share items over your network with other users running the same protocols.

13.5 Check the boxes next to the protocols you want to use for sharing your files.

Table 13.2 File-sharing Protocols

Protocol	Description
AFP	Apple Filing Protocol. This is an older network protocol that Leopard uses for talking to ancient AppleTalk networks.
FTP	File Transfer Protocol. This is a TCP/IP protocol commonly used to transfer files between devices on a network or over the Internet.
SMB	Server Message Block, also called Microsoft Windows Network to former Windows users. This allows Leopard to work seamlessly with a Windows-centric network. Check the boxes next to the accounts you want to enable for SMB sharing. You must enter the password for each account you enable.

Printer Sharing

When you share a printer from your Mac, you aren't physically sharing the printer; you're actually sharing the print queue that you created for the printer in the Print & Fax preferences. This means that when you share a printer, the clients who are sending jobs are sending them to your Mac, not directly to the printer. It's your Mac's responsibility to funnel the job to the printer after it has received it. Check the Printer Sharing check box to enable this feature for Leopard, as shown in figure 13.6.

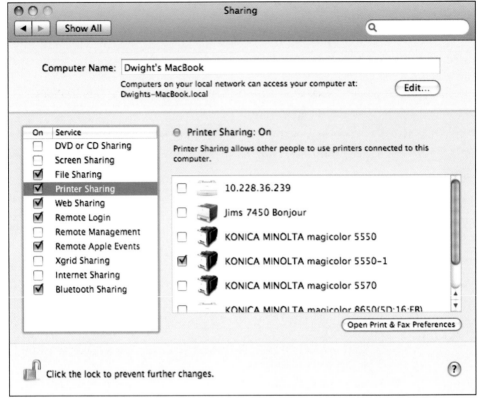

13.6 Share printers you have installed on your Mac using Printer Sharing.

Sharing with Mac OS X users

There's not much involved with sharing printers with other Mac OS X users. Simply check the box next to the printer you want to share in the Printer Sharing pane, and the shared printer will be visible to the user when they go to add a printer. See Chapter 9 for more information on adding a printer.

Sharing with Windows users

To share any printer on your Mac with other computers running Windows:

1. **Check the box next to the printer you want to share in the Printer Sharing pane.**

2. **Enable File Sharing by clicking the File Sharing check box in the Service list.**

3. **Click the Options button in the File Sharing pane.**

4. **Check the Share files and folders using SMB check box.**

5. **Choose which accounts will access the printer, and enter their passwords.**

To add the printer to a Windows PC:

1. **Open the Printers and Faxes control panel if using Windows XP, or open the Printers control panel if running Windows Vista.**

2. **Click the Add Printer button and install a network printer.** See your Windows documentation for instructions on installing a network printer if you're unfamiliar with the procedure.

3. **Select the generic PostScript printer driver during the installation, even if the printer isn't a PostScript printer.** Anybody who understands printer drivers is probably slapping their foreheads at this point, but here's the cool part: When the PC sends a print job, Leopard automatically translates the PostScript code generated by the PC to the code the printer understands. That just goes to further prove how awesome Leopard really is.

 Note The Windows user must be logged in as an administrator account on the PC in order to install the shared printer.

Remote Management

When you first check the Remote Management check box, you are prompted to configure what level of access users of other computers can have to your Mac, as shown in figure 13.7. The options are self-explanatory.

After you enable Remote Management, you can add local users to the access list:

1. **Click the + button under the access list.**

2. **Browse the list of available users, click the user you want, and click Select.**

3. **Configure the access options for this user as you did when you first enabled Remote Management.** You can change these options at any time by clicking the Options button.

13.7 Decide what users can do once they've accessed your Mac.

Sharing through Bluetooth

The Bluetooth Sharing feature, shown in figure 13.8, lets you configure how your Mac will interact and share files with other devices running the Bluetooth protocol.

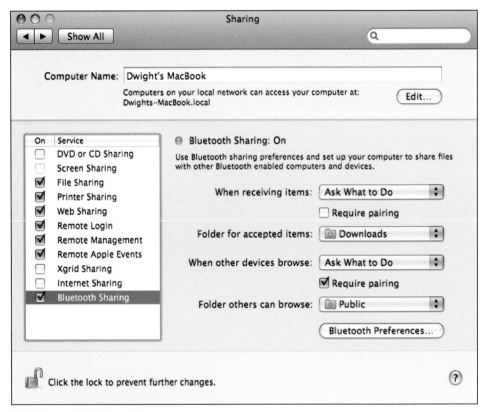

13.8 Bluetooth Sharing options.

Once again, first things first: You must enable Bluetooth on your Mac in order to share files with other devices running the protocol. If Bluetooth is not already on:

1. **Click the Bluetooth Preferences button to open the Bluetooth preferences pane.**

2. **Check the boxes next to On and Discoverable.**

3. **Click the Back button in the upper-left corner of the Bluetooth pane to go back to the Sharing pane.**

Table 13.3 briefly explains the options that are available in the Bluetooth Sharing pane.

Table 13.3 Bluetooth Sharing Options

Option	Functions
When receiving items	Decide how your Mac reacts when another Bluetooth device is trying to send an item to it. Check the Require pairing check box to require a password to be entered before any exchanges take place.
Folder for accepted items	Set the default folder for files received from other devices.
When other devices browse	Determine how your Mac reacts when another Bluetooth device wants to browse your shared folders. Check the Require pairing check box to require a password to be entered before any exchanges take place.
Folder others can browse.	Set the default folder on your Mac that users of other Bluetooth devices can browse.

Note You must pair a device with your Mac in order to exchange files with one another. See Chapter 3 for instructions on pairing Bluetooth devices using the Bluetooth Setup Assistant.

Using Bluetooth File Exchange

Bluetooth File Exchange is the utility you use to browse and exchange files with other Bluetooth devices. Open Bluetooth File Exchange by pressing ⌘+Option+U in the Finder, and then double-click the Bluetooth File Exchange icon.

Send a file from your Mac

To send a file from your Mac to another Bluetooth device:

1. **Choose File ⇨ Send File, or press ⌘+O.**

2. **Browse your Mac for the file you want to send, highlight the file, and click the Send button.**

3. **Select the device you want to send the file to from the list in the Send File window, as shown in figure 13.9, and click the Send button.**

4. **The receiving device may prompt you to allow the incoming traffic from your Mac.** The transfer is complete once the receiving device has received all the data from your Mac.

13.9 Select the device you want to send a file to from the list of available devices.

Browse another Bluetooth device

You can browse another Bluetooth device to find files you want to copy, or to send files from your Mac to a specific location on the device:

1. **Choose File ⇨ Browse Device, or press ⌘+Shift+O.**

2. **Select the device you want to browse from the Browse Files list and click the Browse button.**

3. **Browse the folders on the device from within the Browsing window, shown in figure 13.10.**

4. **If you are sending a file, open the folder on the device in which you want to place the file, and click the Send button.** Browse your Mac for the file you want to send, select it, and click the Send button.

5. **If you want to get a file from the device, find the file, select it, and then click the Get button.** Name the file, choose where to save it, and then click the Save button.

6. **You may also delete a file from the remote Bluetooth device by highlighting the file and clicking the Delete button in the upper-right corner of the Browsing window.**

13.10 Browsing the directories, or folders, on my cell phone.

How Can I Automate My Mac?

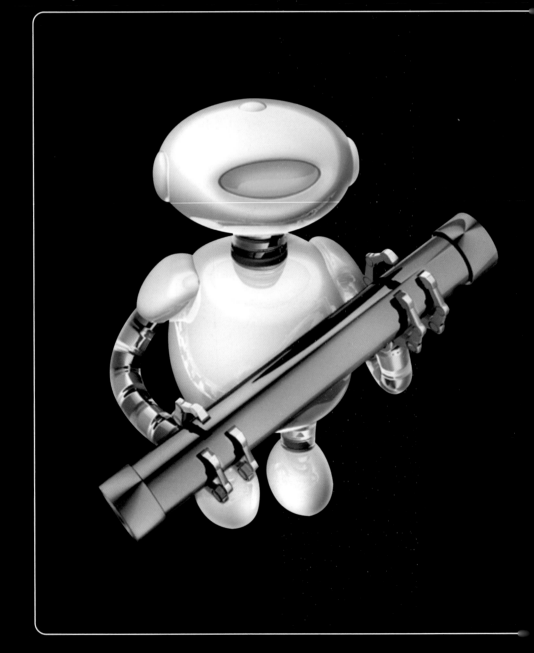

What if you could have your Mac perform daily, routine (and possibly mundane) tasks for you automatically? Sounds pretty tempting, no? Leopard is fully equipped to make your Mac life more enjoyable through automation, using a handy application called Automator. Automator uses actions (another word for steps) to create workflows, which you can run anytime to complete repetitive tasks quickly and easily. Another way that Leopard can help with your Mac housework is with Time Machine, Mac OS X's new backup utility. Time Machine can literally take you back in time to retrieve data that you may have lost in the present.

Getting Around in Automator 276

Using Workflows 277

Recording Your Own Actions 282

Discovering Time Machine 284

Set Up a Backup Disk 285

Select the Files You Want to Back Up 288

Working with Backups 289

Retrieve Information from Time Machine 290

Getting Around in Automator

It's most helpful to know your way around Automator before trying to create workflows and actions. Open Automator by pressing ⌘+Shift+A in the Finder and then double-clicking the Automator icon. When Automator first opens, you must make a selection in the Starting Points window, as shown in figure 14.1.

14.1 Select an item from the list to move onto Automator's main window.

For this example, select Custom and click the Choose button. You are now in Automator's main window; figure 14.2 points out Automator's most important features, and Table 14.1 gives a brief description of each.

Table 14.1 Descriptions of Items in Automator's Main Window

Item	Description
Library column	Lists the applications and other items that are available for you to choose actions from.
Action column	Lists the actions that are available for each application or item in the Library column.
Workflow pane	Allows you to arrange actions in the order they are to be performed.
Description window	Displays a brief explanation of the selected action.
Run	Runs the current workflow.
Stop	Stops the workflow that is running.
Record	Records your keyboard and mouse events to help you create your own custom actions.
Media Browser	Lets you browse your Mac for audio, photos, or videos that you may want to include in your workflows.

Run the current workflow

Open the Media Browser

Stop the currently running workflow

Action column

Record user events

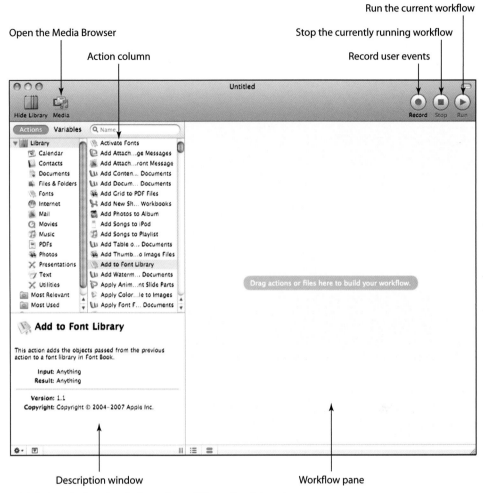

Description window

Workflow pane

14.2 Automator's main window, where all the action takes place.

Using Workflows

Workflows are groups of actions that are combined to help you accomplish a task. When you run a workflow, the actions in it are carried out in sequential order until the last action has been performed. The results, or output, of the first action, become the input for the next action, and so on, until the workflow is completed.

277

Designing a workflow

Building a workflow from scratch is much simpler than you may think. To help you get started with Automator, I've created a new workflow and will walk you through creating that workflow step by step. Here's what I want to do with my new workflow:

1. **First, I want to rename images that I've saved from my camera using Image Capture, to a folder on my desktop called New Pics.** My camera automatically adds "IMG" to the beginning of every file and then numbers them sequentially. I'd like to name the files a little more descriptively, and Automator is the perfect tool to accomplish this task.

2. **Once my files are renamed, I want to open them in Preview so that I can check them out.**

3. **Next, I want my images to automatically print so that I can have a hard copy of each one.**

4. **Finally, I'd like to e-mail my new pictures to friends and family.**

Let's begin building the workflow:

Note

As I mentioned, my camera automatically saves files with an "IMG" prefix at the beginning of every filename, so that's the convention I'll be using in this short tutorial. You may want to adjust the variable in step 3 below to match the default naming conventions of your camera.

1. **Tell Automator what files you want to interact with.** Select Files & Folders from the Library column and then drag-and-drop Find Finder Items into the workflow pane, as shown in figure 14.3.

2. **Choose Other from the Where drop-down menu and select Desktop on the left side of the resulting window.** Click the New Folder button, name the folder New Pics, and then click the Open button.

3. **In the Whose section, leave the Name and contains criteria alone, and enter "IMG" (without quotes) in the text field.** This tells Automator that you are looking for files whose names start with IMG.

4. **Tell Automator that you want to rename the items in the New Pics folder.** Select Files & Folders from the Library column and then drag-and-drop Rename Finder Items into the workflow pane beneath the Find Finder Items action. A caution window appears; click the Don't Add button to proceed.

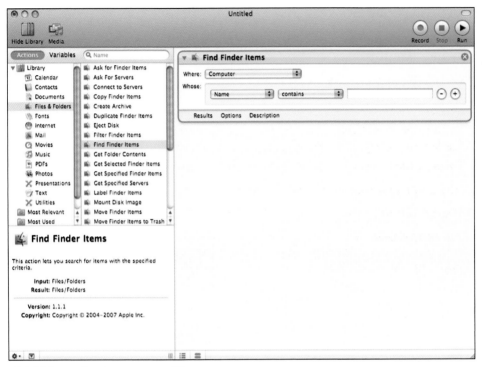

14.3 Adding actions to my new workflow.

5. **Choose Make Sequential from the first drop-down menu, click the new name radio button in the Add number to option, and enter the name you want to begin each of your files with in the text field.** I use *dwightpix* at the beginning of my picture files, as shown in figure 14.4. This action causes Automator to rename all files that start with "IMG" to files that start with *dwightpix* followed by a sequential number. However, I'm not quite finished renaming my files.

6. **Add the date the files were imported to my Mac to the end of my filenames.** Select Files & Folders from the Library column and then drag-and-drop Rename Finder Items into the workflow pane beneath the previous Rename Finder Items action. Click the Don't Add button to proceed as before. The default criteria, shown in figure 14.4, are appropriate for the needs of this example, so nothing needs changed in this action.

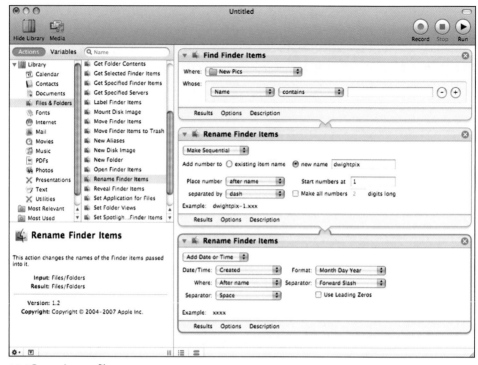

14.4 Renaming my files.

7. **I want my renamed images to open in the Preview application so that I can see how they look.** Select Photos from the Library column, and then drag-and-drop Open Images in Preview to the workflow pane beneath the second Rename Finder Items action. This causes Automator to start the Preview application (if it's not already running) and automatically display the new images in it.

Note You may notice as you drag new actions into the workflow pane that the actions that are already there move down a bit until the action you are dragging is beneath them. This just shows you that you can easily reposition actions in a workflow by simply dragging-and-dropping them into the order you need.

8. **Have Automator print hard copies of the photos automatically.** Select Photos from the Library column and then drag-and-drop Print Images to the workflow pane beneath the Open Images in Preview action. Make any additional adjustments that you deem necessary; for example, I chose to center and scale my images to fit the page, as shown in figure 14.5.

9. **Have Automator open Mail and create a new mail message, automatically attaching the new images to the e-mail so that all you have to do is enter the recipients' addresses and click Send.** Select Mail from the Library column and then drag-and-drop New Mail Message to the workflow pane beneath the Print Images action. Enter any items that you want to automatically be added to your new mail, such as the e-mail address or a subject as shown in figure 14.5.

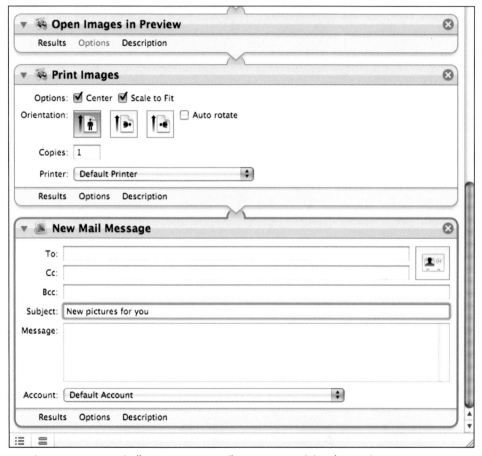

14.5 Automator automatically creates a new mail message containing the new images.

10. **Click the Run button in the upper-right corner to run the workflow.** Automator performs the actions and warns you if there are any problems.

Saving your workflows

You will certainly want to save your workflows so that you don't have to create them every time you need them, which kind of defeats the purpose of Automator. You can save your workflows as workflows, applications, or plug-ins. Table 14.2 gives a brief explanation of each.

Table 14.2 Different Ways to Save Your Workflows

Save As...	Description
Workflow	Simply saves the actions you've brought together as a workflow. You can open the workflow in Automator to run or edit it.
Application	Saving a workflow as an application makes it a stand-alone document. Double-click the workflow application to launch it as you would any other application.
Plug-in	Your workflow is saved as an application-specific plug-in that the application (such as Finder, iCal, or Image Capture) can use to automatically perform tasks.

To save your workflows:

⦿ **Press ⌘+Shift+S to save as a workflow or an application.**

1. Give the workflow a descriptive name, choose where to save it, and then click Save.

2. Choose Workflow or Application from the File Format menu.

⦿ **Press ⌘+S to save an existing workflow that you are modifying.**

⦿ **Press ⌘+Option+S to save as a plug-in.**

1. Give the plug-in a descriptive name.

2. Choose what application the plug-in is for from the Plug-in for drop-down menu.

3. Click Save.

Recording Your Own Actions

The coolest feature in Automator for Leopard is the ability to create your own custom actions based on your keyboard and mouse events. Automator can record your keyboard and mouse events and execute them as part of a workflow.

For Developers and Scripters Only!

Scripters who write their own AppleScripts, or developers who create their own applications, will be delighted to know that they can develop their own actions that are specific to their needs. Xcode, which is an API (application programming interface) distributed by Apple with Leopard, provides all the tools needed for programmers to make unique actions.

You can download the creations of some of these programmers by visiting www.apple.com/downloads/macosx/automator/.

To get started on your custom action:

1. **Open a workflow and click the Record button in the upper-right corner.**

2. **Perform the steps necessary to complete your action.**

3. **Click the Stop button shown in figure 14.6 when you are finished.**

4. **Click the Run button to test your new actions.**

14.6 Automator continues recording your actions until you click the Stop button.

5. **Edit actions in the list by deleting unnecessary actions, changing the timeout setting for each action, or modifying the Playback Speed.**

6. **Save your action as a workflow, application, or plug-in.**

Note You must enable access for assistive devices in the Universal Access preferences. To do so, choose Apple menu ➪ System Preferences, select Universal Access, and then check the Enable access for assistive devices option.

Note Before you start recording, make sure that your Mac is set up exactly the way it needs to be to perform the necessary actions. For example, if you are using an application as part of your action, you will want to have it open before beginning to record.

Discovering Time Machine

One of the Leopard features that Apple is most proud of, and rightly so, is Time Machine. Oh, there have been backup utilities out there made by third-party companies, even a few good ones, but Apple has delivered something above and beyond them in terms of simplicity and information retrieval.

Time Machine backs up your system behind the scenes, allowing you to do your work while it handles its business undetected in the background. Your initial backup will take quite a while, as Time Machine is backing up everything on your Mac's hard disk (again, it all happens in the background, so you can continue to use your Mac). After the initial backup, though, Time Machine continues to back up your files automatically every hour, only backing up items that have changed. Because it is only backing up changed items, the backups are much faster to perform.

Why it's important to back up your files

I wanted to take a small section of this chapter to simply preach to you the doctrine of backing up your computer. You have too many precious memories and too many important documents on your Mac to simply count on it to last forever (yes, even Macs do eventually have issues, as you'll see in Chapter 17). Take a few minutes out of your iLife, and perhaps spend a few dollars for an external hard drive, to get Time Machine up and going. Backing up your data is something that you will simply never regret doing.

Hardware requirements for using Time Machine

Time Machine can back up your data to any of these three configurations:

- **A network volume, such as a file or backup server.** This is a good idea for large networks.

- **An external hard disk, which is my recommendation.** Be certain that the data capacity of the external hard disk is large enough to save all the data on your Mac's hard disk.

- **A partition on your Mac's hard drive if the drive is indeed partitioned.** Partitioning a drive is the act of using a disk utility to divide a single hard disk into several sections, fooling the computer into believing that one disk is actually multiple disks. I do not recommend using this sort of configuration because if your hard disk has a problem, you've lost all of your data in spite of having backed it up.

The Apple Time Capsule

Apple has recently released a new piece of hardware that they call a Time Capsule. A Time Capsule acts as both a wireless network router, like an Airport, and a central backup point for all Macs running Leopard and Time Machine. The Time Capsule automatically backs up every file from every Mac, wirelessly and in the background, eliminating the need to connect an external drive to your Mac. This is one serious backup tool, and I highly recommend getting your hands on one.

Set Up a Backup Disk

There are a couple of steps necessary to get Time Machine started up: You need to format your backup disk, and then you need to tell Time Machine that it can use the disk for its backups.

Formatting a hard disk

You need to format any drive you connect to your Mac before you can use it with Time Machine. To format the disk (see the Caution below before continuing this procedure!):

1. **Open Disk Utility by pressing ⌘+Shift+U, and then double-clicking its icon.**

2. **Connect the drive to your Mac.**

3. **Select the drive in the list on the left of the Disk Utility window.**

4. **Choose the Erase tab near the top of the window, as shown in figure 14.7.**

5. **Set the Volume Format to Mac OS Extended (Journaled).**

6. **Click the Erase button, and then click the Erase button again in the verification window.**

7. **Once the formatting is finished, click the Eject button in the Disk Utility toolbar, and disconnect the hard disk from the Mac.**

Caution If this is a disk you've used before, be sure that you've copied all the data from it before performing a disk format on it. Once the formatting process has started, all data that was on the disk is lost forever.

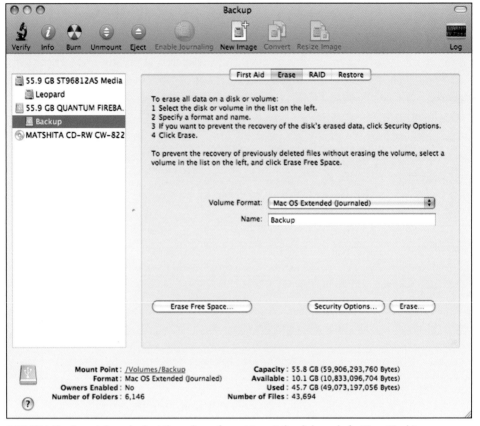

14.7 Click the Erase tab and select the volume format to get the disk ready for Time Machine.

Tell Time Machine about the backup disk

When you first connect an external disk (you may have to format it first) to your Mac, Time Machine detects its presence and asks if you'd like to use this disk for backups. If you say yes, Time Machine sets everything up automatically, and away you go. In most cases, this is fine; you are never bothered about it again, and Time Machine does its duty.

You may be asking why you would say no to the question, if that were the case. Well, if this is a disk you've used in the past, or if it's a drive you want to partition, you may not want Time Machine hijacking it for its sole use. To manually set up a drive:

1. **Open the Time Machine preferences (shown in figure 14.8) by choosing Apple menu ⇨ System Preferences, and then clicking the Time Machine icon.**

14.8 The Time Machine preferences allow you to manually configure how it works.

2. **Click the Choose Backup Disk button.**

3. **Select a disk and click the Use for Backup button.**

4. **Time Machine begins a countdown for when it will perform the first backup, similar to figure 14.9.**

5. **If you want Time Machine to automatically begin backing up everything on the system, just sit back and relax.** However, if you want to only back up a portion of your hard drive, click the On/Off switch on the left side of the Time Machine preferences pane, and jump ahead to the next section in this chapter.

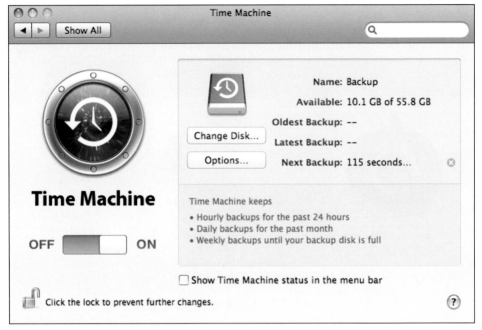

14.9 Time Machine is counting down to its first backup.

Select the Files You Want to Back Up

There may be several good reasons why you don't want Time Machine to back up every file on your Mac, one of which could be that there isn't enough storage space on the backup drive, or perhaps you simply don't want to back up all the information for each user on the computer. Whatever the reason, you need not fear, because I'm about to show you how to exclude information from your backup sessions:

1. **Be sure Time Machine is Off so that it doesn't begin a backup process while you're choosing what not to back up.** Simply click the On/Off switch to toggle it.

2. **Click the Options button in the middle of the preferences pane.**

3. **Click the + button in the lower-left corner of the Do not back up window.**

4. **Browse your Mac for folders and files that you do not want to include in the backup process, select them, and then click the Exclude button to add them to the list, which is shown in figure 14.10.** Refer to the Total included number to see if your backup disk can store that much data. Click Done when finished.

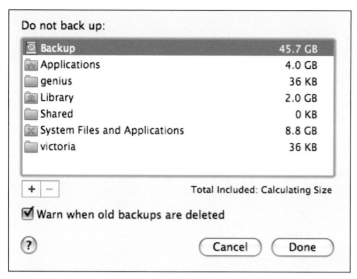

Do not back up:

Backup	45.7 GB
Applications	4.0 GB
genius	36 KB
Library	2.0 GB
Shared	0 KB
System Files and Applications	8.8 GB
victoria	36 KB

Total Included: Calculating Size

☑ Warn when old backups are deleted

Cancel   Done

14.10 You can exclude files from being backed up by Time Machine.

Working with Backups

As mentioned, the entire backup process is handled behind the scenes, but that doesn't mean you can't check out what's going on, and even stop and restart a backup that's already in the works. Open the Time Machine preferences pane to see the progress of a backup procedure.

Manual backup

You don't have to wait for Time Machine to get around to backing up your system; you can start the process right now if you like:

1. **Choose Apple menu ➪ System Preferences, and select the Time Machine icon.**

2. **Check the Show Time Machine status in the menu bar check box.**

Latest Backup: --

Back Up Now
Enter Time Machine

Open Time Machine Preferences...

14.11 Select Back Up Now to back up your information immediately.

3. **Be sure Time Machine is On.** Toggle the On/Off switch, if necessary.

4. **Click the Time Machine icon in the menu bar.**

5. **Select Back Up Now, like I'm doing in figure 14.11.**

Caution When you manually select files to back up, you may not be backing up the preference files and other items necessary for Time Machine to completely restore your Mac, should it fail.

Pause and resume a backup

You can stop and start backup processes if you need to. To pause a backup:

1. **Click the Time Machine icon in the menu bar.**
2. **Select Stop Backing Up.**

To resume:

1. **Click the Time Machine icon in the menu bar.**
2. **Select Back Up Now.** Your backup should begin where it left off. Nothing to it!

Genius You can also use the Time Machine icon in the Dock to begin a backup, to pause or resume a backup, to open the Time Machine preferences, or to browse other Time Machine disks. Control-click, or right-click, the icon in the Dock to see its menu.

Retrieve Information from Time Machine

Now that you know how to back up your system, it's time to learn how to retrieve that information should you ever need to do so. Let's see how to restore individual items and even an entire drive.

Restore individual files

Time Machine lets you restore individual files and folders that you may have lost or simply want to get previous versions of. To do so:

1. **Open Time Machine by clicking its icon in the Dock, or press ⌘+Shift+A and double-click its icon in the Applications folder.**
2. **Time Machine opens and you see a Finder window, similar to that in figure 14.12.**

3. **Use the timeline on the right side of the screen, or the arrow buttons next to it, to navigate through time to the date the item you need was backed up.**

4. **Browse the files in the Finder window to find the item you want to retrieve.**

5. **Select the item in the Finder window, and then click the Restore button in the bottom-right corner of the Time Machine window.** The file is zipped forward in time to today, and Time Machine closes. You have to admit, that's one of the coolest things you've ever seen on a computer!

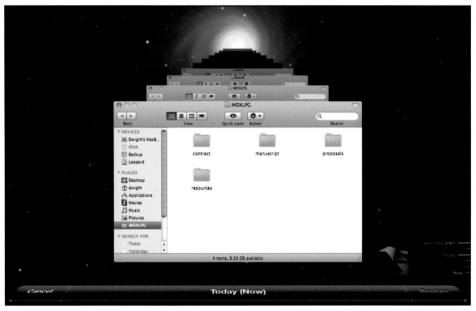

14.12 Traveling through time!

Restore an entire disk

The ability of Time Machine to let you restore an entire disk is worth the price of upgrading to Leopard all on its own. You can save countless hours by not having to reinstall the OS, as well as all the applications you had on the system. To restore a disk:

1. **Connect your backup disk to the Mac.**

2. **Start your Mac using the Leopard installation disk.**

3. **In the Installer application, choose Utilities ⇨ Restore System from Backup in the menu, and then click Continue.**

4. **Choose your backup disk, and then select the backup you want to restore the computer with.**

5. **Follow the instructions from that point to finish the restoration process.** The restoration process can take a while, but not nearly as long as starting from scratch.

Delete Files from Time Machine Backups

What if you want to delete a file from your backed-up folders, instead of restore it? Simple:

1. **Open Time Machine and use the Finder window and timeline to find the item you want to delete from the backup.**

2. **Select the file or folder you want to delete.**

3. **Click the Action menu (which looks like a gear) in the Finder toolbar and select Delete Backup.** To get rid of all references to the item in Time Machine, select Delete All Backups.

UNIX Commands in Terminal?

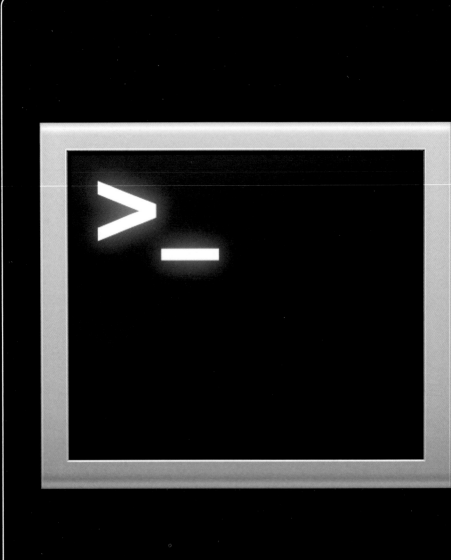

Beneath the beautiful exterior of Leopard beats the heart of a true UNIX beast! But don't act frightened; UNIX feeds off of fear. UNIX is the base software on which the bulk of Mac OS X Leopard rests, and it provides time-tested reliability and stability that is unmatched by any other OS. Most of the functions you perform in Leopard by clicking your mouse or by typing a keyboard shortcut are UNIX commands that you can easily execute through a command line. Windows and Linux users are familiar with the command line concept, but most Mac users have never needed to venture into that territory. I'll attempt to alleviate any command line anxieties in this chapter, as well as introduce some of my more seasoned readers to the Leopard version of a command line interface.

Tinkering with Terminal. 296

Entering UNIX Commands 301

Where to Find Additional UNIX Information 305

Tinkering with Terminal

Terminal is your gateway to entering the command line world of UNIX. In my opinion, in order to even think of yourself as a Mac OS X aficionado, you must have at least attempted some basic UNIX commands using the old-fashioned way. To take a step back in computing time, open Terminal:

1. **Click the Go menu and select Utilities, or press ⌘+Shift+U.**

2. **Double-click the Terminal icon to open a new Terminal window, as shown in figure 15.1.**

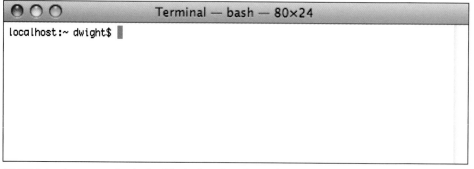

15.1 This is what computing looked like before the advent of the graphical user interface.

Terminal preferences

Terminal, like other applications, can be modified to work the way you want it to. Click the Terminal menu and select Preferences (or press ⌘+,) to open the Preferences window.

Startup

When you first open Terminal, it automatically opens a new Terminal window. The Startup options in the preferences window, shown in figure 15.2, allow you to define the state that Terminal starts up in:

- **Choose what settings to use for the new window, or to open a series of windows called a window group (more on window groups a little later in this chapter).**

- **Determine whether to open Terminal in its default shell, which is called bash, or in a different shell.** A shell is software that allows a user to interact with the UNIX services.

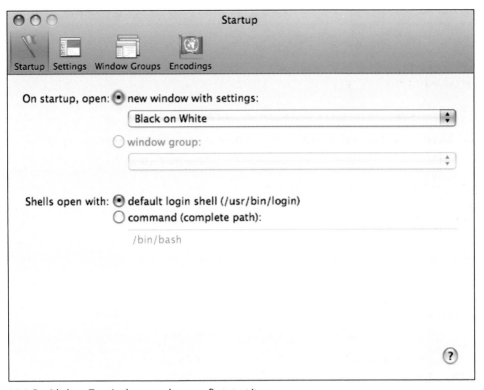

15.2 Decide how Terminal reacts when you first start it up.

Genius

If you are someone who uses Terminal quite a lot (you are an official, card-carrying geek, if that's the case), it's a good idea to keep a shortcut to it in your Dock. That way, the comfort of the command line is within easy reach. I've used Mac OS X for years, and I like to keep the Terminal feature close by my side. You never know when the uncontrollable urge to chmod, mkdir, or ping might strike you!

Settings

The Settings section, shown in figure 15.3, lets you adjust the look and behavior of your Terminal windows. Table 15.1 gives a brief description of what each tab in the Settings section will let you modify.

The list on the left side of the Settings window contains preformatted window settings that you can choose. Set one as your default by highlighting the desired setting and clicking the Default button. Add or delete saved settings by clicking the + or − buttons, respectively.

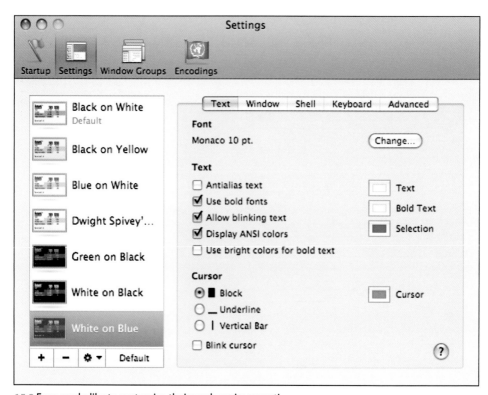

15.3 Even geeks like to customize their work environment!

Table 15.1 Options Available in the Settings Tabs

Tab	Options available
Text	Change the appearance of text, including the font used and the colors designated for certain types of text. You can also control how the cursor is displayed.
Window	Set the default title of windows, as well as what other information appears in the title bar, such as the dimensions of the window or the name of the currently active process. Choose the default background color of windows, the default size of new windows, and how far to allow a user to scroll back.
Shell	Have the shell issue a command by default as soon as a new window is opened, and tell Terminal how to behave when a user exits a shell, and whether it should prompt the user before closing the window.
Keyboard	Assign commands to shortcut keys to make entering commands even faster.
Advanced	Settings allow you to change the Terminal emulation, alarms, and character encodings.

Window Groups

Figure 15.4 shows the Window Groups window, which allows you to manage your window groups. Window groups are useful for users who utilize several windows, allowing them to run multiple tasks during their Terminal sessions.

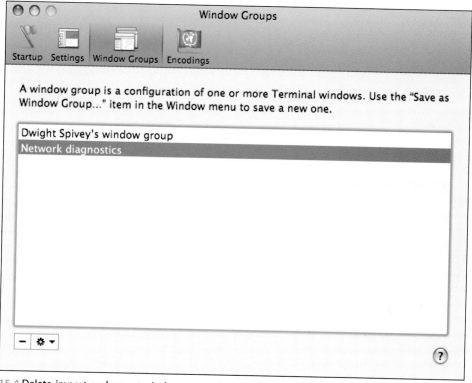

15.4 Delete, import, and export window groups from here.

Creating window groups causes Terminal to keep each window's individual settings intact, so that they are in the same state when you reopen them as they were when you closed them. To create a window group:

1. **Open the windows you will be working with and make sure they are set up in the format that you need.**

2. **Choose the Window menu and select Save Windows as Group.**

3. **Give the window group a descriptive name, like "Network diagnostics," and click the Save button. Check the box in the save window to have this window group open automatically when you first open Terminal.**

Encodings

Figure 15.5 shows the Encodings window of the Terminal preferences. These options allow you to enable and disable international character encodings so that Terminal can display international characters.

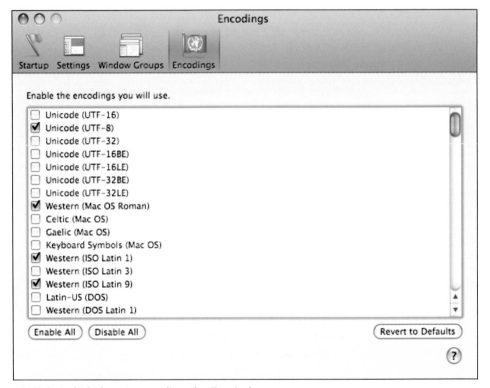

15.5 Select which character encodings that Terminal can use.

Tabbed windows

While some users may prefer to have several Terminal windows open at once, I like the simplicity of having one window running multiple tabs, as shown in figure 15.6.

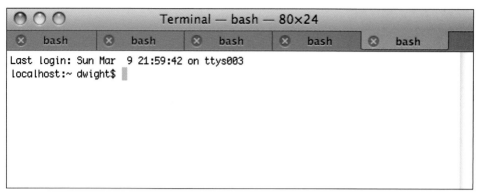

15.6 Tabbed Terminal windows are the way to go for me.

To create a new tab:

1. **Choose Shell ⇨ New Tab.**

2. **Select the setting for the new tab.** For example, choose Basic to select a default shell interface.

Close tabs by clicking the X in the upper-left corner of the tab.

You can also save tabbed windows as a window group by choosing Window ⇨ Save Windows as Group, and giving the group a descriptive name.

Entering UNIX Commands

To effectively navigate in a CLI (command line interface), you need to have an understanding of how UNIX views the structure of your files and folders on the hard drive. UNIX calls each folder on your Mac a directory, and recognizes the disks as volumes. The beginning, or top, level of your startup disk is known as the root directory, which is represented by a / (slash).

Navigating a CLI

Let's begin learning how to get around in UNIX by opening a new window, if you don't have one open already:

1. **Choose Shell ⇨ New Window.**

2. **Select the setting for the new window.**

When you first bring up a Terminal window, it opens in your home directory, which is represented by a ~ (tilde). To move to another directory, type its path on the command line. For example, to move to the root directory of your hard disk, simply type **cd /** and press the Return key (cd stands for "change directory"). To move back from the root directory to your home directory, simply type **cd ~** and press the Return key.

Moving to a subdirectory can be a little trickier; however, knowing where directories are located on your drive will help immensely. Directories are separated by slashes when typing their path. For example, type the following to move to the Utilities folder on your hard drive, and press Return:

```
cd/Applications/Utilities
```

Common commands

You can bend Leopard to your will using the Terminal just as you can with the mouse. Entering commands in the CLI executes functions that range from listing items in a directory to performing diagnostics on your network. As you just saw in the previous section, entering and executing a command is as simple as typing it and pressing Return; that's it!

What's Up, Man?

There are literally hundreds of UNIX commands at your disposal in Leopard, and each one of those commands could have several options that further expand their abilities. Needless to say, there's simply no way for me to explain the functions of all those commands here, but fear not; there's a UNIX command that can tell you everything you need to know about all the other commands: man. In a Terminal window, type **man**, followed by the name of the command you need more information about, and press Return to see the man (or manual) page for that command. A command's man page describes what the command can do and what options are available for it.

When you first open the man page for a command, you can only see a few lines of the page. To navigate through the man page:

- **Press the up and down arrows on your keyboard to scroll up or down one line at a time.**
- **Press the space bar to move to the next page.**
- **Press Q to exit the man page.**

Table 15.2 lists some of the most commonly used UNIX commands and gives a brief explanation of the functions they perform.

Table 15.2 Common UNIX Commands

Command	Function
ls	Lists files in the current directory.
ls –a	Lists all files, including hidden files, in the current directory.
cd	Changes directories; type this command, followed by the path of the directory you want to change to.
man	Displays the manual page for a command.
su	Stands for "superuser," and temporarily enables the root user account, discussed later in this chapter. Type **su** followed by the command you want to invoke as the superuser, and then press Return. Enter the password for the root account when prompted.
mv	Moves or renames a file. Type **mv** followed by the name of the file (and in some cases, the path to the file) you want move, and then enter the path and name of the file you want to move it to. This action creates a new file in the new location, and deletes the original.
rm	Deletes a file. Enter the command followed by the path and name of the file you want to delete.
rm –r	Deletes a directory and all of its contents. To use this command, type **rm –r** *directory name*, and press Return.
pwd	Displays the path to the directory you are currently working in.
cp	Copies a file. Type **cp** followed by the path and name of the file you want to copy, and then enter the path and name of the file you want to copy it to. This action creates a new file in the new location, but also retains the original.
mkdir	Creates a new directory. Type **mkdir**, and then enter the path and name of the new directory.

It's a bird! It's a plane! It's superuser!

There is a very special account that you can use both in Terminal and in Leopard that is separate and above all others: the superuser, or root, account. The root user is the end-all and be-all account that has the final say over every other account on the system, including administrator accounts.

Apple hides this powerful account from most users, and for good reason: If you are using the root user account and make just the right mistake at just the right time, you can totally junk your Mac. As a matter of fact, the root account is disabled by default in Leopard. However, there are some things you can do with root, such as access folders of other user accounts, that you just can't do with an administrator account. If you are feeling especially brave, you can enable the root account by following these steps:

1. **In the Finder, press ⌘+Shift+U to open a Finder window directly into the Utilities folder.**

2. **Double-click the Directory Utility icon.**

3. **When Directory Utility opens, click the lock in the bottom-left corner of the window, and then enter an administrator account name and password.**

4. **Choose Edit and select Enable Root User.**

The default password for the root account is blank, and this simply won't do. To change the password:

1. **Choose Edit ⇨ Change Root Password from the menu.**

2. **Enter a password in the Password field, like I'm doing in figure 15.7, and retype the password in the Verify field.** Click OK when finished.

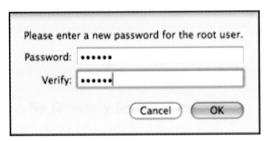

15.7 Creating a password for the root, or superuser, account.

Expand the Abilities of Leopard by Using X11

Because the Leopard version of UNIX, Darwin, is a fully compliant and certified UNIX variant, it can compile and run the full gamut of your UNIX applications. There are thousands of applications, many of them using graphical user interfaces, that you can run side-by-side with your Mac OS X applications using X11, also known as the X Window System. X11 is an optional installation that can be performed with your Leopard installation disk. Apple has an excellent online resource for discovering X11 and learning how to use it to expand your Mac OS X Leopard experience; check it out at http://developer.apple.com/opensource/tools/runningX11.html. Some X11 applications of note include OpenOffice.org and Fink.

Where to Find Additional UNIX Information

UNIX adds a whole other dimension to Leopard that many regular users will never discover, but believe me, there are hidden treasures in UNIX that you may find well worth discovering. Here are some additional resources to learn more about UNIX and how to utilize its commands and applications alongside your other Mac OS X applications and utilities:

- **www.apple.com/macosx/technology/unix.html**
- **http://images.apple.com/macosx/pdf/L355785C_UNIX_TB.pdf**
- **www.apple.com/opensource/**
- **http://developer.apple.com/opensource/**
- **www.unix.org**

All of these links are accurate at the time of this writing. The Internet is chock-full of more UNIX goodness, so feel free to scour it for all the command line enlightenment you can stand.

Can I Install Windows on My Mac?

Now that all new Macs are equipped with Intel processors, you can install Windows XP or Vista on your Mac just as you would on any other Intel-based PC. If you are switching over from a Windows computer to the wonderful world of Mac, having Windows installed on your Mac can make the transition a little smoother. However, if you are like every other Windows convert I know, you will find yourself booting up into Windows less and less as you become more familiar with Leopard.

Understanding Boot Camp 308

Using Boot Camp to Install Windows 309

Choosing a Startup Disk 313

Removing Windows from Your Mac 315

Understanding Boot Camp

Boot Camp is simply a tool provided with Leopard that helps step you through the process of installing Microsoft Windows on your Mac. It is a very simple utility but one that performs some very big jobs, such as:

- **Partitioning your hard disk.**
- **Booting from the Windows installation disc.**
- **Installing drivers in Windows that you need in order to use the hardware that comes with your Mac, such as your built-in camera (if you have one).**

Benefits of installing Microsoft Windows

If you're a long-time Mac fan, you may be dubious about the title of this section, but former Windows users probably already understand the upside of having Windows at your fingertips. Here are a few of the most obvious benefits:

- **Some companies use software that runs only on Windows.** If you work for one of those companies but are one of the smart folks who insist on having a Mac, you can have the best of both worlds.

- **Windows converts probably have a lot of Windows-only software, including games, that they don't want to just trash because they now have a Mac.** Boot Camp enables them to keep their software.

- **On increasingly rare occasions, you may run across a Web site that only works with a Windows operating system version.** Those sites are no longer off-limits to Mac users.

- **Some new Mac users may have printers that only work with Windows (this is also becoming increasingly rare).** Installing Windows ensures that they won't have to chuck the printer, which can be pretty painful if you have a stockpile of consumables (such as toner and ink) tied up in the device.

What you need in order to install Windows

Here are the requirements that must be met before installing Windows on your Mac:

- **At least 10GB of space available on your hard drive.**

- **Your Mac must have an Intel processor.**

- **You must install all firmware updates available for your Mac.** Run Software Update (choose Apple menu ➪ Software Update), or go to the Apple support Web site for your particular Mac model, to find out if there are any updates for your computer.

- **A Mac OS X Leopard installation disc.**

- **At least 1GB of memory if you are installing Windows Vista.**

- **A Windows installation disc.** You can install Windows XP Home or Professional editions, or Windows Vista Home Basic, Home Premium, Business, or Ultimate.

Note You must install a 32-bit version of Windows. If you are installing Windows XP, it must be Service Pack 2. You cannot install versions prior to Service Pack 2 and upgrade after the fact; the install disc must contain Service Pack 2 already.

Using Boot Camp to Install Windows

Open the Boot Camp Assistant to get started:

1. **From within the Finder, press ⌘+Shift+U to open the Utilities folder.**

2. **Double-click the icon for Boot Camp Assistant to see a window like that in figure 16.1.**

3. **Click the Print Installation & Setup Guide button to do just that, assuming you have a printer.** This guide is very helpful, and you need to print it if you can.

4. **Click Continue.**

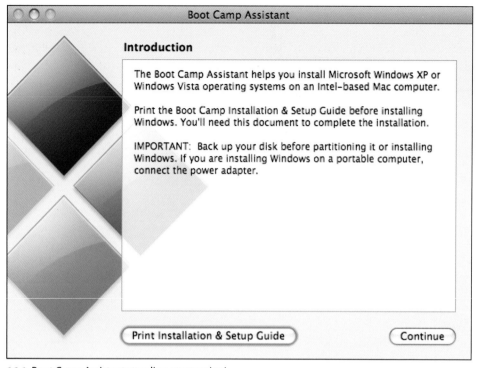

16.1 Boot Camp Assistant standing at attention!

Caution When I said the Print Installation & Setup Guide was "very helpful" in step 3, what I meant to say was "print it or don't continue with this chapter." This chapter is only meant as a brief tour of installing Windows, not a comprehensive guide. The Setup Guide is 26 pages long and is chock-full of information that you must have before continuing any further. If you can't print it, have it running on another Mac or view it from the Apple support Web site on a different computer at www.apple.com/support/bootcamp/.

How to partition your hard disk

Boot Camp Assistant now wants to help you partition your Mac's hard disk. Partitioning your disk essentially marks off a section of your hard drive and fools Leopard into thinking your Mac has two hard drives installed instead of one.

Note If you already partitioned your Mac's drive at some other time, you may simply see a window asking if you want to create or remove a Windows partition or start the Windows installer. Because you are installing Windows in this chapter, choose to start the Windows installer and click the Continue button.

At this point, you need to decide how much of your Mac's hard disk to allocate to Windows. There is no set number that I can recommend to you for the size; it depends entirely on your needs. Vista calls for at least 16GB of drive space to install it and XP needs at least 2GB's. Keep in mind that you will also need additional space to install applications and to store files. To divide the disk, drag the button between the Mac OS X and Windows boxes to the left or right to increase or decrease the size for each partition, as shown in figure 16.2.

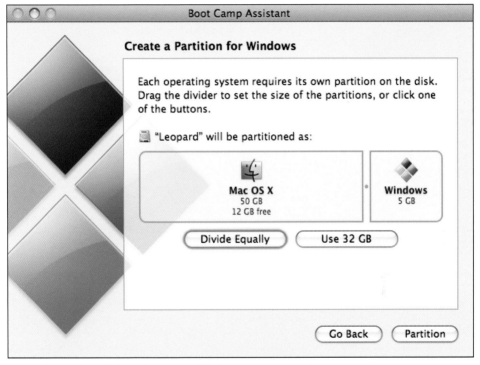

16.2 Partition your disk to make room for Windows on your Mac.

If you have a lot of Windows applications that you plan on installing, you might do well to click the Divide Equally button. Click the Use 32GB button if you want to automatically set the Windows partition to that amount. You would do so if you were using the FAT format when installing Windows and needed to use the maximum amount of disk space that this format allows.

1. **Set the size of your Windows partition and click the Partition button.** Boot Camp Assistant checks your hard disk for any potential problems and then continues the process.

the Windows installation disc. Do so, and then click the Start Installation button, as shown in figure 16.3.

○ ○ ○   Boot Camp Assistant

Start Windows Installation

Insert your Windows installation disc and click Start Installation.

You'll need an authentic 32-bit Microsoft Windows XP Home Edition or Professional with Service Pack 2 or later, or Windows Vista Home Basic, Home Premium, Business, or Ultimate disc.

After you have installed and set up Windows, insert your Mac OS X Leopard install disc to install additional drivers and other software for Windows.

Go Back   Start Installation

16.3 Click the Start Installation button to begin installing Windows.

Windows installation

By now, your Mac should have booted into the Windows installer disc, which is where I pick up:

1. **Follow the instructions on your computer for installing Windows, being sure to follow along with the Boot Camp Installation & Setup Guide you printed earlier.**

2. **At a certain point, you are asked which partition to install Windows on.** Be certain to choose the one labeled BOOTCAMP! This is key to your success or failure.

3. **Select the partition format you want to use for Windows (either NTFS or FAT32).** If you're installing Vista, NTFS is your only option. If you install XP, consider using FAT32; you can easily transfer files between the Mac and Windows partitions because Leopard can natively read the FAT32 file system, but not NTFS.

4. **Once Windows is installed, your Mac reboots into Windows.**

5. **Eject the Windows installation disc by choosing the Start menu in the bottom-left corner and selecting My Computer.** Click the drive containing the Windows installation disc to highlight it, and then click the Eject this disk option in the Systems Tasks (the upper-left corner of the window).

6. **Insert your Mac OS X Leopard installer disc; the Boot Camp installer program runs.** Follow the instructions on your screen and never cancel any part of the installation! Remember to read the guide! Your Mac restarts when the installation is completed and you have finished your Windows installation process.

Note
If you are prompted by a message saying the software hasn't passed Windows Logo testing, click the Continue Anyway button.

Don't Be Afraid to Ask for Help!

When you first boot your Mac into Windows following the Boot Camp installation, you see the Boot Camp Help window. Use this resource! It has invaluable information on how to use your Mac and its hardware, such as the keyboard, with Windows software. There are some differences when using a Mac compared to using PC hardware, but nothing that you can't easily overcome by reading through a Help window.

Choosing a Startup Disk

Now that you have a Mac with two operating systems on it, you need to decide which one will be its default: Leopard or Windows? You can easily select either of the two disks to be your default startup disk, and you can just as easily switch between the two operating systems.

From Windows

To select a startup disk from within Windows:

1. **Click the Start menu and select Control Panel.**

2. **Choose Classic view to see all the control panels that are installed.**

3. **Double-click the Boot Camp icon.**

4. **Under the Startup Disk tab, shown in figure 16.4, select the operating system that you want to boot into by default, and then click OK.** Click the Restart button if you want to reboot right now.

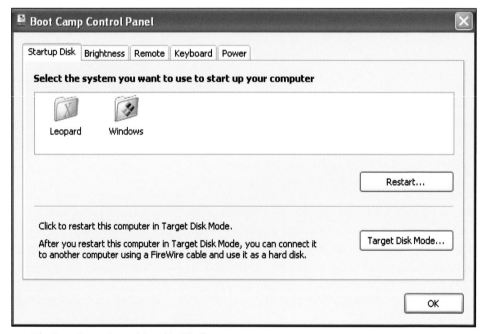

16.4 The Boot Camp Control Panel in Windows.

From Leopard

To select a startup disk from within Leopard:

1. **Choose Apple menu ⇨ System Preferences.**

2. **Click the Startup Disk icon.**

3. **Select the operating system that you want to be your default from the list, shown in figure 16.5.** Close the System Preferences, unless you'd like to reboot the Mac now, in which case you would click the Restart button.

16.5 Select the disk partition you want your Mac to boot into by default.

Removing Windows from Your Mac

Once you get tired of Microsoft's operating system taking up a large chunk of your hard drive, you may want to know how to safely remove it. Easy enough:

1. **Open the Boot Camp Assistant by pressing ⌘+Shift+U from within the Finder and double-clicking its icon.**
2. **Click Continue.**
3. **Select the Create or remove a Windows partition option and click Continue.**
4. **Click the Restore button to completely wipe out your Windows partition and restore your Mac's drive back to a single partition.**

Do You Have Any Troubleshooting Tips?

Macs have a well-earned reputation for being as rock-solid reliable as it gets in the tech realm, but nothing, not even Cupertino engineering, lasts forever. Things happen, and hopefully with this chapter I'll be able to point you to the help you need, if not lend a hand in resolving the issue altogether.

Problem Solving 101 . . . . **318**

Make Sure You Are Up-to-Date **318**

Startup Issues **319**

Isolating Software Troubles **322**

Permissions Problems **323**

When All Else Fails, Reinstall **325**

Problem Solving 101

Most issues with your Mac are fairly simple to resolve. As a matter of fact, the simplest resolution to most problems is to simply restart your Mac. Restarting is something that most computer users have had to do at some point, and it's always the first recourse to take when you notice quirky things beginning to happen. To restart your Mac:

1. **Choose Apple menu ⇨ Restart.**

2. **Leopard asks if you are sure you want to restart (see figure 17.1).** Click the Restart button to restart the computer.

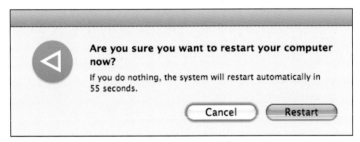

Are you sure you want to restart your computer now?

If you do nothing, the system will restart automatically in 55 seconds.

Cancel   Restart

17.1 Press the Restart button to perform the oldest troubleshooting trick in the book.

Hopefully your woes are gone once your Mac boots back up; if not, the rest of this chapter should help you get to the heart of the matter.

Make Sure You Are Up-to-Date

There could be a bug in your operating system or application software that is causing your problems. Check to be sure you are using the latest versions of your Mac's firmware and Leopard by running Software Update:

1. **Choose Apple menu ⇨ Software Update.**

2. **If Software Update finds new versions of your firmware or software, install them to see if this resolves your issues.**

If the problems you are experiencing are related to a particular application, visit the Web site of the application's developer to see if there are any updates to the software or if there are any known issues with it. Table 17.1 lists the addresses of some of the most popular Apple software vendors and a list of their more popular products.

Table 17.1 Third-party Apple Software Vendors

Company	Popular applications	Support site address
Adobe	Photoshop, InDesign, Illustrator, Acrobat	www.adobe.com/go/gn_supp
Quark	QuarkXPress	www.quark.com/service/desktop/support/
Microsoft	Word, Excel, PowerPoint, Entourage	https://www.microsoft.com/mac/default.mspx
Mozilla	Firefox, Thunderbird	http://support.mozilla.com/
Intego	VirusBarrier, FileGuard	www.intego.com/support/
Intuit	TurboTax, Quicken, QuickBooks	www.intuit.com/support/
FileMaker	FileMaker Pro, Bento	http://filemaker.com/support/index.html
Roxio	Toast, Popcorn	www.roxio.com/enu/support/default.html

Startup Issues

When your Mac won't start, it's a pretty scary time. I won't insult your intelligence by telling you there's nothing to worry about, but most of the time this can be solved with a few quick-and-easy steps. If you told me you had startup issues, the first question I would ask you is if the Mac literally won't power up, or if it is getting hung up in the boot process. Let's take it from there.

Your Mac won't power up

Here a few questions and tips to try if your Mac simply won't power up at all:

- **Is the power cable connected?**

- **Does the power outlet you are connected to work with other devices?**

- **If you are using a laptop, is the power adapter connected or are you running off the battery?** Is the battery charged? Will the Mac work with the power adapter connected?

- **Is the Mac itself powering up, but the display isn't coming on?** If so, you could have a bad display. Try connecting another display to your Mac to determine if that is the issue. If a new display doesn't work, or if your display works with another computer, your Mac's video card could be having problems.

- **Have you added any devices (such as an external hard disk) or parts (such as memory) to your Mac, either internally or externally?** If so, remove or reconnect the device or part and try to boot again. You may have a defective device, cable, or part.

● **If all else fails, you should try to reset the System Management Controller, or SMC.**
There are three ways to reset the SMC, depending on the model of Mac you have:

   ● **For Mac Pros, iMacs, and Mac minis, shut down the computer and remove all its cables (mouse, keyboard, power cord, everything).** After waiting at least 15 seconds, reconnect only the power cable, mouse, and keyboard (in that order) and then push the power button.

   ● **For MacBooks and MacBook Pros, remove the battery and unplug the power adapter if it is connected.** Hold the power button down for at least 5 seconds and release. Install the battery and connect the power adapter, and then press the power button.

   ● **For MacBook Air, connect the power adapter to the computer.** Holding down the Shift, Option, and Ctrl keys on the left side of the keyboard, press the power button once. Wait at least 5 seconds before pushing the power button again to turn on the computer.

Note

If you have a PowerPC Mac, you need to reset the Power Management Unit, or PMU. Search the Apple Web site for instructions on how to do so for your particular model.

Your Mac is hung at startup

Believe it or not, sometimes it is even more maddening to start up your Mac but not be able to boot into Mac OS X than it is simply not being able to turn on the computer at all. All sorts of things can occur: You may see a folder with a blinking question mark, the screen may be stuck at the gray Apple logo with the spinning gear, a blue screen may appear but nothing happens past that point, and so on. These issues can hopefully be resolved by following one of these next few steps:

● **Force your Mac to restart.** Hold down the power button for several seconds until the Mac turns off. Restart the Mac and see if it boots normally.

● **Reset the parameter RAM, which is also known as zapping the PRAM.** Leopard stores information about your Mac in the PRAM, such as speaker volume levels, time zone settings, display settings, and the like. Restart your Mac and immediately hold down the ⌘+Option+P+R keys simultaneously. Continue to hold down all four keys until you've heard your Mac's startup sound at least two times (give it three, just for good measure). Release the keys after the second or third startup sound, and hopefully you will be able to start up normally.

- **Start up your Mac in Safe Mode by holding down the Shift key immediately after the startup sound, and don't let go until you see the gray Apple logo.**

- **Boot your Mac using your Leopard installation disc, and select Disk Utility from the Utilities menu.** Click the icon of your hard drive in the left column of the list, and click the Repair Disk button in the lower-right corner of the window. Once the repair is completed, reboot your Mac to see if it starts normally.

If you're still having no luck getting your Mac started up at this point, it's time to take some drastic measures. Contact Apple technical support at this point, as your Mac may need a bit more hands-on expertise.

Handy startup keyboard shortcuts

Apple has come up with a toolbox of startup keyboard shortcuts that allow you to start up your Mac and perform specific tasks, such as choosing a different startup disk. Table 17.2 lists the shortcut key combinations and the tasks they facilitate.

Table 17.2 Startup Keyboard Shortcuts

Task performed	Key combinations
Start up from a disc	Insert the disc into your Mac's optical drive and hold down the C key until the disc begins to boot.
Choose a startup disk	Press and hold Option as soon as you hear the startup sound. Release the button after you see available startup disks. Select the disk you want to boot from.
Start in Safe Mode	Hold the Shift key as soon as you hear the startup sound, and don't release it until you see the spinning gear under the gray Apple logo.
Start up in Target Disk mode	Press and hold T immediately after the startup sound.
Zap the PRAM	Press and hold ⌘+Option+P+R immediately at startup, before you hear the startup sound.
Start in Single User mode	Press ⌘+S immediately after the startup sound.
Start up in Leopard instead of Mac OS 9	If you have an older PowerPC Mac with Mac OS 9 and Mac OS X installed on the same disk, you can force the Mac to boot into Mac OS X by holding down ⌘+X at startup.
Eject a disc at startup	Hold down the mouse button or the eject button on your keyboard at startup.

Isolating Software Troubles

You're typing away in your favorite word processor, and all of a sudden you see the "spinning wheel of death," the application crashes, and you've lost about an hour's worth of non-stop typing because you forgot to save your document as you were going along. Or you are performing a banking transaction in your favorite Web browser when the browser freezes on you, and you find out that your transaction was lost in the process of your browser crashing. What to do if you have an application that just won't behave? I've taken the liberty of listing some questions and tips for troubleshooting a software issue:

- **Have you installed the latest updates for your software?** If not, visit the Web site of the application developer to see if there are any updates.

- **Did the issue occur only after you installed an update (either an application or a Mac OS X update)?** Check with the application developer for any known issues with the update.

- **Do you experience problems with only one document?** There may be an element in that particular document, such as a font or graphic, that is corrupted and causing the issue. Try creating a new document; copy and paste elements from the old document into the new one and see if your issues are resolved.

- **Do you get a specific error message?** If so, consult the application's documentation or the manufacturer's Web site for help in interpreting the message.

- **Is the issue related to a software/hardware combination, such as a certain scanner or camera with a particular application?** For example, if you have a problem with Image Capture crashing when you try to import images from your camera, check to see if you can import images with some other application. If other applications also have this issue, then see if another camera will work. If other applications do not exhibit the problem, it's quite likely that the single misbehaving application is the culprit.

- **Discard the application's preferences files.** Consult your application's documentation or contact the manufacturer to find out where the application stores its preferences in Leopard. When you restart the application, new preferences files are created.

- **Is the application frozen?** If so, force the rogue application to quit by pressing ⌘+Option+ESC. Select the offending application from the list in the Force Quit Applications window and click the Force Quit button.

Unfortunately, if the issue at hand hasn't cleared up by now, you may need to reinstall the application. Again, be sure to contact the manufacturer or read the documentation that the application came with to see if there are any special instructions that you need to follow to properly reinstall the application.

Permissions Problems

Every single file in Mac OS X has a set of permissions assigned to it, which tells Leopard exactly who can access the file and how they can use it. Sometimes these permissions can get a little out of sorts and need to be repaired in order for your Mac to function in its normally spectacular way. Here are some symptoms to look for:

- **You are unable to empty a file from the Trash.**
- **An application can only be launched by one user account, even though it is installed for use on all accounts.**
- **You cannot open a document that you know you should to be able to open.**
- **The Finder may restart when you are trying to change permissions for a file.**
- **You are unable to open folders on your Mac or the network that you are supposed to have access to.**
- **An application crashes when you try to print from it.**

There are several other issues that may be related to permissions problems as well, but these are the most common.

Repairing permissions is thankfully an easy task to accomplish:

1. **From within the Finder, open Disk Utility by pressing ⌘+Shift+U and double-clicking its icon.**

2. **Select the drive that contains the files with the permissions issues.**

3. **Click the Repair Disk Permissions button in the lower-left corner of the First Aid tab, and the process of repairing the permissions will begin, as shown in figure 17.2.**

Note You can also run Disk Utility from the Leopard installation disc, which is especially helpful if you can't boot up with the disk in question. Boot your Mac using the installation disc, choose Utilities ⇨ Disk Utility, and run the repairs as described in the previous steps.

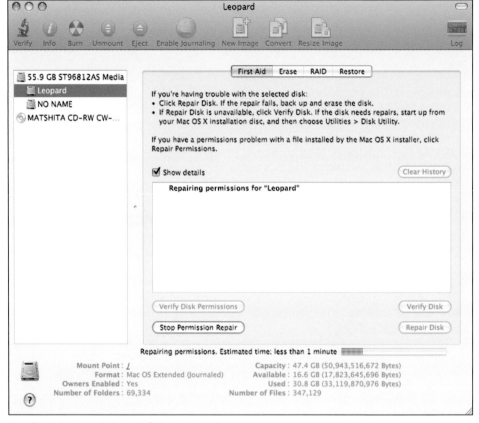

17.2 Restoring permissions to their proper states.

When All Else Fails, Reinstall

When the dust settles and you've done all that I've mentioned already — and you may have even dug further into the issues than this book does — but the Mac still won't work properly, it's time to completely back up and reinstall Leopard. See Chapter 14 for help on backing up your system, and Chapter 1 for instructions on installing Leopard over an existing copy of Mac OS X.

Index

A

A button, 120
Account Setup window, 119
Accounts icon, 241, 249
Accounts pane, 107–108, 148
Accounts preferences window, 241
Accounts tab, 64, 107, 108, 119
Accounts window, 243, 246, 248
Acrobat, 188, 319
Action button, 105
Action menu, 291
activity logs, 258–259
Activity Monitor, 42
Add Account window, 107, 108
Add button
    application assignment to spaces and, 27
    bookmarks and, 90
    folder sharing and, 265
    for mailboxes, 105
    printer installation and, 180, 181
    for Widget creation, 216
Add Printer button, 269
add printer window, 180
Add to Library window, 131
adding/removing
    album cover artwork, 129
    Desktop pictures, 198
    devices, troubleshooting and, 319
    Dock items, 22

e-mail/chat restrictions, 257
Finder sidebar items, 205
Finder toolbar items, 203, 204
iSync devices, 81–82
Login Items, 248
mailbox criteria, 115
New Message window items, 111
playlist criteria, 133
printers, 179–180, 253, 269
search attributes, 31
Smart Group conditions, 72
spaces, 25
Spotlight searches and, 27
Terminal settings, 298
users, from permissions list, 18
Web sites, allowable, 255
Address Book
    AutoFill feature and, 99
    creating contacts in, 69–72
    exporting contacts from, 74
    function of, 41
    groups in, 71–72
    importing contacts to, 73–74
    map feature of, 77–78
    opening, 69
    overview of, 59
    preferences for, 74–77
    Widgets and, 211
Address Book Archive, 74
Address Book icon, 69

Address Book window, 70, 71

Adjust Colors window, 171

administrator account

    capabilities of, 240

    creating accounts by, 241

    new account setup and, 244

    password reset and, 243

    printer sharing and, 269

    root account and, 303, 304

    settings modification and, 251

Adobe, 160, 167, 185, 187–188, 319

adult Web sites, 254

Advanced button, 230

Advanced pane, 100

Advanced preferences

    for iCal, 64–65

    for installation, 8–10

    for iTunes, 137–139

    for QuickTime, 232

    for Safari, 100–101

    for Terminal, 298

Advanced tab, 15

AIM account, 118

AirPort, 42, 230, 263

AirPort Base Station, 42

alarm, 63, 64, 65, 67

Animate opening applications check box, 23

AOL Instant Messenger, 118

Appearance icon/menu, 194

Appearance pane, 97

Appearance preferences pane, 194–197, 196

Apple Events, 263

Apple Filing Protocol (AFP), 267

Apple menu. See also System Preferences

    applications and, 44

    Desktop and, 11

    functions of, 12

    Recent Items on, 196

    restarting computer and, 318

    software updates and, 309, 318

Apple Remote Desktop, 263

Apple TV, 138

AppleScripts, 283

AppleTalk protocol, 178, 180, 181

Application Assignments window, 27

applications, See also names of specific

    applications

    Calculator, 37

    Chess, 37–38

    common commands for, 45

    Dictionary, 38, 211, 255

    DVD Player, 38–39

    Font Book, 39–40

    frozen, 322

    keyboard shortcuts for, 45

    limit access to, 252–253

    link file types to, 162

    navigating, 44–47

    opening/closing, 44

    overview of, 35–36, 40–41

    reinstalling, 323

    Stickies, 40

    workflows and, 282

Applications folder

    Chess and, 37

    display of, 36

    iChat and, 119

    opening, 18, 36, 119

    printer utilities and, 175

    Simple Finder and, 250, 251

    Stacks and, 46

    Time Machine and, 290

archive installation, 6–7

Attachment button, 111

attachments, e-mail, 111–112

audio books, 134

audio chats, 121

Audio MIDI Setup, 42

AutoFill feature, 98–99

automatic login, 247

Automatic Task drop-down menu, 151, 152

Automatically set up account check box, 107, 108

Automator

    designing workflows in, 278–281

    function of, 41

    navigating in, 276–277

    overview of, 275

    recording actions in, 282–283

    saving workflows in, 282

Automator icon, 276
Automator's main window, 276–277
Autosaving, 56

B

Back to My Mac, 229
backing up. *See also* Time Machine
   Address Book, 74
   importance of, 284
   installation and, 7
   mailboxes, 116
   TextEdit preferences and, 56
   Time Capsule and, 285
   Windows installation and, 310
backup server, 284
battery status, 226
Bento, 319
bitmap (BMP), 160
Bluetooth
   enabling, 79
   function of, 42
   Internet/network and, 230
   iSync and, 79–81
   keyboard/mouse and, 227
   sharing preferences and, 263
   sharing through, 270–273
Bluetooth Preferences button/pane, 270
Bluetooth Setup Assistant Introduction window, 80
Bluetooth System Preferences window, 79, 80
Bluetooth tab, 227
Bonjour protocol, 178, 180, 181, 264
bookmarks
   creating, 89–90
   defined, 89
   importing/exporting, 92
   installation and, 6
   organizing, 90–92
   Preview preferences and, 163, 164
   Safari preferences and, 97, 98
Bookmarks pane, 97
Bookmarks window, 92
Boolean operators, 32

Boot Camp (Assistant)
   functions of, 42, 308
   hard drive partition and, 8, 310–312
   opening, 309
   removing Windows with, 315
Boot Camp Control Panel, 314
Boot Camp Help window, 313
Boot Camp icon, 314
Boot Camp Installation & Setup Guide, 312
broadband Internet connection, 120
Browse button, 272
Browsing window, 272
Buddy List, 118, 119–120, 121
Buddy List window, 119, 121
Buddy Picture, 148
burning CDs, 133, 138, 205, 253

C

cable
   Ethernet, 177
   FireWire, 43, 230
   printer, 174, 177
   startup problems and, 319, 320
   USB, 73, 78, 174, 177
Calculator, 37, 209, 211
CalDAV servers, 64
calendar. *See* iCal
Calibrate button, 226
camera, digital. *See* Image Capture; Photo Booth
Camera button, 143, 144, 145, 147
Cancel Sync button, 83
CandyBar, 209
Cascading Style Sheet, 100
cautionary notes
   on backup procedure, 285, 290
   on device synchronization, 81
   on folder customization, 208
   on importing contacts, 74
   on installation, 6, 7
   on Login Items, 249
   on master password, 224
   on print dialogs, 185
   on printer compatibility, 174

on printer driver, 175
on security options, 223
on synchronization history, 85
on Windows installation guide, 309
CD labels, 133
CD/DVD drive, 263
CDs, burning, 133, 138, 205, 253
CDs & DVDs preferences pane, 225
cell phones, 78, 80, 83, 230, 273
Change All button, 162
Change button, 53
Change picture check box, 199
Change Settings button, 101
chatting. See iChat
Check Now button, 233
Check the applications to allow window, 252
Chess, 37–38
Choose Backup Disk button, 287
Choose button, 116, 198, 246, 276
Choose File button, 111
Clock, 11, 12, 232
color customization, 43, 195, 206–207, 225, 226
Color pop-up menu, 200
color profiles, 42, 151, 186, 226
Color tab, 226
ColorSync, 42
Columns view, 17
command line. See UNIX
Comma-separated (CSV) format, 73
Common UNIX Printing System, 183
Computer Name field, 262
Connect to Server window, 205
connecting devices, 319. See also iSync
Console, 43
contacts, 82, 83. See also Address Book
Content tab, 254
Continue Anyway button, 313
Control Panel, 269, 314
cookies, 100
Cover Flow view, 17, 129
cover page options, 187
Create Account button, 242
Create button, 107, 109

creating
Address Book contacts, 69–72
To Do items, 116–117
e-mail account, 106–109
icons, custom, 151
keyboard shortcuts, 227–228
mailboxes, 114
PDFs, 187–189
playlists, 131–133
print queue, 178–182
user accounts, 241–246
videos, 144
Web pages/sites, 148, 151, 229
Widgets, 215–216
window groups, 299
cropping images, 171
CUPS, 183
custom installation, 6–7
Customize button, 110, 221, 254
Customize Toolbar sheet, 203, 204, 205
customizing. See preferences; System Preferences
customizing Mac
Appearance preferences pane and, 194–197
color modification and, 194
Desktop picture and, 197–199
Finder and, 202–207
icons and, 207–209
overview of, 193
recently used items and, 196
screen saver and, 199–201
scrolling options and, 195–196
Widgets and, 209–210

D
Darwin, 305
Dashboard. See also Widgets
Exposé preferences and, 24
function of, 41
hot corner and, 201
opening, 209–210
Dashboard Widgets Web site, 214, 215
Data Change Alert, 85
Data Change Alert window, 84
date/time settings, 232–233

Default button, 180, 298
Delete button, 273
deleting. *See also* adding/removing
    backed-up files, 292
    bookmarks, 91, 164
    browsing history items, 96
    calendar events, 65
    To Do items, 65
    downloaded list items, 97
    fields, 76
    files, with UNIX, 303
    folders, from Privacy List, 29
    images from camera, 148, 151, 153–154
    login items, 248, 249
    PDF pages, 166
    user accounts, 240, 245, 246
    Web articles, 98
    Widgets, 213
    window groups, 299
Desktop
    customizing, 197–199
    Finder and, 11, 14
    function of, 12
    iChat file transmission and, 124
    picture for, 197–199
    removable media and, 21
    Simple Finder, 251
Desktop & Screen Saver icon, 197
Desktop & Screen Saver pane, 199
Desktop & Screen Saver preferences
    pane, 197, 198
Desktop tab, 197, 198
Destination Paper Size pop-up menu, 186
Develop menu, 101
device window, 156
Devices menu, 150
Dictionary, 38, 211, 255
DigitalColor Meter, 43
Directory, 43
Directory Utility icon, 246, 304
Directory Utility window, 246
disabling
    automatic login, 222
    fonts, 39
    hot corners, 201

international character encodings, 300
keyboard shortcuts, 227
remote control infrared receiver, 223
screen saver, 201
synchronization, 85, 128
Widgets, 212
Disk icon, 11, 12
Disk Utility
    formatting hard disk and, 285
    functions of, 43
    partitioning hard drive and, 8, 9
    troubleshooting and, 321, 323, 324
Disk Utility toolbar, 285
Disk Utility window, 8, 285
Display Calibrator Assistant's Introduction
    screen, 226
Display tab, 225–226
Do not back up window, 288
Dock
    adding/removing items and, 22
    applications and, 44
    Desktop and, 11
    divider line of, 22
    e-mail alerts on, 113
    Finder and, 204
    function of, 12, 22
    hiding, 23
    preferences and, 22–23
    Preview icon on, 160
    Simple Finder and, 250
    Stacks and, 46
    System Preferences icon on, 179, 194
    Terminal and, 297
    Time Machine icon on, 290
    user account limitations and, 253
Dock Preferences window, 23
Document drop-down menu, 154
documents, 323. *See also* TextEdit
Documents folder, 251
Documents stack, 11, 12
Done button, 204
Don't Add button, 278
DOS, 50
Download All button, 152

Download button, 152
Download Folder drop-down menu, 152
Download Some button, 152, 153
Download To drop-down menu, 151
downloads
    Bonjour, 264
    iTunes store and, 137
    Podcasts, 134
    printer software, 175, 176
    for QuickTime, 232
    Safari preferences and, 96, 97
    screen savers, 199
    software updates, 175
    Widget, 214–215, 216
    WMV Components disk image, 93
Downloads stack, 11, 12
Drag Backdrop Here window, 147
drag-and-drop function
    Address Book groups and, 71
    backdrops and, photo/video, 147
    for bookmark organization, 90
    Dock display and, 22
    Finder sidebar and, 205, 206
    Finder toolbar and, 204
    for image transfer, 153
    for Mail attachments, 111
    for Mail customization, 106, 111
    to move Widgets, 209
    for playlists, 131
    to preview files, 160
    for printing, 184
    for rearranging PDF pages, 167
    removable media and, 21
    Spotlight preferences and, 29
    for Spring-loaded folders/windows, 14
    workflow design and, 278, 279, 280, 281
drivers
    administrator account and, 240
    printer, 174–176, 180, 181, 269
    for Windows, 308
DVD drive, 4
DVD Player, 38–39
DVDs, 43, 205, 225, 253, 263

E

Edit button, 62, 70, 99
Edit List button, 221
Edit menu, 166, 304
Edit Picture window, 246
editing
    Address Book contacts, 70
    Address Book groups, 72
    calendar events, 62–63
    images, 167–171
    language list, 221
    PDFs, 165–167
    recorded actions, 283
Effects button, 123, 145, 146, 147
Eject button, 285
Eject icon, 21
ejecting removable media, 21
e-mail, 29, 70, 75. See also Mail
Enable Parental Controls check box, 249
Enable Spaces check box, 25
enabling
    assistive devices access, 283
    Bluetooth, 79
    device sharing, 156
    file-sharing protocols, 267
    FileVault feature, 224
    Finder path bar, 203
    international character encodings, 300
    Parental Controls, 249–250
    printer sharing, 267–268
    private browsing, 92–93
    root account, 245, 304
    syncing, 85
    Widgets, 212
Encodings window, 300
Energy Saver preferences pane, 226–227
Entourage, 73, 319
Erase button, 285
Erase tab, 285, 286
error message, 322
ESPN, 211
Ethernet interface, 174, 176–177, 226, 230, 263
Excel, 319

Exchange servers, 75, 108
Exclude button, 288
Expert Mode check box, 226
Export Bookmarks window, 92
exporting
    Address Book contacts, 74
    Address Book options and, 76
    bookmarks, 92
    calendar, 66–67
    window groups, 299
Exposé, 23–24, 41
Exposé & Spaces icon, 24, 25
Exposé & Spaces preferences window, 24
Exposé tab, 24
Extensible Markup Language (XML), 50
extensions, file, 15, 18

F

Fan mode, 46
fast user switching, 247
FAT format, 311, 313
file extensions, 15, 18
File Format menu, 49, 282
file formats. See also Portable Document Format
    (PDF) files
    Address Book and, 73, 74
    calendar sharing and, 67
    FAT, 311, 313
    HTML, 50, 56
    Preview supported, 160
    for scans, 156
    TextEdit and, 49–50, 54
File menu
    Address Book, 69, 71–74
    applications and, 44
    Bluetooth File Exchange, 271–272
    Calculator and, 37
    calendar and, 60, 68
    Finder, Info window and, 18
    iChat, file sharing and, 124
    Image Capture, printing and, 148
    Mail, import mailboxes and, 116
    Preview, 160–161
    Safari, 92, 216
    TextEdit, 48, 51, 183–184, 188

file sharing, 263, 264–267
File Sharing check box, 264, 268
File Transfer Protocol (FTP), 267
FileGuard, 319
Filemaker, 319
FileVault, 224, 242
Find Next button, 53
Finder
    activating, 204
    applications and, 36, 44
    Automator access from, 276
    Desktop and, 11
    Exposé and, 23, 24
    function of, 10, 13
    image information and, 151
    importance of, 10
    information access and, 17–18
    navigating in, 16–21
    preferences and, 13–15
    Preview and, 160
    Quick Look feature and, 19–20
    removable media and, 21
    searching with, 29, 30–31
    Simple Finder, 250–252
    Spotlight and, 29, 30
    Stacks and, 46
    troubleshooting and, 323
    viewing options for, 16–17
Finder Preferences window, 14, 15
Finder window(s)
    background of, 206–207
    backup file deletion and, 291
    columns in, 202
    components of, 12–13
    customizing, 194, 202–207
    opening, 30
    path bar in, 202, 203
    Photo Booth and, 144
    removable media and, 21
    search attributes and, 31
    sidebar in, 205–206
    Time Machine and, 290–291
    toolbar in, 203–205
Fink, 305
Firefox, 101, 319

firewall, 101, 224
FireWire, 43, 230, 263
First Aid tab, 323
Flight Tracker, 211
Flip4Mac, 93–94
folders
    Bluetooth sharing and, 271
    for bookmarks, 90, 91, 92
    customizing, 207
    for e-mails, 114
    Finder preferences and, 14
    Finder toolbar and, 205
    Finder window and, 12
    function of, 12
    Go menu and, 18
    installation and, 6
    sharing, 265–266
    for snapshots, 144, 151
    workflow design and, 278
Font Book, 39–40
fonts
    appearance preferences and, 196
    Safari preferences and, 97
    Terminal settings and, 298
    TextEdit and, 51–52, 54
Fonts button, 112
Fonts window, 51–52
Force Quit Applications window, 322
Force Quit button, 322
Format for pop-up menu, 183
Format menu, 8, 76
Formats tab, 221, 222
formatting
    documents, 50–53
    e-mail content, 112
    hard disk, 285–286
    photos, 151
Forward button, 113
Full Screen mode, 19, 129–130
function keys, 23–24, 26
functional limitations, 252–253

G

G5 processor, 4
games, 37, 134, 211, 308

General pane, 95–96
General tab
    Finder preferences and, 14
    iCal preferences and, 63–64
    iTunes preferences and, 135, 139
    for Preview preferences, 163
    security options and, 222–223
Get button, 273
Get Info window, 20
Get Mail button, 113
Go menu
    Address Book and, 69
    applications and, 36, 44
    folder access and, 18
    iCal and, 60
    iSync and, 81
    Preview and, 160
    root account and, 246
    Terminal and, 296
    TextEdit and, 183
    utilities and, 44
Google, 199, 211, 214
Google Maps, 78
Google Talk, 118
Grab, 43
grammar check, 52–53
Grapher, 43
graphic artists, 160
Graphics Interchange Format (GIF), 160
Greeking, 164
Grid mode, 46–47
Group by pop-up menu, 258

H

hard disk/drive
    backups and, 284
    external, 284
    formatting, 285–286
    installation and, 5, 7
    partitioning, 8–9, 284, 308, 310–312
    RAID Utility and, 43
    Stacks and, 46
    system requirements and, 4
    Windows on Mac and, 309

Hard Drive menu, 175, 213
Helpful Tips button, 234
Hide check box, 248
Hide Toolbar button, 12, 13
hiding
    album cover artwork, 118
    To Do items, 64
    Dock, 23
    file extension, 18
    Finder sidebar, 12, 206
    Finder toolbar, 12, 204
    keyboard shortcut for, 45
    Login Items, 248
    mail activity, 105
    profanity in Dictionary, 255
High Dynamic Range (HDR), 160
Highlight Color menu, 194
history, Web browsing, 96, 97
Home page, Web, 96
Hot Corners, 201
HotSync Manager, 83
HotSync reminder, 85
HyperText Markup Language (HTML), 50, 56

I

iCal
    adding events in, 61–62
    editing events in, 62–63
    function of, 41
    information types in, 62–63
    managing calendar in, 60–61
    new calendar and, 60
    opening, 60
    overview of, 59
    preferences for, 63–65
    printing calendars in, 68–69
    sharing and, 65–67
    subscribing to calendars and, 67–68
    synchronization options and, 82, 83
    Widgets and, 209, 211
iCal Advanced Preferences tab, 64–65
iCal preferences window, 63
iCal window, 60, 61

iChat
    account setup and, 117–119
    advanced, 122–124
    Buddy List and, 119–120
    chatting in, 120–122
    function of, 41
    overview of, 103
    Parental Controls and, 256–257
    Photo Booth and, 148
    send/receive files in, 123–124
iChat icon, 119
iChat Theater, 124
icons
    creating, 151
    customizing, 151, 207–209
    Directory Utility, 304
    sizing, 16, 23
    Terminal, 296
Icons view, 16
ICS format, 67
iDisk, 205, 229
iLife application suite, 148, 149, 154
Illustrator, 319
iMacs, 320
Image Capture
    deleting images and, 153–154
    device connection to, 150
    device sharing and, 156–157
    function of, 41, 141, 148
    image transfer and, 150–152
    opening, 149
    preferences for, 149–150
    scanning and, 154–156
Image Capture Device Browser, 156
images. See also Photo Booth
    color adjustment of, 170–171
    cropping, 171
    for Desktop, 197–199
    editing, 167–171
    for Finder background, 206, 207
    information on, 168
    Preview and, 159, 160, 167–171
    resizing, 168–169, 208
    resolution of, 155, 169

rotating, 169–170
for user accounts, 246–247
Images tab, 163
IMAP servers, 108
Import Bookmarks window, 92
Import button, 92
importing
bookmarks, 92
with Image Capture, 150
images, 148
to iTunes, 130–131, 138
window groups, 299
Incoming Mail Server window, 108
InDesign, 185, 319
Info window, 18, 162, 208
Information button, 213, 214
Information tab, 151
infrared receivers, 223
Input Menu tab, 222
Inspector, 20
Install button, 5, 7, 10, 214
Install Mac OS X window, 5
Install Summary window, 5, 7
installation. *See also* printing; setup and
administrator account and, 240
custom, 6–7, 8–10
system requirements for, 4
upgrading option and, 4–6
Windows on Mac, 309–313
of WMV Components disk image, 93–94
of Xcode developer tools, 8, 9–10
Installed Updates tab, 233
Installer application, 291
installer icon, 175, 176
instant messaging. *See* iChat
Intego, 319
Intel processor, 4, 307, 309
International preferences pane, 220–221
Internet. *See also* downloads; Web pages/sites
Parental Controls and, 254–256
QuickTime preferences and, 232
security settings and, 224
sharing preferences and, 263
Widgets and, creating, 215–216

Internet addresses
for Apple support, 309
for Bonjour download, 264
for calendar subscribing, 68
for icon modification, 209
for instant messaging account, 118
for MobileMe, 229
for software support, 319
for supported devices, 78
for UNIX resources, 305
for Widget downloads, 216
for WMV Components disk image, 93
for X11 information, 305
Internet Explorer, 101
Internet Protocol (IP) Printing, 177, 178, 180–181
Internet Service Provider (ISP), 106, 107, 108
Intuit, 319
IP button, 180
iPhones, 138
iPhoto
book's focus and, 149, 159
iChat Theater and, 124
image touch-up with, 154
Mail attachments and, 111
Photo Booth and, 148
Preview image editing and, 167
iPods, 134, 138
iSync
add device to, 81–82
Bluetooth and, 79–81
data change alert and, 83–84
function of, 41, 78
Palm OS devices and, 83
preferences for, 84–85
supported devices and, 78
synchronization options and, 82–83
USB devices and, 81
iSync icon, 81, 85
iSync Preferences window, 84
iSync window, 81, 83
iTunes
burning CDs in, 133
creating playlists in, 131–133
Full Screen mode in, 129–130

iTunes *(continued)*
  importing music to, 130–131
  overview of, 127
  preferences for, 135–139
  user interface of, 128–129
  Widgets and, 211
iTunes Library, 129, 131, 135, 136, 137
iTunes Store, 134–135, 137

J

Jabber, 118
Joint Photographic Experts Group (JPEG), 160

K

Keep button, 214
Keyboard & Mouse preferences pane, 227–228
Keyboard Shortcuts tab, 227
keyboard shortcuts/keystrokes
  for Address Book, 70, 71, 74
  for bookmark, new, 90
  for calendar, new, 60
  for calendar event, new, 61
  common, for applications, 45
  creating, 227–228
  for documents, 48, 51, 53
  for DVD Player functions, 39
  for e-mail, receiving, 113
  for Finder background, 207
  for finding text on Web site, 94
  for folder access, 18
  for importing music, 131
  for Internet browsing, 88, 97
  for iSync device, new, 81
  to open Applications folder, 36, 44, 119, 183
  to open Automator, 276
  to open Calculator Paper Tape window, 37
  to open Dashboard, 209–210, 212
  to open Device Browser, 156
  to open Disk Utility, 285
  to open Finder window, 144, 204
  to open Image Capture, 149
  to open Info window, 162, 208
  to open Preview, 160

  to open Utilities, 296, 304, 309
  for pasting, 208
  for PDF annotating, 166
  for PDF markup, 165, 166
  for PDF sidebar, 167
  for playlists, new, 131, 132
  for printing, 133, 148, 184
  retrieving, 228
  for rotating images, 169
  for saving Preview files, 161
  for saving workflows, 282
  for selecting all, 51
  for space navigation, 26
  for Spotlight functions, 29, 32
  for Stacks, adding, 46
  for startup, 321
  Terminal settings and, 298
  for TextEdit preferences, 53
  Windows and, 45
Keyboard tab, 227
Keychain Access, 43

L

Labels tab, 15
language, 5–8, 211, 220–221
Language tab, 221
laptop computer, 6, 226, 319
layout options, 186
Leopard installation disc, 321, 324
Lightweight Directory Access Protocol (LDAP), 77
Lightweight Directory Interchange Format (LDIF), 73
Limit computer use to check box, 258
Limit iChat check box, 257
Limit Mail check box, 257
links, Web, 53, 89, 97
Linux, 187, 261, 295
List view, 17
lock icon, 241
login
  automatic, 222, 223
  for iTunes, 129
  sharing preferences and, 263
  to user account, 246–249

Login Items, 247–249
Login Options button, 246
login window, 247
Logs tab, 258–259

M

Mac minis, 320
Mac OS 9, 321
Mac OS X 10.2, 4
Mac OS X Leopard installation disc, 309, 312, 313
Mac OS X Tiger, 27
Mac Pros, 320
MacBook Air, 320
MacBooks (Pros), 320
Magnification check box, 23
Mail
    Address Book file formats and, 73
    backups and, 116
    composing/sending mail in, 110–112
    creating account and, 106–109
    forwarding mail and, 113
    main window of, 104–105
    navigating in, 104–106
    organizing mail and, 113–117
    overview of, 103
    Parental Controls and, 256–257
    Photo Booth and, 148
    receiving mail and, 113
    replying to mail and, 113
    RSS feeds and, 117–118
    toolbar for, 105–106
    workflow design and, 278, 281
Mail & iChat tab, 256–257
Mail icon, 113
Mail window, 114
Mailbox pane, 105, 114
mailboxes, 114–115
Manage Widgets button, 212, 214
Managed by Parental Controls account, 249
MBOX format, 116
media, removable, 21, 43, 205
Media Browser, 276

Media Keys, 232
memory, 4, 85, 150, 223, 309
menu bar
    battery status in, 226
    clock in, 232
    on Desktop, 11
    functions from, 12
    Help access from, 44
    iSync preferences and, 85
    spaces and, 26
    Time Machine icon in, 290
    Time Machine status in, 289
Message Viewer, 113
Messages tab, 123
metadata, 27
Microsoft, 319. *See also* Windows
Microsoft Windows Network, 267
MIDI devices, 42
MIDI files, 232
Migration Assistant, 43
MIME settings, 232
MobileMe, 229
Mouse Keys, 235
Mouse tab, 227
movies/videos
    Automator and, 276
    creating, 144
    Image Capture and, 150
    infrared receiver and, 223
    iTunes functions and, 129
    from iTunes Store, 134
    music, 134
    Photo Booth and, 144, 147–148
    Playback preferences and, 136
    sharing, 229
    streaming and, 232
    Web Gallery and, 229
    Widgets and, 211, 213
    Windows Media and, 93
Mozilla, 319
multiple users, 247
music videos, 134

N

naming/renaming
  bookmarks, 91, 92
  e-mail account, 107
  Finder viewing options and, 18
  mailboxes, 114, 115
  PDF document, 188
  playlists, 131
  in Preview, 161
  scanned files, 155
  shared devices, 156
  window groups, 300
  workflow design and, 278, 279–280
navigating
  in applications, 44–47
  in Automator, 276–277
  command line interface, 301–302
  in Finder, 16–21, 203, 205
  in Mail, 104–106
  in Safari, 88–89, 100
  in Spaces, 26
  Widgets and, 215
network
  backups and, 284
  Energy Saver and, 226
  Firewall settings and, 224
  installation and, 6
  preferences for, 229–231
  printer and, adding, 269
  printer setup and, 174, 177–178
  Sharing Only account and, 241
  supported connections and, 230
Network preferences pane, 229–230
Network Settings check box, 7
Network Utility, 43
new accounts window, 242
New Document tab, 53–55
New Folder button, 278
New Mailbox window, 114
New Message button, 110
New Message window, 110, 111
new name radio button, 279
New Note window, 116
New Oxford American Dictionary, 38

Note button, 116
Notes, 115, 116, 117
NTFS format, 313
Number of Recent Items pop-up menu, 196

O

ODBC Administrator, 43
Only allow selected applications check box, 252
Open and Save tab, 53, 55–57
Open button, 48, 73, 160, 278
Open Database Connectivity, 43
Open dialog, 160
Open Print Queue button, 181
Open Speakable Items Folder button, 234
OpenDocument Text, 50
OpenOffice, 47, 50, 305
optical drive, 263
Optional Installs folder, 8
Options button
  file-sharing protocols and, 267
  for Image Capture, 151
  installation and, 7
  printer sharing and, 268
  Remote Management and, 269
  for screen saver, 200
  search attributes and, 31
  Time Machine and, 288
options pop-up menu, 185
Options tab, 226, 229
Outgoing Mail Server window, 109
Outlook, 73
oval button, 204, 206
Overview button, 155
Oxford American Writer's Thesaurus, 38

P

Page Setup dialog, 183, 186
Pages, 47
pairing devices, 80, 271
Palm Desktop software, 83
Palm OS, 78, 83
paper feed options, 187
paper handling options, 186
Paper Size pop-up menu, 183

Paper Tape function/window, 37
Parental Controls
    account types and, 240
    activity logs and, 258–259
    application/function limitation and, 252–253
    Dictionary and, 255
    enabling, 249–250
    importance of, 254
    Mail/iChat and, 256–257
    new account setup and, 244
    time limits and, 257–258
    Web sites and, 254–256
Parental Controls icon, 249, 250
Parental Controls preferences, 250
Parental preferences, 138
Partition button, 311
Partition tab, 8
partitioning hard drive, 8–9, 42, 284, 286, 308,
    310–312
Password Assistant window, 243
Password check box, 156
password(s)
    to awaken computer, 222, 223
    for Bluetooth sharing, 271
    changing, 253
    creating, 241, 242, 243
    for e-mail account, 107
    hints for, 242, 247
    Keychain Access and, 43
    to login to account, 246
    to login to Mac, 222, 223
    master, 224
    PDF security options and, 190
    printer installation and, 176
    printer sharing and, 269
    to remove Widgets, 213
    root account and, 246, 303, 304
    Safari preferences and, 99
path bar, 202, 203
PDAs, 78
PDF button, 188
PDF Save dialog, 189
PDF Security Options window, 188
PDFs. See Portable Document Format (PDF) files

permissions problems, 323–324
phone button, 121
phone number formats, 76
Photo Booth
    function of, 41
    Mail attachments and, 111
    main window of, 142
    overview of, 141
    printing from, 148
    special effects and, 123, 144–147
    taking snapshots with, 143–144
    using photos/videos and, 147–148
Photo Booth pane, 148
Photo Browser button/window, 111
photography, digital, 160. See also Image Capture;
    Photo Booth
Photoshop, 160, 167, 319
Photoshop Document (PSD), 160
plain text format, 50, 54, 56
Playback preferences, 136
playlists, 131–133
plug-in, 282
Plug-in for drop-down menu, 282
Pocket PCs, 78
Podcast Capture, 43
podcasts, 134, 136
POP servers, 108
Popcorn, 319
pop-up blocking, 100
Portable Document Format (PDF) files
    annotating, 165, 166
    deleting pages from, 166
    marking up, 165
    overview of, 159
    Preview preferences and, 164
    Preview supported files and, 160
    print options and, 187–189
    rearranging pages in, 167
    security options for, 188–189
Portable Network Graphics (PNG), 160
PostScript printer driver, 269
power failure, 226
Power Management Unit, 320
PowerPC G4, 4

PowerPC Mac, 320, 321
PowerPoint, 319
PRAM, 320
preferences. *See also* System Preferences
    for Address Book, 74–77
    for calendar, 63–65
    for chess, 38
    for Dock, 22–23
    for Exposé, 24
    for Finder, 13–15
    for Image Capture, 149–150
    for iSync, 82–83, 84–85
    for iTunes, 135–139
    for Mail toolbar, 105–106, 111
    for Preview, 162–164
    for Safari, 95–101
    for Simple Finder, 251
    for Spaces feature, 25–26
    for Spotlight, 29–30
    for Terminal, 296–300
    for TextEdit, 53–57
    troubleshooting and, 322
    for Widgets, 213–214
Preserve Users check box, 7
Preview
    file types supported by, 160
    Finder viewing options and, 18
    function of, 41
    image resizing in, 208
    image viewing/editing in, 167–171
    Inspector feature and, 20
    opening files in, 160–161
    overview of, 159
    PDF editing in, 165–167
    preferences for, 162–164
    saving files in, 161
    workflow design and, 278, 279
Preview Preferences window, 163
previewing scans, 155
Print & Fax icon, 179
Print & Fax pane, 181
Print & Fax preferences, 179, 263, 267
Print & Fax System Preferences pane, 174

Print button, 133, 184
print dialog, 184, 185
Print Installation & Setup Guide, 309, 310
print servers, 177
Print Using pop-up menu, 180, 181
Printer Sharing check box, 263, 267
Printers (and Faxes) control panel, 269
printing
    calendars, 68–69
    CD labels, 133
    documents, 183–189
    overview of, 173
    printer compatibility and, 174
    setup and, 174–182
    sharing preferences and, 263, 267–269
    snapshots, 148
    troubleshooting and, 323
    user account limitations and, 253
    utilities for, 175
    Windows on Mac and, 308
    workflow design and, 278, 280
Privacy list, 29
processor, 4, 42, 307, 309
profanity, 255
programming
    Calculator and, 37
    Develop menu and, 101
    Image Capture Information tab and, 151
    plain text format and, 50
    tools for, installation and, 8
    Xcode and, 283
    XML format and, 50
Protocol pop-up menu, 180
Publish button, 66
publishing calendar, 65–66

Q

QuarkXPress, 185, 319
Quick Look, 19–20, 205
Quick Look button, 19
QuickBooks, 319
Quicken, 319
QuickTime (Player), 41, 93, 124, 231–232

R

RAID Utility, 43
Random Access Memory (RAM), 4, 223
Random order check box, 199
raster graphics, 160
RAW format, 160
Reader, 187
Recent Items, 12
Record button, 283
Recycle Bin, 12
refresh rates, 225
reinstalling Leopard, 325
Reminders, 117
remote control access, 223
remote management, 263
Remote Management check box, 269
Remove button, 164
Remove Now button, 98
removing. *See* adding/removing; deleting
renaming. *See* naming/renaming
Rendezvous protocol, 178
Repair Disk button, 321
Repair Disk Permissions button, 323
Reply button, 113
Require pairing check box, 271
Reset Sync History button, 85
resizing images, 168–169, 208
resolution, 155, 169, 225, 226
Restart, 12
Restart button, 5, 247, 314, 315, 318
Restore button, 291, 315
Restore Defaults button, 228
restoring
    disk, 291–292
    files, 290–291
    mailboxes, 116
    permissions, 324
Restrict button, 258
Results window, 13
Rich Text Format (RTF), 49, 50, 54, 56
root account, 244–245, 303–304
root directory, 301
rotating images, 170–171
router, 224

Roxio, 319
RSS (Really Simple Syndication) feeds, 105, 117–118
RSS preferences pane, 97–98
Run button, 281, 283

S

Safari
    bookmarks and, 89–92
    browsing in, 88–89
    finding text and, 94–95
    Google Maps and, 78
    overview of, 87
    preferences for, 95–101
    printer driver downloads and, 176
    private browsing and, 92–93
    RSS feeds and, 117
    site browser limitations and, 101
    Status bar and, 89
    user interface of, 88–89
    video viewing and, 93–94
    Web archive format and, 50
    Windows Media files and, 93–94
Safari icon, 216
Safe Mode, 321
Save As dialog, 161
Save As window, 66
Save button, 31, 48, 66, 273, 300
Save dialog, 49, 188
saving
    Address Book contacts, 70
    Address Book exports, 74
    Address Book groups, 72
    documents, 48–49, 56
    downloaded files, 96
    PDF document, 166, 167, 188
    in Preview, 161
    Terminal tabbed windows, 301
    workflows, 282
Scan button, 155
Scan Mode drop-down menu, 154
Scan To Folder drop-down menu, 155
scan window, 154
scanning, 148, 149, 154–156, 160

Scheduled Check tab, 233

scheduler options, 187

screen saver, 199–201

Screen Saver tab, 199

screen sharing, 263

scripters, 283

scrolling options, 195–196

Search field, 12–13, 28, 38, 88, 105

Search text field, 28, 30

searching/finding. *See also* Spotlight

    e-mails, 105

    filtering, 31–32

    with Finder, 29, 30–31

    Finder toolbar and, 205

    with Image Capture, 148

    in iTunes, 129

    for screen savers, 199

    snapshots, 144

    text on Web site, 94–95

    for Widgets, 214

Secure Shell (SSH) in Terminal, 263

security options

    login and, 247

    for PDF documents, 188–189

    Safari and, 99–100

    System Preference settings and, 222–224

Security Options button, 188

Security pane, 99

Security preferences pane, 222

Select a Destination screen, 7

Select button, 97, 207, 265

Send button, 110–111, 113, 123, 271–272

Send Invitation button, 77

Server Message Block (SMB), 267

Set button, 246

Set date & time automatically check box, 232

Set Up New Device button, 80, 227

Settings window, 298

Share button, 124

Share files and folders using SMB check box, 269

Share my devices check box, 156

Shared folder, 251

Shared Folders window, 265

sharing

Address Book preferences and, 77

Bonjour and, 264

calendar, 65–67

devices, 156–157

files, 264–267

    with Image Capture, 148

    iTunes Library, 135, 137

    iTunes preferences and, 136

    overview of, 261

    printers, 267–269

    Remote Management, 269

    Spotlight searches and, 28

    System Preferences and, 262–263

    through Bluetooth, 270–273

    via MobileMe, 229

Sharing & Permissions, 18

Sharing button, 156

Sharing icon, 262

Sharing Only account, 241

Sharing pane, 270

Sharing preferences window, 262, 264, 266, 268

shell, 296, 298

Shell menu, 301

Show activity for pop-up menu, 258

Show All button, 249

Show Cookies button, 100

Show Databases button, 100

Show Develop menu, 101

Show profiles for this display only check box, 226

Show Spaces in menu bar check box, 26

Show Stationery button, 111

Show Time Machine status in the menu bar

    check box, 289

Show with clock check box, 199

Shut Down, 12

Shut Down button, 247

sidebar

    in Finder window, 12–15, 21, 202, 205–206

    in Preview, 164, 166, 167

Sidebar tab, 15

Silicon Graphics Image (SGI), 160

Simple Finder, 250–252

Simple Finder window, 251

Size box, 8

Size slider, 23
Ski Report, 211
Sleep button, 247
sleep mode, 12, 201
slide shows, 148, 151
Smart Groups, 72
Smart Mailbox, 105, 114
Smart Playlists, 132–133
smart quotes, 54
SMTP server, 109
Snapshot mode, 142
software installation, 240
software license agreement, 5, 7
Software License Agreement window, 10
software updates, 233, 309, 318, 322
Sound Check option, 137
sound preferences, 228–229
Source pane, 134, 135
Spaces
    application assignment and, 27
    function of, 25, 41
    hot corners and, 201
    navigating in, 26
    preferences for, 25–26
Spaces icon, 26
Spaces tab, 25, 27
special effects
    for closing Widgets, 210
    minimizing function and, 23
    for Photo Booth, 144–147
    with video chats, 123
speech preferences, 234–235
Speech Recognition tab, 234
Spelling and Grammar dialog, 53
spelling check, 52–53
Spotlight
    Desktop and, 11
    efficiency of, 27–28
    Finder and, 30–31
    Finder viewing options and, 18
    flexibility of, 30
    function of, 12
    keyboard shortcuts for, 32
    preferences for, 29–30
    speeding up, 32

Spotlight Comments, 18
Spotlight icon, 28
Spotlight Search fields, 28
Spring-loaded folders/windows, 14
Stacks, 46–47
standard accounts, 240
Standard Install on "Leopard" window, 10
Start Installation button, 312
Start menu, 12, 313, 314
Starting Points window, 276
Startup Disk icon, 314
startup disk preferences, 235
Startup Disk tab, 314
Stationary feature, 111
Statistics bar, 12
Stickies, 40, 211
Stocks, 211
Stop button, 144, 283
streaming, 232
Subscribe button, 67
subscribing to calendars, 67–68
superuser account, 244–245, 303–304
Sync Devices button, 83
synchronization, 75, 138. See also iSync
System Management Controller, 320
System Preferences
    account picture and, 148
    appearance preferences and, 194
    Apple menu and, 12
    Bluetooth and, 79
    CD/DVD options and, 225
    date/time and, 232–233
    Desktop picture and, 197
    display and, 225–226
    Energy Saver and, 226–227
    Exposé and, 24
    function of, 41
    hardware and, 225–229
    iChat account and, 118
    international options and, 220–222
    keyboard/mouse and, 227–228
    MobileMe and, 229
    network and, 229–231
    opening, 220
    overview of, 219

System Preferences (continued)
  Parental Controls and, 249
  personal options and, 220–224
  printer installation and, 174, 179
  QuickTime and, 231–232
  screen saver and, 199
  security options and, 222–224
  sharing and, 262–263
  Simple Finder and, 250
  software updates and, 233
  sound and, 228–229
  Spaces and, 25
  speech and, 234–235
  Spotlight and, 29
  startup disk and, 235
  startup disk choice and, 314
  Time Machine and, 287, 289
  universal access and, 235
  user accounts and, 240, 241
System Preferences icon, 179, 194
System Preferences window, 194, 220, 249
System Profiler, 43
System tab, 251, 252

T

Tab button, 70
tabbed browsing, 88–89
tabbed chatting, 123
Tab-delimited format, 73
Tabs pane, 97
Tagged Image File Format (TIFF), 160
"Take account online" check box, 109
technical support, 321
template for Address Book, 76
Terminal
  function of, 43
  opening, 296
  preferences for, 296–300
  tabbed windows in, 300–301
  UNIX commands and, 301–305
Terminal icon/window, 296
Test button, 199
text chats, 120–121
Text File format, 73

TextEdit
  file formats and, 49–50
  fonts and, 51–52
  formatting documents and, 50–53
  function of, 41, 47
  new document and, 48
  opening, 48, 183
  opening existing document in, 48
  preferences for, 53–57
  printing and, 183–189
  saving documents and, 48–49
  selecting text and, 51
  spelling/grammar check in, 52–53
TextEdit icon, 48
thesaurus, 38
thumbnail bar, 147–148
thumbnails, 166, 167
Thunderbird, 73, 319
Tile Game, 211
Time Capsule, 285
Time Limits tab, 257–258
Time Machine
  file selection and, 288–289, 290
  formatting hard disk and, 285–286
  function of, 41
  hardware requirements for, 284
  information retrieval and, 290–292
  manual drive setup and, 286–288
  manual startup and, 289
  monitoring backup and, 289
  opening, 290
  overview of, 275, 284
  pause/resume backup and, 290
Time Machine icon, 287, 289, 290
Time Machine preferences pane, 287, 289
Time Machine window, 291
time zone, 232
To Do button, 116
To Dos, 116–117
Toast, 319
toolbar
  Dictionary, 38
  Disk Utility, 285
  Finder, 12, 13, 16, 202–205, 292

in Fonts window, 52
Mail, 105–106, 111
Spotlight Search fields in, 28
Tools menu, Preview
    image color adjustment and, 171
    image resizing and, 168
    image rotation and, 169
    PDF annotating and, 166
    PDF markup and, 165
Trackpad, 235
Trackpad tab, 227
Trash
    Desktop and, 11
    Dock and, 22
    for e-mails, 114
    Finder preferences and, 15
    Finder toolbar and, 205
    function of, 12
    troubleshooting and, 323
Trash icon, 22
troubleshooting
    Console and, 43
    Image Capture Information tab and, 151
    permissions problems, 323–324
    reinstallation and, 325
    restarting computer and, 318
    software, 322–323
    software updates and, 318
    startup issues, 319–321
TurboTax, 319
Turn On FileVault button, 224
TV shows, 134

U

Unit Converter, 211
Universal Access, 100, 235, 283
UNIX
    CLI navigation and, 301–302
    command function data and, 302
    common commands of, 302, 303
    overview of, 295
    plain text format and, 50
    resources on, 305
    Terminal and, 43, 296–301

upgrading
    installation options and, 4–6
    to Quick Time Pro, 232
    software updates and, 233, 309, 318, 322
Upload button, 153
USB connection, 81, 174, 176, 177, 180
Use for Backup button, 287
Use random screen saver check box, 199
Use Simple Finder check box, 251
Use TWAIN UI button, 156
user accounts. See also Parental Controls
    creating, 241–246
    installation and, 6
    logging in to, 246–249
    Migration Assistant and, 43
    overview of, 239
    photo for, 148
    picture for, 246–247
    printer sharing and, 269
    Remote Management and, 269
    root account, 244–245, 303–304
    sharing preferences and, 265–266
    Simple Finder and, 250–252
    troubleshooting and, 323
    types of, 240–241
    UNIX commands and, 303
user name, 99, 163, 242, 243
utilities
    function of, 42–43
    for icon modification, 209
    listed, 42–43
    overview of, 35–36, 42
    for printer, 175
Utilities folder, 18, 302, 304, 309
Utilities menu, 291, 321

V

vCard, 70, 73, 74, 76
Vertical/Horizontal scrollbar and arrows, 13
video backdrops, 146–147
video button, 121
video card, 319
video chats, 120, 121–122
videos. See movies/videos

View menu
    Finder, 203–204, 207
    Preview, PDF sidebar and, 166
View Options window, 207
VirusBarrier, 319
VoiceOver Utility, 43, 235, 247
Volume control, 11, 12
Volume Scheme, 8

W

Weather, 209, 211
Web archive format, 50
Web browsers, 96, 101, 319. *See also* Safari
Web Clip, 211
Web Clip icon, 216
Web Clip Widget window, 216
Web Gallery, 229
Web pages/sites. *See also* downloads; Internet;
    Internet addresses
    creating, 148, 151, 229
    filtering, 254–255
    HTML format and, 50
    plain text format and, 56
    Windows-only, 308
    XML format and, 50
Web Sharing check box, 263
WebDAV server, 65
Welcome screen, 5, 7
Welcome to Mail screen, 106–107
Where drop-down menu, 278
white space, 56
Widget manager window, 212
Widgets
    creating, 215–216
    finding additional, 214–215
    managing, 212–213
    opening/closing, 209–210

    preferences for, 213–214
    supplied with Leopard, 210–211
    uninstalling, 213
Wikipedia, 38
window groups, 296, 299–300
Window Groups window, 299
Window menu, 299
Windows
    Bonjour protocol and, 264
    Boot Camp Assistant and, 42
    keyboard shortcuts and, 45
    on Mac, 307–315
    partitioning hard drive and, 8
    Recycle Bin and, 12
    sharing and, 261, 267, 268–269
    Start menu and, 12
    UNIX and, 295
Windows Explorer, 10
Windows installation disc, 308, 309, 312, 313
Windows Media, 93–94
Windows XP/Vista, 269, 307, 309, 311, 313
wireless network adapter, 177, 230
Word, Microsoft, 47, 50, 319
word processor. *See* TextEdit
workflows, 277. *See also* Automator
World Clock, 209, 211

X

X Window System, 305
X11 utility, 43, 305
Xcode developer tools, 8, 9–10, 283
Xgrid server, 263

Y

Yahoo!, 75
Yellow Pages, 211

The Genius is in.

978-0-470-29052-1

978-0-470-29050-7

978-0-470-38108-3

978-0-470-29169-6

978-0-470-29170-2

The essentials for every forward-thinking Apple user are now available on the go. Designed for easy access to tools and shortcuts, the *Portable Genius* series has all the information you need to maximize your digital lifestyle. With a full-color interior and easy-to-navigate content, the *Portable Genius* series offers innovative tips and tricks as well as savvy advice that will save you time and increase your productivity.

Available wherever books are sold.

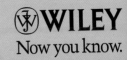
WILEY
Now you know.